Rose Guide to
Discipleship

PUBLISHING

Carson, California

Register your Rose Publishing book at www.rose-publishing.com/register to receive a FREE Bible reference download.

Credits

Contributing Editor Len Woods

Design by Sergio Urquiza

All Scripture quotations, unless otherwise indicated, are taken from the Holy Bible, New International Version®, NIV®. Copyright ©1973, 1978, 1984, 2011 by Biblica, Inc.™ Used by permission of Zondervan. All rights reserved worldwide. www.zondervan.com The "NIV" and "New International Version" are trademarks registered in the United States Patent and Trademark Office by Biblica, Inc.™

Other Bible quotes from:

The Scripture quotations marked (ESV) are taken from the ESV® Bible (The Holy Bible, English Standard Version®) copyright © 2001 by Crossway, a publishing ministry of Good News Publishers. ESV® Text Edition: 2011. The ESV® text has been reproduced in cooperation with and by permission of Good News Publishers. Unauthorized reproduction of this publication is prohibited. All rights reserved.

The Scripture quotations marked (NASB) are taken from the NEW AMERICAN STANDARD BIBLE®, Copyright © 1960, 1962, 1963, 1968, 1971, 1972, 1973, 1975, 1977, 1995 by The Lockman Foundation. Used by permission.

Scripture quotations marked (NLT) are taken from the Holy Bible, New Living Translation, copyright © 1996, 2004, 2007 by Tyndale House Foundation. Used by permission of Tyndale House Publishers, Inc., Carol Stream, Illinois 60188. All rights reserved.

The Scripture quotations marked (TLB) are taken from the Living Bible copyright © 1971 by Tyndale House Foundation. Used by permission of Tyndale House Publishers Inc., Carol Stream, Illinois 60188. All rights reserved. The Living Bible, TLB, and the The Living Bible logo are registered trademarks of Tyndale House Publishers.

Photos are from www.shutterstock.com and www.lightstock.com

Library of Congress Cataloging-in-Publication Data

Names: Woods, Len, author.
Title: Rose guide to discipleship.
Description: Carson, California : Rose Publishing, Inc., 2016.
Identifiers: LCCN 2016004729 (print) | LCCN 2016025756 (ebook) | ISBN 9781628623581 | ISBN 9781628623598 ()
Subjects: LCSH: Discipling (Christianity) | Spiritual formation.
Classification: LCC BV4520 .W635 2016 (print) | LCC BV4520 (ebook) | DDC 248.4--dc23
LC record available at https://lccn.loc.gov/2016004729

Printed in the United States of America
October 2016, 1st printing

Contents

Quick Start Guide

Use the forms in the Appendix, to get off to a good start. You'll find a series of helpful worksheets, forms, guidelines, etc.

- ▷ "How to Create a Flexible Discipleship Program" provides tips on designing your discipleship program to meet the specific needs of the members of your group.

- ▷ "Discipleship Snapshot" is a personal assessment tool for each participant.

- ▷ "Guidelines for Disciplers and Group Leaders" includes tips on facilitating discussion.

- ▷ "What to Expect in a Discipleship Group" is a handout for group participants.

- ▷ "Discipleship Participant Form" is a sign-up form for the discipleship course or small group.

If you are an individual working through these materials, it is still recommended that you complete the "Discipleship Snapshot" to help you see how and where you might need to focus your attention, your study, and your prayers.

What Is Discipleship?

The word "gospel" comes from the Greek word *euangélion*, which simply means "good news."

The Greek word *disciple* means "student" or "learner." In New Testament times, a disciple entered into a master-apprentice relationship with his teacher. A disciple's hope was to acquire his mentor's wisdom and skills, and to imitate his life. The leader's expectation was that, once trained, his disciple would repeat the process.

Jesus began his public ministry by urging people to "Repent and believe in the gospel" (Mark 1:15, NASB). He then called those who were responsive to his message to become his devoted followers. Approaching some simple fishermen, he said, "Follow Me, and I will make you become fishers of men" (Mark 1:17, NASB).

A Definition of *Disciple*

A disciple is a person who follows Jesus—to *know* Jesus and his teaching; to *grow* more like Jesus; and to *go* for Jesus, serving others and making new disciples.

According to Jesus, discipleship alters every facet of life: our beliefs (knowing), our essential nature (growing), and our actions (going). Using Christ's words from Mark 1:17, the chart at the bottom of the page shows how discipleship affects every facet of a disciple's life.

Jesus' unlikely band of 12 disciples spent three amazing years with him. They listened to his authoritative words. They observed his awe-inspiring miracles. Christ invested huge amounts of time in his followers. He trained them and introduced them to a life of humble servanthood. He modeled for them how to love (John 13:33–34). Slowly but surely, their lives were radically transformed by watching and imitating.

After his death and his resurrection, and just before returning to heaven, Jesus called his followers together and commissioned them to help others learn to follow him:

> "All authority in heaven and on earth has been given to me. Therefore go and make disciples of all nations, baptizing them in the name of the Father and of the Son and of the Holy Spirit, and teaching them to obey everything I have commanded you. And surely I am with you always, to the very end of the age" (Matthew 28:18–20).

"Follow me"	"I will make you become"	"Fishers of men"
Knowing	Growing	Going
New truth	New character	New mission
Information	Transformation	Multiplication
Head	Heart	Hands

6

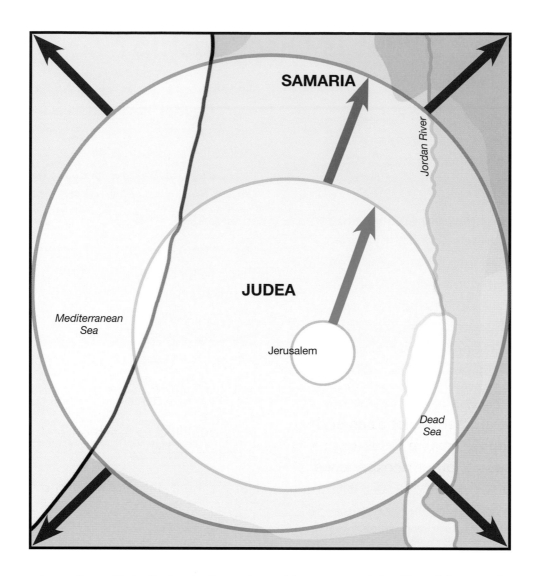

With the coming of the Holy Spirit in Acts 2, and because of the faithfulness of these disciples, the gospel of Jesus spread like wildfire. The church of Jesus expanded from Jerusalem, into Judea, Samaria, and to the ends of the earth (Acts 1:8). (See map.)

This story continues all the way up to the present day. We get to join in the great mission of calling on people everywhere to repent, believe in the gospel, and follow Jesus by faith.

Five Traits of a Disciple

A disciple's life is marked by five traits:

1. **Trust**: Disciples believe the gospel and—by faith—follow the Son of God.

   The essence of the spiritual life is *faith* (Hebrews 11:6). Understood correctly, faith is less a noun (something we "have"), and more a verb (something we "exercise"). Disciples trust God. They take him at His word. They live, not on the basis of what culture recommends or what *seems* right, but according to what God has said.

2. **Love**: Disciples live in healthy community with the people of God.

The greatest commandment, Jesus said, is to love God wholeheartedly and to love others sacrificially (Mark 12:28–34). It is only a lifestyle of love that shows the world we are Christ's followers (John 13:34–35). In fact, without love, our spiritual efforts are as worthless as a clanging cymbal (1 Corinthians 13).

3. **Learning**: Disciples are shaped and guided by the Word of God.

Disciples of Jesus study and embrace the teachings of Jesus. We hunger to know the Lord and understand his Word better and better. But we seek biblical/theological knowledge not as an end in itself. Rather, we acquire God's truth and *take it to heart* in order to experience life change.

4. **Life Change**: Disciples are yielded to and transformed by the Spirit of God.

Jesus' original call in Mark 1:17 was to "Follow me . . . " [in order to] "become" [something they weren't]. Likewise as we follow Jesus—as we internalize God's Word, submit to his Spirit, encounter trials, live in authentic but messy community, and engage in spiritual practices that open us up to God's transforming presence—Christ's character is formed in us (Galatians 4:19).

5. **Service**: Disciples are devoted to and engaged in the mission of God.

Disciples serve like Jesus, choosing daily to "give their lives away" (Mark 10:45). This means using the resources, abilities, and opportunities God gives to further *his* kingdom (Acts 20:24). Christ's servants share the gospel message boldly, clearly, and humbly . . . with neighbors near and far. And as we become better disciples of Jesus, we also seek to make and serve other disciples of Jesus.

The apostle Paul repeated this idea to Timothy when he said:

"And the things you have heard me say in the presence of many witnesses entrust to reliable people who will also be qualified to teach others" (2 Timothy 2:2).

Here is a real-life picture of the New Testament model for discipleship.

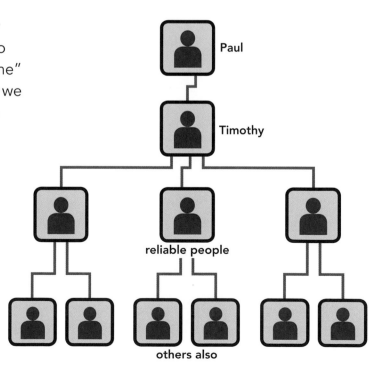

How to Use This
Thirty-Topic Discipleship Training Guide

If you spend much time around church, you'll hear people speak of their faith journey, their attempts to walk with the Lord, their desire to grow spiritually. You'll likely hear church leaders use words and phrases like sanctification, Christian education, and spiritual formation.

The hope and goal behind all such talk is discipleship—learning to follow Jesus Christ in order to become like him.

Becoming "disciples who make disciples" is the mission (and ministry model) Jesus gave his church (Matthew 28:18–20). This is why congregations offer catechism classes, Sunday school departments, small group ministries, special seminars, weekend retreats, etc.

The Bible clarifies for us what discipleship is and isn't:

Discipleship Is	Discipleship Is Not
The essential mission of Jesus Christ	An optional program of the church
A lifelong process	A short-term project
Fundamentally transformational	Primarily informational
Something we do with others	Something we do by ourselves
For *every believer* in Christ	For a few special "super saints"

Who should use this resource?

In bypassing the religious elite and choosing regular people (i.e., fishermen, tax collectors, etc.) to be his original disciples, Jesus demonstrated that discipleship is for everyone. With that in mind, *Rose Guide to Discipleship* was written for anyone who wants to grow in his or her faith. Do you and some others in your church want to both become and make disciples? This resource will help you do just that.

What makes this book a unique and helpful tool?

> ▶ It is *foundational*—equipping users with a solid, basic biblical foundation, for a lifetime of following Christ.

▷ It is *comprehensive* (without being overwhelming)—comprised of 30 essential discipleship topics/lessons. Each topic can be used on its own. Each is a stand-alone lesson.

▷ It is *practical*—suggesting clear, everyday ways to live as Christ intended.

▷ It is *transferrable*—designed so that participants can turn around and take others through the same material.

▷ It is *creative*—utilizing Rose Publishing's proven ability to use charts, diagrams, and other visuals to explain biblical truths and clarify difficult spiritual concepts.

▷ It is *group-friendly*—intended for one-on-one discipling relationships, men's or women's groups, for small groups, and Bible study classes.

Can I use this on my own?

Certainly an individual could work through this resource alone, and be challenged and blessed. But if you have another Christian nearby, a group of two or more is recommended. A careful study of the life of Jesus shows that he favored an interpersonal and group approach to disciple-making.

In the Bible, we see Jesus ministering to people in various group sizes:

▷ **Large groups:** Jesus taught the Sermon on the Mount to a large crowd on a mountainside (Matthew 5—7) and he miraculously fed a crowd of more than 5,000 people with just five loaves of bread and two fish (Mark 6:30–44).

▷ **One-on-one:** On other occasions, Jesus spent time ministering to individuals one-on-one, such as Nicodemus (John 3), the unnamed Samaritan woman at Jacob's well (John 4) and Zacchaeus (Luke 19).

▷ **Small groups:** Jesus spent the bulk of his time training his small group of 12 disciples. And out of that group, Jesus invested much time in an even smaller circle of three: Peter, James, and John. The inescapable conclusion? While there are times we need to be alone with Christ, we also need to be with the people of God in large and small group settings. Learning to follow Jesus happens best when we worship, study, and serve *together*. You'll get more out of this resource if you find a friend (or several others) who will agree to work through it with you.

In creating (or joining) such an authentic, close-knit community of disciples, you'll find:

▷ A forum in which to cultivate spiritual friendships

▷ Fellow travelers (and strugglers) for the spiritual journey ahead

▷ Support for the hard times of life

▶ A setting in which you can encourage others

▶ A safe place to wrestle with the biggest questions of life

▶ A circle of trust in which to discuss questions and pray about problems

▶ Partners with whom you can serve and minister

Where should we start?

If you are preparing to lead personal disciples, a class, or a small group through this discipleship course, look through the materials at the end of *Rose Guide to Discipleship*. In the Appendix, you'll find a series of helpful worksheets, forms, guidelines, etc.

▶ "How to Create a Flexible Discipleship Program" provides tips on designing your discipleship program to meet the specific needs of the members of your group.

▶ "Discipleship Snapshot" is a personal assessment tool for each participant.

▶ "Guidelines for Disciplers and Group Leaders" includes tips on facilitating discussion.

▶ "What to Expect in a Discipleship Group" is a handout for group participants.

▶ "Discipleship Participant Form" is a sign-up form for the discipleship course or small group.

If you are an individual working through these materials, it is still recommended that you complete the "Discipleship Snapshot" to help you see how and where you might need to focus your attention, your study, and your prayers.

Now, if you're ready to get started on the great adventure of following Christ, let's begin!

CHAPTER 1:

Believing the Gospel

Topic 1: A Radical Message

The Uniqueness of the Gospel of Jesus

"For I am not ashamed of the gospel,
because it is the power of God that brings
salvation to everyone who believes: first to
the Jew, then to the Gentile."

—Romans 1:16

In all the history of the world there has never been anyone like Jesus. He, and his life were so extraordinary and impacted the world so strongly, that time itself changed! Our calendar is based on when he was born. We count the years since his birth and call it AD—an abbreviation for *Anno Domini*, which is Latin for "in the year of our Lord." We refer to all history before Jesus was born as BC—an abbreviation for "before Christ."

What was so important about Jesus? It was his radical message of love—what we call the gospel.

> The word "gospel" comes from the Greek word *euangélion*, which simply means "good news."

Over the centuries, the gospel of Jesus has spread through the world like wildfire. Millions of people have called themselves "Christians," naming themselves for Jesus, the Christ. They do so to show their devotion and because they want to imitate and follow him, to be Christ-like.

So what is it that inspires this type of devotion? How does this so-called "gospel of Jesus" uniquely offer hope to a world so full of trouble and bad news?

The word "gospel" comes from the Greek word *euangélion*, which simply means "good news." For example, in ancient times, a herald might proclaim to hearers the "gospel" of a military victory, the birth of a royal child, or some other joyous announcement. In the Bible, the word "gospel" takes on added spiritual and eternal significance.

In the Old Testament, anticipating the dark years of the Babylonian exile, God moved the prophet Isaiah to encourage mourning Jews of a coming day when a God-sent messenger would "bring good news to Zion" (Isaiah 40:9). This anointed messenger, Isaiah foretold, would not only rescue the people of God (61:1–4), but also restore the perfect rule of God.

In the New Testament this good news of God is immediately associated with the person of Jesus. Luke shows Christ beginning his public ministry by reading those very words of Isaiah and declaring them fulfilled (Luke 4:16–21, Isaiah 61: 1–2a). In other words, Christ was claiming to be the one about whom Isaiah prophesied. The gospel is the ancient promises of God realized in the person of Jesus Christ!

This is the reason the "evangelists," the gospel writers Matthew, Mark, Luke, and John, all focus on Jesus—his words and works. This is why the apostle Paul repeatedly referred to the "gospel of Christ" (Romans 15:19; 1 Corinthians 9:12; Galatians 1:7). *Jesus is the gospel!* He embodies God's good news. Through his death and resurrection, Jesus made the way for us to have a relationship with God and experience his love forever.

Old Testament Promises   New Testament Good News

G-O-S-P-E-L

Romans 1:16, the memory verse for this session makes the critical point that salvation—right standing with God, forgiveness, new/eternal life—is found only in the gospel of Jesus:

> "For I am not ashamed of the gospel, because it is the power of God that brings salvation to everyone who believes: first to the Jew, then to the Gentile" (Romans 1:16).

Let's break that good news down using the easy-to-remember acrostic G-O-S-P-E-L.

The gospel is about **G**od.

The gospel is about **O**urselves.

The gospel is about a **S**avior.

The gospel is **P**owerful.

The gospel must be **E**mbraced.

The gospel is **L**ife-altering.

Next, we'll look more closely at the first four letters, *G, O, S,* and *P*. We'll unpack letters *E* and *L* in "Topic 2: Coming to Faith."

14

Bible Study

When we put our faith in Christ, an amazing transformation takes place. We become brand-new creations (we'll talk more about this in "Topic 3: All Things New"). This change is spiritual. It is actual and real. It is internal, fundamental, and essential. It affects our basic nature. Theologians call this regeneration. Jesus called it being "born again" (John 3).

The **gospel** is about **G**od.

1. Take a few minutes to slowly read Psalm 103. What does this beloved prayer/song reveal about God's nature?

_____

_____

_____

2. Psalm 103 describes God as "compassionate and gracious, slow to anger, abounding in love." Does this match what you heard about God in your younger years? Based on your experience, which of these descriptions is easiest to accept? Which is more difficult?

_____

_____

_____

3. Speaking of Jesus Christ, the apostle John wrote: "No one has ever seen God. But the unique One [Jesus], who is himself God, is near to the Father's heart. He has revealed God to us" (John 1:18, NLT). What does Jesus reveal to us about God?

_____

_____

The **gospel** is about **O**urselves.

4. Read Romans 3:10–18, 23 and Romans 6:23. According to these verses, why do we need a savior?

_____

_____

Many people today believe we humans are basically okay—maybe even divine. But the Bible tells us that we all come into this world as naturally self-centered rebels against God. As sons and daughters of Adam and Eve, we have inherited their sin nature, and we each have sinned in thought and deed. Every last one of us has an innate tendency as well as a long track record of wanting what we want rather than what God wants for us.

The Bible tells us the penalty for such rebellion against God is death. At the most basic level, death is separation. When we die physically, our souls are separated from our bodies, and we are separated from our loved ones. Spiritual death is the ultimate consequence of sin. It means separation from God and the life he gives.

> C. S. Lewis said that we are not "basically decent" folks who need a bit of improvement. We are rebels who need to lay down our arms.

As spiritually dead people (see Ephesians 2:1), we do not have the power to "pull ourselves up by our own bootstraps."

5. What do you think total surrender looks like? Why do you think it is difficult to do?

_____

_____

_____

The Bible makes it clear we are incapable of self-rescue. That's not good news. It's terrible news—in fact, the worst news ever . . . until we remember . . .

The **gospel** is about a **Savior.**

God has not left us alone in our helpless, hopeless state (remember his love?). God sent a Savior!

6. Read Isaiah 53:1–6. This is a continuing description of the one the prophet identified as the bringer of good news. What does this passage say about Christ? What did his death accomplish? What would have happened if he hadn't died?

_____

_____

_____

_____

© Bristol Works, Inc.   www.rose-publishing.com   May be reproduced for classroom use only, not for sale.

16

The penalty for sin is death. We deserved to die. But the Bible says Jesus acted as our substitute. He voluntarily took the punishment we deserved because of our sin. "He was pierced for our transgressions" (Isaiah 53:5). Christ died, so that we might live.

His triumphant cry from the cross ("It is finished!" John 19:30) means that humanity's debt to God because of sin has been "paid in full." The tearing of the veil in the temple at that precise moment (Matthew 27:51) indicated that access to God was now possible for humankind because the problem of sin had been solved by Jesus.

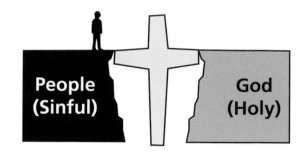

In the cross of Christ we see vividly portrayed the awfulness of sin and the justice of God. But we also have a stunning reminder of the love of God. In the resurrection of Jesus, we have undeniable evidence of his authority and power over sin and death.

The **Gospel** is **P**owerful!

7. Read our memory verse again, Romans 1:16. The Greek word translated as "power" is the word *dunamis*. This is the word from which we get our English word "dynamite." How is the gospel like "spiritual dynamite"?

_____

_____

_____

_____

8. Second Corinthians 5:17 says, "Therefore, if anyone is in Christ, the new creation has come: The old has gone, the new is here!" What does it mean to be a new creation in Christ?

_____

_____

_____

_____

Knowing these truths is critical. But merely knowing them is not enough. We must take them to heart. We must exercise faith. (We'll talk more about this in "Topic 2: Coming to Faith.")

What's in a Name?

Ten Names of Jesus that Show How and Why He Is God's Good News

Name	Reference	Significance
Immanuel	Matthew 1:23	Since Jesus is "God with us" we do not have to reach up for God or go on a religious search for him; in Christ, God has come down to seek us (Luke 19:10).
Jesus	Matthew 1:21	"Jesus" is the Greek form of the Hebrew name *Yeshua*, which means "The Lord is salvation." Jesus came into the world not only to draw near to and seek sinners but to save them (Luke 19:10). We don't have to try to save ourselves—and we couldn't even if we tried!
Lamb of God	John 1:29, 36	The Old Testament provides a very strict set of rules required in order for people to be considered "right" with God. One of these rules involved the sacrifice of lambs as a sign of repentance for sins (Numbers 6:14). But Jesus, through his death and resurrection, made it possible for us to be forgiven of our sins and to know God (Matthew 27:51; Romans 5:1–2). Jesus is the perfect sacrificial lamb for all time (Hebrews 7:26–29).
Gate	John 10:9	Jesus is the gateway to God, the entryway to new, abundant, eternal life. Christ's disciples do not have to search for other paths or wonder if they are on the right road.
Prince of Peace	Isaiah 9:6	Disciples of Jesus do not have to fear that God is angry with them (or hostile toward them). Jesus came to end the conflict between God and humanity by giving himself as a peace offering. In Christ we have eternal peace with God, not based on anything we do, but based on what Christ has done for us (Romans 5:1).
Light of the World	John 8:12	Because Jesus is the radiance of God's glory, we do not have to stumble in darkness (John 8:2). In fact, as disciples we get to shine the light of God so that others might also see eternal truth (Matthew 5:16).
Pioneer and Perfecter of Faith	Hebrews 12:2	Jesus is the perfecter of faith in us, completing the work he began (Philippians 1:6). We do not have to fret or fear. The life of faith is not about trying harder but trusting more deeply. It's not about us changing ourselves but allowing Jesus to change us from the inside out.
Shepherd	1 Peter 2:25	In a confusing and frightening world, Jesus is the one who, as a faithful shepherd, guides us, provides for us, and protects us.
Resurrection and the Life	John 11:25	We do not have to fear the grave. Those who believe in Jesus will live on, even after this life. Through his death and resurrection, Jesus defeated death for all who believe in him (1 Corinthians 15:55–57).
Lord of Lords	Revelation 19:16	Jesus is the sovereign, all-powerful ruler. He has promised to come again to restore the world and rule over all things forever.

Which of these names represent a way in which Jesus has impacted your life? Which name(s) represent a way in which you need Jesus? When you pray, try calling Jesus by that name.

Take-Home Reflections

Transformation

We began this session by talking about bad news. We then asked the question, why is the gospel of Jesus worth considering? Hopefully the answer is clear: Only the gospel reveals the heart of God to come to us, to rescue us from our brokenness, and to powerfully transform us. Only the gospel is able to meet the deepest needs of every man, woman, boy and girl in the world. Only the good news of Jesus brings the hope our souls most crave.

What's the Difference?

Author Philip Yancey tells of a time when a group of religious scholars convened in England for a comparative religion symposium. A lively debate over various theological concepts began and worked its way into a discussion of Christianity's unique contribution among world religions. C. S. Lewis wandered into the room, and when the topic was revealed to him, Lewis quickly put an end to the debate. "Oh, that's easy," he said. "It's grace."[1]

"Grace" is the beautiful biblical word that means "undeserved favor." And Lewis was right. *Grace* is the great distinctive of the gospel. It's grace that makes Christianity unique among the world's religions. No wonder the apostle John described Jesus as being "full of grace and truth" (John 1:14).

---

1   Philip Yancey, *What's So Amazing About Grace?* (Grand Rapids, MI: Zondervan, 1997), 45.

Life Application

An important part of discipleship is learning how to apply God's truths to your life. Below are just a few ways you can start thinking about what you've learned and apply it to your daily life.

1. Memorize our memory verse:
   "For I am not ashamed of the gospel, because it is the power of God that brings salvation to everyone who believes: first to the Jew, then to the Gentile" (Romans 1:16).

2. Write about your own experience with Christ. When did he become a real person to you, more than just an idea or a historical figure?

3. Watch the news on television, or read it in the newspaper or online. Think about how the gospel of Jesus could bring hope to each crisis, crime, or tragedy.

4. Wrestle with one or two of the following:

   ▶ How do we reconcile God's holy nature (and righteous wrath towards sin) with his love?

   ▶ Is the cross more about the love of God or the judgment of God? Is it more about the beauty of grace or the ugliness of sin?

   ▶ What have been the most powerful effects of the gospel in your own life?

Topic 2: Coming to Faith

How to Begin a Relationship with God

"Yet to all who did receive him [Jesus], to
those who believed in his name, he gave
the right to become children of God."

—John 1:12

In "Topic 1: A Radical Message," we saw, that to a rebellious world full of sin and suffering, brokenness and bad news, God sent his eternal son. We noted therefore that the gospel isn't just a message. It's a man—the God-man Jesus! The good news is that we can be brought into a right relationship with God—we can know God! . . . through Jesus.

Using the acrostic G-O-S-P-E-L, we began unpacking the great truths about God's epic plan to rescue the world from sin and death. Thus far in our exploration of Jesus Christ and his mission, we have seen:

The gospel is about **G**od.

The gospel is about **O**urselves.

The gospel is about a **S**avior.

The gospel is **P**owerful.

The gospel must be **E**mbraced.

The gospel is **L**ife-altering.

In short, we want to look at what it means to come to genuine faith in Christ.

When Jesus began his public ministry, he called on people to "Repent and believe the good news!" (Mark 1:15).

- The Greek word translated "repent" in the New Testament comes from two Greek words that, taken together, mean literally "to change the mind."

- The Hebrew word translated "repent" in the Old Testament means "to turn back."

This is what repentance is: a changing of one's mind about God, about one's own condition, about what it takes to come into a relationship with God. Repentance is a change of mind that results in a life change.

> Repentance is a change of mind
> that results in a life change.

A repentant person realizes: "My sin is real. I am separated from a good and holy God. I deserve his judgment. I am in trouble. However, Jesus claims to be the way—the only way—to the Father. I can see that he is my only hope. I cannot save myself, but Jesus can save me. And he wants to."

It's been said that repentance has less to do with emotion and more to do with insight. Repentance is waking up to the truth of who God is, who we are, and what Jesus has done for us—and responding accordingly. Repentance means re-thinking our lives. God promises he will renew our minds so that we seek what is good and righteous—more and more each day.

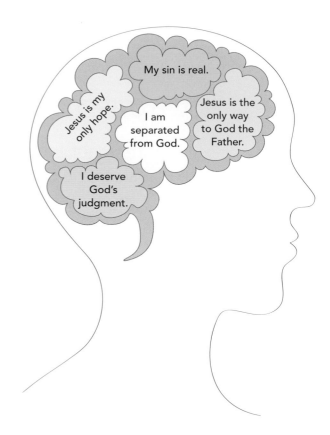

Bible Study

The gospel must be Embraced.

1. Read John 1:12, our memory verse for this topic. What does it mean to receive Jesus? What does it mean to believe on his name?

_____

_____

_____

2. James 2:19 challenges people who merely believe there is a God: "You believe that there is one God. Good! Even the demons believe that—and shudder." Why isn't it enough to merely acknowledge that there is a God? What does it look like when someone embraces the gospel and believes as is described in John 1:12?

_____

_____

_____

Some beliefs have no effect on our lives. Believing it is important to get a flu shot is not the same as actually letting a nurse jab you in the arm with a syringe full of flu vaccine. Believing in God the way he wants us to is more than nodding at a list of theological facts.

In the physical realm we exercise trust when we rest our full weight on a chair. We depend on, rely on, that chair to support us completely. In the spiritual realm, we exercise trust when we place our full confidence and hope in Christ. We rest fully on what he's done for us. We stop trusting in anyone or anything else to make us right with God. We trust in Jesus alone.

A massive wildfire, whipped along by strong winds, was consuming everything in its path. One family, seeing the impossibility of outrunning the inferno, left their home. In a nearby meadow, they lit a backfire that quickly consumed several acres of dry grass. With time running out, they then lay down in the midst of the freshly burned area and covered themselves with earth.

Almost immediately, the towering blaze reached the edge of the smoldering meadow, and swept around it, continuing its destructive path. The family was saved because they understood that the only safe place would be a place where the fire had already burned.

The gospel tells us the fire of God's wrath (because of human sin) has already touched down at one particular point in history. When it did, it completely consumed an innocent man hanging on a cross. It did not burn a large area, but it finalized God's work of judgment.

The good news is that we can be forgiven when we trust in the one who bore God's judgment for sin on the cross. Jesus is our "burned-out area." He is the one and only safe hiding place for sinners.

One word for this kind of trust-filled belief is "faith." Read the story in the sidebar for an example of what this kind of faith is like.

The most obvious way to express faith in God is through prayer, through simply talking to God. That can be done silently or out loud. You can do it privately or with a more mature Christian. If you sense God drawing your heart to Jesus, respond! Tell God what is taking place in your soul.

Understand there is no magical "salvation prayer." The words you speak to God aren't nearly as important as the heart behind them. Admit to God your sin and need for forgiveness. Tell God that you are placing your faith in Jesus, that you are trusting in all that he has done for you. Then thank God for the great promise of the gospel. Thank him for giving you new life through Christ.

3. If you have put your trust in Christ, what were the circumstances? If you haven't, what holds you back?

_____

_____

_____

For those who *do* believe in Christ . . .

The gospel is Life-altering.

4. Read 1 Peter 2:9–12 and 3:15. According to these passages, how should a follower of Jesus live in a world full of bad news?

_____

_____

5. How has your faith in Christ altered your life?

_____

_____

6. This topic is titled "Coming to Faith." Consider the following verses that speak of faith:

> ▶ "The apostles said to the Lord, 'Increase our faith!'" (Luke 17:5).

> ▶ "Let your roots grow down into him, and let your lives be built on him. Then your faith will grow strong in the truth you were taught, and you will overflow with thankfulness (Colossians 2:7, NLT).

> ▶ "We hope that your faith will grow so that the boundaries of our work among you will be extended (2 Corinthians 10:15, NLT).

From what you've read about faith in these verses, what can you say about how faith works in a believer's life?

_____

_____

Faith in Christ isn't the finish line of the spiritual life; it's only the beginning. We "repent and believe the good news" (Mark 1:15). Then as disciples, we heed Jesus' call to "Follow me"

(Mark 1:17). This requires ongoing trust. In a sense we keep coming to faith, or at least coming back to faith, every day, for the rest of our lives.

The gospel is glorious and beautiful and mind-boggling. It is mysterious and miraculous. How difficult it is to wrap our hearts and minds around God's grace. But we can experience it by faith.

The Difference Genuine Faith Makes

When we trust in Jesus we go . . .	
From being lost Isaiah 53:6; Mark 6:34	**To being found** Matthew 18:12; Luke 15
From being spiritually blind John 9:39–41; 2 Corinthians 4:4	**To having spiritual vision** Luke 4:18-19; 24:31; John 9:39
From being dirty or impure Romans 6:19; 1 Thessalonians 4:7	**To being clean and pure** Hebrews 9:14; 1 John 1:9
From being foolish and ignorant of God Acts 3:17; 17:23; Ephesians 4:18; 1 Timothy 1:13	**To knowing God in wisdom** Luke 1:77; 1 Corinthians 2:12; Ephesians 1:8, 17; James 1:5
From being at war with God (his enemy) Romans 5:10; Colossians 1:21	**To being at peace with God (his friend)** John 15:14–15; Romans 5:1
From being children of wrath Ephesians 2:3	**To being beloved children of God** John 1:12; Romans 8:15; Galatians 4:6; 1 John 3:2
From being under God's condemnation and wrath Romans 1:18; 2:5; 5:18	**To being justified and pardoned by God** Romans 5:18
From being spiritually dead Romans 5:12; Ephesians 2:1, 5	**To being spiritually reborn and made alive** John 3; 5:24–26; Ephesians 2:5
From being in darkness Matthew 4:16 John 3:19; Acts 26:18; Romans 13:12; Ephesians 5:8	**To being in light** John 8:12; Ephesians 5:8; Colossians 1:13
From owing God a debt Colossians 2:14; 1 Peter 1:19	**To being ransomed and redeemed** Matthew 20:28; 1 Corinthians 6:20; 7:23; Hebrews 9:15
From being enslaved to sin/in bondage John 8:34; Romans 6:6, 16–18, 20, 22	**To being free** John 8:36; Romans 6:18, 22; Galatians 5:1, 13
From being an alien to God's kingdom 1 Peter 2:11; Hebrews 11:13	**To being a citizen of heaven** Philippians 3:20

Take-Home Reflections

We all sin. I have sinned. I'm not perfect and I'm not proud of everything I've done. The Bible says we deserve death for our sins (Romans 3:23). But the good news is that God sent Jesus, not ultimately to teach or preach or heal (though he did all those things). God sent his son to die. At the cross, God was both righteous Judge and loving Father. The very payment he required for sin, he supplied. The crucified Jesus took our terrible punishment. The resurrected Jesus offers a full pardon and new life to all who will trust in him.

Despite our sin, God loves us just as we are and promises to forgive us our sins and make us clean. All we have to do is accept this amazing gift of grace.

Have you trusted Jesus for salvation? Is he *your* way, your truth, your life?

Life Application

An important part of discipleship is learning how to apply God's truths to your life. Below are just a few ways you can start thinking about what you've learned and apply it to your daily life.

1. Memorize our memory verse:

   "Yet to all who did receive him, to those who believed in his name, he gave the right to become children of God" (John 1:12).

2. Read John 3 and 4. Notice how Jesus interacted, first with a respected Jewish religious leader, then with a Samaritan woman with a history of failed relationships.

3. Wrestle with one or two of these questions:

   ▷ What would you say to a child who asked you to explain faith?

   ▷ Based on John 1:12, is every person on earth a child of God? Why or why not?

   ▷ How can a person tell if his or her faith is growing?

   ▷ Do you think that there is a difference between believing things *about* Jesus and believing *in* Jesus? How might these two be related?

Topic 3: All Things New

Understanding Who You Are in Christ

"Therefore, if anyone is in Christ, the new
creation has come: The old has gone, the
new is here!"

—2 Corinthians 5:17

Who doesn't love new stuff? The smell of a new car. The joy of making a new friend. The fun of discovering a great new restaurant or ideal vacation spot.

New means different. It hints of surprise and tantalizes us with the possibility of breaking out of old ruts. *New* almost always means an upgrade—thus the overused marketing phrase "new and improved."

The promise of the gospel is that faith in Christ brings new (and improved!) life— right here and right now.

▶ A lot of people see religious faith as being mostly about one's *past*: "For much of my life I lived in terrible ways. But then I heard the good news of Jesus. I trusted him, and he forgave all my sins."

▶ Or they see salvation as being primarily a *future* thing: "Because of Jesus, when I die, I'm going to heaven!"

While both of these things are true, there's also the fact that salvation has incredible implications for everyday life in the present!

Theologians like to say that salvation has three aspects:

Salvation from the
PENALTY
of sin
(the doctrine of
justification)

Salvation from the
POWER
of sin
(the doctrine of
sanctification)

Salvation from the
PRESENCE of sin
(the doctrine of glorification—i.e., in the life to come, when we finally meet Christ face-to-face.
See 1 John 3:2.)

It is this second aspect we primarily want to concentrate on in this study. We want to look at the phenomenal changes brought on by "so great a salvation" (Hebrews 2:3). The gospel doesn't only address our former lives, and it doesn't merely provide eternal life when we die. The gospel is also about new life *now*.

So Great a Salvation!

Salvation through Jesus Christ brings staggering benefits, but among the more obvious blessings are

▶ a new life

▶ new standing with God

▶ a new identity

▶ a new nature (and thus new desires and new struggles!)

▶ a new power to live as we should!

Key Terms about Salvation

Term	Meaning	Scripture
Condemnation	Humans, because of their sinful nature and actions, deserve divine wrath/eternal judgment. Without Christ, we are all *condemned* because of our sin.	Romans 8:1
Redemption	God paid the price to recover us from our slavery to sin. God *redeemed* us from being condemned.	Acts 20:28; Ephesians 1:7
Imputation	God "charges" a believer's sin to Christ's "account" and credits that person's "spiritual account" with Christ's righteousness. God *imputed* our guilt to Christ.	Romans 5:12–19
Justification	God declares condemned sinners "not guilty" by virtue of his grace and their faith in Christ. They have been *justified*.	Romans 5:1; Galatians 2:16
Regeneration	God grants spiritual life to those who are spiritually dead. Their lives have been *regenerated*, given new life.	John 3:5; Titus 3:5
Conversion	God enables sinners to experience *conversion* and turn from sin to God.	Acts 15:3; 26:18
Reconciliation	God restores his rebellious creatures into a right relationship with himself. We are *reconciled* with God.	Romans 5:10; Colossians 1:21–22
Adoption	God *adopts* us and makes us his children—members of his forever family—by his grace and through our faith.	Romans 8:15; Galatians 4:5; Ephesians 1:5
Sanctification	God's work throughout a believer's life of making believers holy, like Christ. We have been *sanctified* by Christ's sacrificial death.	Romans 6:19; Hebrews 12:14
Glorification	God's perfect finish, after death, of the work he began in us at the time of regeneration. Once *glorification* takes place, we will sin no more.	1 John 3:2

Bible Study

New Life

1. Read Ephesians 2:1–10. What does it mean that non-believers in Christ are "dead in . . . transgressions and sins" (v. 1)? How does it make you feel to know that apart from Christ, we are "separated from the life of God" (Ephesians 4:18), but that when we trusted in Jesus, "God . . . made us alive with Christ" (Ephesians 2:4–5)?

_____

_____

New Standing with God

2. Read Romans 5:1–21. In the same way we all became sinners as the result of the actions of one man (Adam), we can be justified before God through the acts of another (Jesus). What are some of the things these verses tell us we can enjoy as a result of our new standing with God?

_____

_____

New Identity

When we accept Christ we are given new names, a new identity. We are now beloved, accepted, forgiven, chosen—we are children of God.

3. Read Romans 8:5–17.

a. Read verses 14–16 again. What does it mean that we are children of God?

_____

_____

b. Now read verse 17 again. As an heir of God and co-heir of Christ what does this verse say we share in with him?

_____

_____

Who Does God Say We Are?

The New Testament describes the new identity of a disciple using a variety of word pictures. Which of these new identities suits you best and why?

Disciples are called or likened to:	Scripture	Meaning
Fishers of men	Matthew 4:19	We are called to "fish for people" with the net of the gospel.
Salt	Matthew 5:13	We are to live in a way that makes people thirsty to know God; we are to act as a preservative in a corrupt society.
Light	Matthew 5:14–16	In a dark world, we reflect God's nature and shine for him.
Branches	John 15:5	As branches connected to the Vine, Jesus, we bring his blessing/fruitfulness to the world.
Stewards/ Servants	1 Corinthians 4:1–2	We are managers of God's good news, gifts, resources, and blessings—ultimately responsible and accountable to him.
Ambassadors	2 Corinthians 5:20	We are representatives of Christ's kingdom to the lost people of this world.
Saints/Holy people	Ephesians 1:1	We are God's holy ones—by virtue of what Christ has done for us.
Citizens of heaven	Philippians 3:20	Our allegiance is to God and his kingdom—not this world.
Soldiers	2 Timothy 2:3–4	We are engaged in a battle—not against people—but the spiritual forces of evil.
Athletes	2 Timothy 2:5	We are to live self-controlled lives and train ourselves to be godly.
Farmers	2 Timothy 2:6	We sow God's word faithfully in order to reap an eternal harvest.
Living stones, a spiritual house	1 Peter 2:5	We are God's dwelling place; his modern-day temple.
A priesthood	1 Peter 2:9–10	We may draw near to God—and we have the privilege of helping others do the same.
Foreigners, exiles	1 Peter 2:11	This world is not our home. We are only passing through.

New Nature

4. Our memory verse for this lesson says:

"Therefore, if anyone is in Christ, the new creation has come: The old has gone, the new is here" (2 Corinthians 5:17).

How would you explain this idea to an eight-year-old kid?

_____

_____

_____

_____

5. Read and ponder these two passages:

▶ "I have been crucified with Christ; and it is no longer I who live, but Christ lives in me; and the life which I now live in the flesh I live by faith in the Son of God, who loved me and gave Himself up for me" (Galatians 2:20, NASB).

▶ "For you died, and your life is now hidden with Christ in God. When Christ, who is your life, appears, then you also will appear with him in glory" (Colossians 3:3–4).

The great reformer Martin Luther once said, "The moment I consider Christ and myself as two, I am gone." What do you think he meant by this? Why is a believer's union with Christ so important?

_____

_____

_____

_____

New Desires (and New Struggles)

6. Consider these two statements from the apostle Paul:

▶ "So I find this law at work: Although I want to do good, evil is right there with me. For in my inner being I delight in God's law; but I see another law at work in me, waging war against the law of my mind and making me a prisoner of the law of sin at work within me" (Romans 7:21–23).

▶ "For the flesh desires what is contrary to the Spirit, and the Spirit what is contrary to the flesh" (Galatians 5:17).

In 2 Corinthians 5:17, Paul said believers in Christ are brand new creations. If that's true, why do we still have evil desires in us?

_____

_____

_____

_____

_____

It has been said that sanctification, growing more like Christ, is not really the process of becoming something new. Rather, sanctification is the lifelong process of becoming who we are in Christ. It is learning to live from our new, true hearts. And we do this despite still having our old, unredeemed "flesh," which is incapable of transformation or upgrading (see John 3:6; 6:63; Romans 7:18).

New Power

7. Choose an area of your life with which you are experiencing some difficulty (your marriage, a tough family situation, a broken friendship, a struggle with temptation or addiction, a need to forgive someone, etc.). Now read and consider these two passages:

   ▶ Ephesians 3:16 says, "I pray that out of his glorious riches he may strengthen you with power through his Spirit in your inner being."

   ▶ Second Peter 1:3 promises, "His divine power has given us everything we need for a godly life through our knowledge of him who called us by his own glory and goodness."

   How can the prayer and the promise in the verses above help you with the problem situation you chose?

_____

_____

_____

_____

Take-Home Reflections

The Spirit's Work in Our Transformation

The Holy Spirit . . .	
Enlightens our minds	Jeremiah 31:34; 1 Corinthians 2:9–10; Ephesians 1:17–18; 1 John 2:27
Purifies our emotions	Romans 5:5; 8:15; 2 Corinthians 7:10–11
Empowers our wills	Romans 8:13; 1 Corinthians 15:10; Galatians 5:16
Sensitizes our consciences	2 Corinthians 7:10–11; Hebrews 10:22; 1 Timothy 1:5
Satisfies our longings	Isaiah 55:1–2; John 4:13–14; 2 Corinthians 3:6
Expresses our needs	Romans 8:26

New life in Christ, new standing with God, a new identity, a new nature (and thus new desires and new struggles!), plus a new power to live as we should . . . what a mind-boggling list! It sounds too good to be true.

But it is true—all this and more. And this fact of being a new creation means you can't go on living the way you used to live because, well, you're no longer the person you used to be! As a child of God, you have a brand new nature that contains divine spiritual DNA—meaning the desire to do right *is* within you (whether you feel it or not).

We will never live as Jesus calls us to live until we see ourselves as Jesus sees us. Identity determines activity.

According to the promise of the gospel, if you have put your trust in Jesus, you have been utterly, absolutely, completely transformed. Do you dare believe it?

Life Application

An important part of discipleship is learning how to apply God's truths to your life. Below are just a few ways you can start thinking about what you've learned and apply it to your daily life.

1. Memorize our memory verse:

   "Therefore, if anyone is in Christ, the new creation has come: The old has gone, the new is here" (2 Corinthians 5:17).

2. Read Paul's letter to the Romans in one sitting.

3. Bounce one of these questions around (over coffee or lunch) with your discipleship partner or group:

   ▶ How can a person embrace their new identity in Christ and begin to focus on a new way of living?

   ▶ What are the implications of the Bible's claim that Jesus Christ is life itself (see John 11:25; 14:6; Colossians 3:4; cf. John 10:10)? Is guilt more a subjective feeling or an objective condition or state? Why?

   ▶ How could it be that the death of a Jewish-carpenter-turned-rabbi on a Roman cross on a Friday afternoon some 2,000 years ago makes it possible for a person today to be "acquitted by God" on all counts of sinfulness?

   ▶ In what specific ways do you struggle to see yourself as Christ sees you?

   ▶ Where do you see newness in your life because of Christ? Where would you like to see more newness?

4. Meditate each morning and evening on the affirmations under "In Christ I am . . ." You might even say them aloud.

Because of my trust in the person and work of Jesus Christ, the following things are true of me (even if I don't sense them or feel them):

In Christ I am . . .

▶ Chosen by God! (Ephesians 1:3–8)

▶ Forgiven of all my sins—past, present and future! (Colossians 1:13–14)

▶ Justified—I am righteous in the sight of God! (Romans 5:1)

▶ Free from any and all condemnation! (Romans 8:1–2)

▶ Bought with a price—I belong to God! (1 Corinthians 6:19–20)

▶ A brand-new creation—my old life is no more! (2 Corinthians 5:17)

▶ God's child! (John 1:12)

▶ Born of God and the evil one cannot touch me! (1 John 5:18)

▶ More than a conqueror—eternally secure in the love of God! (Romans 8:31–39)

▶ United with/joined to Christ forever! (1 Corinthians 6:17)

▶ A friend of Jesus! (John 15:15)

▶ Seated with Christ in the heavenly realm! (Ephesians 2:6)

▶ A citizen of heaven! (Philippians 3:20)

▶ Complete in Christ! (Colossians 2:9–10, NASB)

▶ Hidden with Christ in God! (Colossians 3:1–4)

▶ A branch of Jesus Christ, able to bear fruit for God! (John 15:16)

▶ A member of Christ's body! (1 Corinthians 12:27)

▶ Given direct access to God's throne of grace! (Hebrews 4:14–16)

▶ Able to approach Almighty God with freedom and confidence! (Ephesians 3:12)

▶ God's "masterpiece," created for good works! (Ephesians 2:10, NLT)

▶ A dispenser of grace to others in the body of Christ! (1 Peter 4:10)

▶ Able to accomplish whatever God asks me to do! (Philippians 4:13)

▶ Guaranteed that God works for my good in all life's circumstances! (Romans 8:28)

▶ Sure that God will complete the good work he has begun in me! (Philippians 1:6)

Topic 4: Assurance of Salvation

Being Sure That You're Right with God

"This is the testimony: God has given us eternal life, and this life is in his Son. Whoever has the Son has life; whoever does not have the Son of God does not have life. I write these things to you who believe in the name of the Son of God so that you may know that you have eternal life."

—1 John 5:11–13

Bill Bright, the founder of Campus Crusade for Christ (now known as Cru), once said:

"Surveys indicate that 50 percent of the church members in the United States are not sure Christ is in their lives. These are good people. Often, they have served faithfully in the church for years. And yet, they still have no assurance of Christ's abiding presence, no confidence that, if they died today, they would go to be with the Lord. . . .What about you? If you were to die today, are you absolutely sure, beyond a shadow of a doubt, you would go to heaven?"[2]

As followers of Jesus, one of our greatest needs is the confident assurance that we are right with God, that our sins are forgiven, that we are children of God.

Perhaps you struggle with this question of your status with God, or your eternal destiny. If so, this lesson is for you. And even if you are "absolutely sure," it's essential to understand this issue thoroughly, so that you can help explain this truth to other confused believers.

2   Bill Bright, "Transferable Concepts: How You Can Be Sure You Are a Christian," *Cru.* https://www.cru.org/train-and-grow/transferable-concepts/you-can-be-sure-you-are-a-christian.html.

Five Common Reasons Christians Doubt their Salvation

Reason	The Doubt	The Truth
#1: Fluctuating feelings	Many people experience a delighted sense of freedom and closeness with God when first understanding and embracing the good news of Jesus. Typically, however, this joy fades away. And for many that sense of God's nearness also fades away. Without these feelings to assure them, they question if anything happened at all.	Following Christ involves learning to live by what God says is true (faith), not by what seems to be true (our feelings). See Romans 1:17; 2 Corinthians 5:7; and Galatians 2:20 for more on living by faith.
#2: Struggles in life	Some new Christians mistakenly assume that receiving Christ will bring an end to their worldly troubles (e.g., medical, financial, occupational, etc.). When their problems don't go away, they wonder if their salvation is real.	Nowhere does the Bible guarantee an easy life for God's people. In fact, it suggests just the opposite is true. As C. S. Lewis said, "If you want a religion to make you feel really comfortable, I certainly don't recommend Christianity."[3]
#3: Falling back into sin or old habits	Salvation (i.e., the new birth—John 3) means we receive new life, new standing with God, a new nature, a new identity, new desires, and new power. We are new creations (2 Corinthians 5:17)! And yet we still have an unredeemed human nature, we live in a fallen world filled with temptation, and our minds are not yet fully renewed. We remain vulnerable to sinful impulses. And when we yield to them, we doubt that we have become "new" at all.	Our failures don't suggest we're not believers; they indicate our continuing need for Jesus. Regret over sin and the desire to change show that you are God's child. We won't be perfect in this life (Philippians 1:6), but we can expect to make progress as we walk by the Spirit (Galatians 5:16).
#4: Attacks by the evil one	When we stumble and fall, we hear a voice in our head that tells us "A true child of God would never do such a thing," "See there, your heart isn't really changed!" or similarly condemning statements.	That condemning voice we hear is not God's voice—it's the voice of the enemy, Satan, the father of lies (John 8:44). Satan seizes every opportunity to attack us (Ephesians 6:16). Take up your shield of faith and ignore that voice!
#5: Losing sight of grace	Legalism is the devilish lie that we are responsible to live good lives and thereby "maintain our salvation." This system of "works righteousness" denies God's grace and asserts that we can earn salvation through our good deeds. When we know we haven't been good enough, we doubt our standing with God.	The gospel of grace says that we didn't do anything to earn or deserve salvation and we can't do anything to preserve right standing with God. (Galatians 3:2–3). Instead, we trust in a grace that is freely given (Ephesians 2:8-9).

3   C. S. Lewis, *God in the Dock*, (Grand Rapids, MI: Wm. B. Eerdman Publishing Co., 1970).

Bible Study

1. What are some typical responses when people are asked if they know *for sure* that they are right with God and destined to spend eternity with him?

_____

_____

_____

2. Look closely at these verses:

   ▶ "This is the testimony: God has given us eternal life, and this life is in his Son" (1 John 5:11).

   ▶ "For the wages of sin is death, but the gift of God is eternal life in Christ Jesus our Lord" (Romans 6:23).

   ▶ "For it is by grace you have been saved, through faith—and this is not from yourselves, it is the gift of God—not by works, so that no one can boast" (Ephesians 2:8–9).

   a. What do these verses say about salvation and eternal life?

   _____

   _____

   b. These verses contrast the idea of a *gift* with that of a *wage* you earn. How would you explain the difference between these two concepts?

   _____

   _____

   c. Why is it important that the Bible says salvation is a gift? What does this mean in your own life? Have you ever tried to "earn" God's grace? Explain.

   _____

   _____

   _____

3. Now take a moment to examine these verses:

▶ Jesus, in speaking about himself: "I am the way and the truth and the life. No one comes to the Father except through me" (John 14:6).

▶ Jesus, while praying: "Now this is eternal life: that they know you, the only true God, and Jesus Christ, whom you have sent" (John 17:3).

▶ The apostle Peter, in preaching about Jesus: "Salvation is found in no one else, for there is no other name under heaven given to mankind by which we must be saved" (Acts 4:12).

▶ The apostle John, in writing about Jesus, the Son of God: "He who has the Son has life; he who does not have the Son of God does not have life" (1 John 5:12).

a. What do these verses say about the source of eternal life?

_____

_____

_____

b. In light of these passages, how do you respond to commonly heard statements like: "I believe there are many ways to God" or "It doesn't really matter *what* you believe as long as you are sincere" or "It is narrow and arrogant for Christians to claim that Jesus is the only way to God!"?

_____

_____

_____

c. Why do you think people have a hard time understanding and accepting that salvation cannot be earned through good works, but is found only in Jesus?

_____

_____

_____

38

4. Carefully read these verses:

> ▶ "I write these things to you who believe in the name of the Son of God so that you may know that you have eternal life" (1 John 5:13).

> ▶ "Very truly I tell you, whoever hears my word and believes him who sent me has eternal life and will not be judged but has crossed over from death to life" (John 5:24).

a. What does it mean to believe in Christ?

_____

_____

_____

b. What does John 5:24 mean when it says that we will have "crossed over from death to life"? What kind of life transformation might we see?

_____

_____

_____

c. If we put our trust in Christ, what can we be absolutely sure about? (Hint: Re-read 1 John 5:13.)

_____

_____

_____

d. If you were to die, and God were to say to you, "Why should I let you into heaven?" what would be a good biblical response based on your study here?

_____

_____

_____

_____

Take-Home Reflections

Three Amazing Truths about Eternal Life

1. Eternal life is a GIFT (1 John 5:11; Romans 6:23; Ephesians 2:8–9; John 3:16).

2. Eternal life is found only in a RELATIONSHIP WITH CHRIST (1 John 5:12; John 14:6; 17:3; Acts 4:12).

3. Eternal life is a CERTAINTY for those who trust in Christ (1 John 5:13; John 5:24).

Life Application

An important part of discipleship is learning how to apply God's truths to your life. Below are just a few ways you can start thinking about what you've learned and apply it to your daily life.

1. Memorize our memory verse:

   "This is the testimony: God has given us eternal life, and this life is in his Son. Whoever has the Son has life; whoever does not have the Son of God does not have life. I write these things to you who believe in the name of the Son of God so that you may know that you have eternal life" (1 John 5:11–13).

2. Share with one other person (a spouse, coworker, child, neighbor, friend, etc.) the concepts in this lesson—how he or she can be absolutely sure of being in right relationship with God.

3. Consider how you would answer this objection:

   "This idea of *assurance* is a dangerous teaching! If you go around telling people they can know for sure they have eternal life, what will keep them from living any old way they want!?"

4. How can we help someone who is struggling with doubts such as the ones listed on page 35? Have you ever struggled with similar doubts? Having doubts motivates us to ask questions. Where can we go to find answers or get wise advice?

CHAPTER 2:

Becoming a Disciple

Topic 5: A Disciple Learns

The Bible Guides Us

"All Scripture is God-breathed and is useful for teaching, rebuking, correcting and training in righteousness, so that the servant of God may be thoroughly equipped for every good work."

—2 Timothy 3:16–17

We get our English word "disciple" from the Latin word *discipulus*, which means "pupil." This corresponds to the New Testament noun *mathētēs* (from a Greek verb that means "to learn"). In short, the most basic and literal meaning of "disciple" is "student." *A disciple is first and foremost a learner.*

> **The disciple's goal is to become Christ-like.**

However, learning in the time of Christ was different than it is now. Being a student in the first century required being *physically with* one's mentor. With no Internet and no online courses available, you couldn't watch YouTube videos of your rabbi or receive the latest blog posts of your teacher via email. Sages and scholars in that day weren't tweeting their wisdom or posting pithy sayings on social media. All of which means, if you wanted to know what your teacher was thinking and saying, you had to tag along behind him. You literally had to follow him. Otherwise you'd surely miss an important lesson or an essential truth.

The gospels show the first disciples following Jesus— to *know* Jesus and his teaching; to *grow* more like Jesus; and to *go* for Jesus, serving others and making new disciples. Two thousand years later, that's still a good definition of discipleship.

> ## A Definition of *Disciple*
> A disciple is a person who follows Jesus—to *know* Jesus and his teaching; to *grow* more like Jesus; and to *go* for Jesus, serving others and making new disciples.

So discipleship involves *knowing, growing,* and *going.* We can compare these three areas of discipleship to the head, heart, and hands of a disciple. The idea of "Knowing" is symbolized by the head, while "growing" is symbolized by the heart, and finally, "going" is symbolized by hands. (Though we don't walk on our hands, the hands are a better symbol for this concept than feet would be, as the idea of "going on mission" is more tied to serving others than walking somewhere.)

Though broken into three different concepts, we can't draw sharp boundary lines between the "head, heart, and hands" aspects of following Christ. These categories bleed over into one another and depend on each other. *Healthy discipleship is always integrated.*

▶ Head—Beliefs that don't penetrate our hearts to help us *grow* or alter our behavior so that we *go* and serve are worthless.

▶ Heart—*Growing* in the faith can't be separated from *knowing* truth and *going* on mission to serve.

▶ Hands—Serving the Lord effectively is tied together with *knowing* God's truth and *growing* to have the right heart attitude.

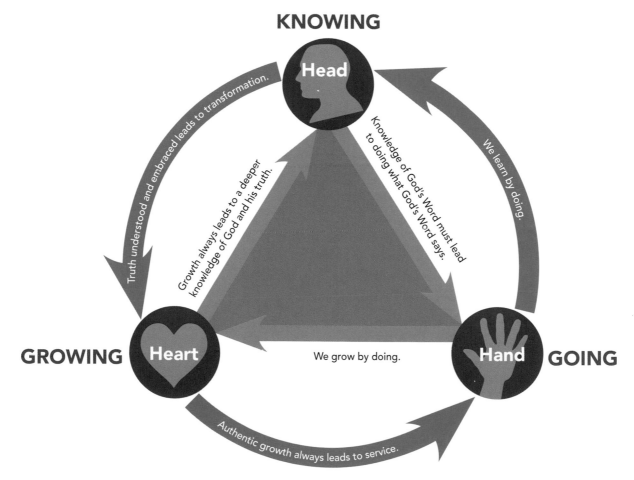

Though each relies on the other, we will examine these three areas individually in three separate sessions. In this session we want to get an overview of the *knowing*, or head, aspect of discipleship. A follower of Christ is a student of Christ. He or she must learn certain things.

Bible Study

1. Consider these passages from the gospels. They all show Jesus helping his followers grasp God's eternal truths. He did this largely through teaching:

   ▶ "Now when Jesus saw the crowds, he went up on a mountainside and sat down. His disciples came to him, and he began to teach them" (Matthew 5:1–2).

   ▶ "Jesus answered, 'My teaching is not my own. It comes from the one who sent me'" (John 7:16).

   ▶ After an extended time of teaching in the Upper Room the night before his death (see John 13–16), Jesus looked toward heaven and prayed *to* his Father *for* his disciples, "Make them holy by your truth; teach them your word, which is truth" (John 17:17, NLT).

   What did Jesus want his disciples to know about his teaching? From whom did it come?

   _____

   _____

   _____

   _____

   _____

Jesus taught his followers God's Word. Why? Because the ancient Scriptures are a revelation of God. They reveal:

   ▶ what God is like (Isaiah 46:8–10)

   ▶ why the world is broken (Genesis 3)

   ▶ how we can know God personally (Acts 17:27, 1 John 4:10)

   ▶ how broken people like us can find wholeness and enjoy lives full of significance and purpose (John 10:10, 2 Corinthians 5:17)

It's easy to forget that the "Bible" Jesus read and taught from was only the Old Testament (the New Testament documents weren't written until after the death of Christ). Consider Psalm 119, the longest chapter in the Old Testament. It's a beautiful collection of meditative prayers about the wonder of God's revelation.

Ten Names for God's Word in Psalm 119

Names	Meaning
Law(s)	The Hebrew word is *torah*, which means instruction, and may refer to the whole Pentateuch—the first five books of the Old Testament
Testimony(ies)	One of God's regulations, a rule, or standard for conduct
Judgment(s)	A divine judicial decision, binding law or ruling
Commandment(s)	A clear, authoritative order from God
Statutes	Literally "things inscribed;" this refers to enacted laws that set limits or boundaries
Precepts	Divine orders
Word	The general term for God's revelation—the utterance of God
Saying	Sometimes translated "promise"
Way(s)	The way of life required by God's good and wise moral law
Path(s)	Used interchangeably with "way"

In this one psalm, we see that God's Word reveals his holy nature and can lead his people into a life that is blessed and protected. It is even more than that. It's a love letter, a lamp, light, and so much more. As the psalm points out, the Scriptures give a follower of Jesus:

- power against sin (vss. 3, 11, 101, 165)

- freedom (v. 45)

- direction and guidance (vss. 105 and 130)

- stability (v. 89)

- peace (v. 165)

- hope (vss. 114 and 147)

- delight (vss. 16, 24, 35, 47, 77, 92, 174).

2. Take a moment to read what the gospel writer Mark said about Christ's way of teaching his followers:

- "[Jesus and his disciples] went to Capernaum, and when the Sabbath came, Jesus went into the synagogue and began to teach" (Mark 1:21).

- "Once again Jesus went out beside the lake. A large crowd came to him, and he began to teach them" (Mark 2:13).

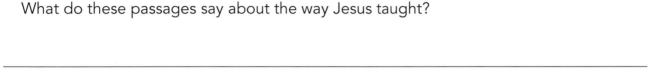

▶ "He taught them by telling many stories in the form of parables" (Mark 4:2, NLT).

▶ "Now learn a lesson from the fig tree. When its branches bud and its leaves begin to sprout, you know that summer is near" (Jesus, speaking in Mark 13:28, NLT).

▶ "Take my yoke upon you and learn from me, for I am gentle and humble in heart, and you will find rest for your souls" (Jesus, speaking in Matthew 11:29).

What do these passages say about the way Jesus taught?

_____

_____

_____

_____

Reading the gospels, we see Jesus was a master teacher. He understood that people learn in different ways. Some people learn best through hearing, others by seeing, and still others through hands-on experience. For these reasons, Jesus taught in a variety of ways:

▶ Publicly (Luke 21:37) and privately (Luke 10:38–39)

▶ Through lectures (Matthew 5–7)

▶ Telling stories (Luke 15)

▶ Turning common, life experiences into teachable moments (Matthew 15:32–38; Luke 21:2–3; John 4)

▶ Using object lessons (Matthew 18:2)

▶ Using examples from history (Matthew 12:40; Luke 13:4).

> Discipleship is the pursuit of whole-life *transformation*, not just biblical or theological *information*.

Underscoring the brilliance of Jesus' teaching methods, modern educational researchers have discovered that the deepest learning involves a combination of reading, studying, listening, discussing, watching, participating, testing, experimenting, etc.

Disciples grasp this, too. They see their knowledge of Jesus deepen as they study and put into practice God's Word.

3. What are the primary ways God has helped you gain knowledge of Christ and his truth?

_____

_____

_____

_____

_____

_____

After his crucifixion and resurrection and just before his return to heaven, Jesus, the master teacher, gathered his "students" and told them to go and make disciples of all the nations. "Teach these new disciples to obey all the commands I have given you" (Matthew 28:20a, NLT). Do you see it? The taught ones were to become teachers themselves.

That's precisely what they did! This first generation of disciples began to pass on the things they had learned from Jesus. In Acts 2, we read that all the believers "devoted themselves to the apostles' teaching" (v. 42). That's still the pattern. We learn . . . then we share what we've learned with others (2 Timothy 2:2).

4. In 2 Timothy 3:16–17, our memory verses for this lesson, we see how and why knowing God's Word is so important. Reread this passage. What sticks out to you in these verses?

_____

_____

_____

_____

_____

_____

In summary, a disciple is a student. A disciple follows Jesus in order to learn—to learn *about* him and to learn *from* him.

Take-Home Reflections

Getting into the Word . . . and Getting the Word into Us

Colossians 3:16 urges "Let the word of Christ dwell in you richly" (ESV). How does this happen in our lives? How do we become people who know the truth of God—not merely in a cerebral or academic way, but in a deeply personal way that brings honor to God, blessing to others, and joy to our own souls? Take a few minutes to work through this list and evaluate your own habits when it comes to knowing Christ and his teaching.

Way to learn and internalize God's Word	My experience—positive or negative	My future plan
1. Hearing God's Word read Via audio Bible MP3s, at church, through responsive readings, etc.		
2. Listening to communicators teach or preach God's Word At church, conferences, online, etc.		
3. Reading God's Word on my own Carefully, regularly, prayerfully; perhaps even reading through the entire Bible		
4. Discussing God's Word With a community of spiritual friends; small groups, Sunday School settings, etc.		

Way to learn and internalize God's Word	My experience—positive or negative	My future plan
5. Studying God's Word Reading, learning—then practicing—how to accurately unpack, interpret, and apply a Scripture passage		
6. Memorizing God's Word Hiding the truth of God in my heart and mind so that I can recall it at anytime		
7. Trusting God's Word Believing the promises and claims of God when he seems absent or life seems hopeless		
8. Paying close attention to how others live out God's Word in everyday life situations In giving, serving, sacrificing, forgiving, etc.		
9. Teaching God's Word Sharing with others, formally or informally, Scriptural truth that has impacted me		
10. Reflecting on God's Word Meditating, pondering, and praying over the things God has revealed; letting them govern my heart and mind		

What surprises you most about this exercise? What's the biggest takeaway for you?

_____

_____

_____

_____

Life Application

An important part of discipleship is learning how to apply God's truths to your life. Below are just a few ways you can start thinking about what you've learned and apply it to your daily life.

1. Memorize our memory verse:

   "All Scripture is God-breathed and is useful for teaching, rebuking, correcting and training in righteousness, so that the servant of God may be thoroughly equipped for every good work" (2 Timothy 3:16–17).

2. Read Psalm 119 carefully and make a list of all the blessings and benefits that come to the disciple who learns to follow the Word of God.

3. Wrestle with one or two of these questions:

   ▶ Here are two old teaching sayings: "More is caught than taught" and "I hear, I forget; I see, I remember; I do, I understand." What do these statements mean?

   ▶ Jean-Pierre de Caussade said, "God instructs the heart, not by ideas but by pains and contradictions." What does this mean? How does this insight apply to the disciple who seeks to know God and His truth?

   ▶ What would you tell a friend who said, "Help me! I'm realizing my knowledge of Christ is impersonal and academic. It makes no real difference in my life. How can I have a real relationship with Jesus?"

4. Improve your Bible study skills with *How to Study the Bible* resources from Rose Publishing. *How to Study the Bible* has concise steps for personal preparation, descriptive resources and reference information, and a step-by-step approach for inductive Bible study that teaches students to dig deeper into God's Word. These materials are available as an easy-to-use pamphlet, a wall chart, or a PowerPoint®. Go to www.rosepublishing.com for more information.

Topic 6: A Disciple Grows

Becoming More Christ~Like

"Being confident of this, that he who began a good work in you will carry it on to completion until the day of Christ Jesus."

—Philippians 1:6

You go to your 20-year reunion and, for the most part, it's what you expected: People acting like their lives are better than they really are. Balding classmates trying to one-up each other. Ex-cheerleaders still trying to bask in their high-school glory days. You smile and shake your head. But then, you talk with Eddie, the biggest, most obnoxious jerk from your graduating class. He's had a spiritual conversion. Now, he's humble and genuine. You are stunned at the change.

The next week, while waiting for your daughter to finish her dance class, you're scrolling around on social media on your smart phone. Someone's posted a link to a video about a young woman with a horrific

past. As she tells her story, you marvel at how full of joy she is. When she talks convincingly about the Lord giving her the grace to let go of her bitterness and forgive her abuser, you find yourself wiping away tears, genuinely touched by her story.

The promise of the gospel is more than a clean slate with God and the promise of heaven when we die. The gospel gives us radical new life *now*. Being a disciple of Jesus is stepping into that new life, following Jesus, experiencing his transforming presence. "Follow me," Jesus said, "and I will make you become . . . " (Mark 1:17, ESV). In other words, "If you pursue me, expect your life to change."

Accept the gospel. → Follow Jesus. → Experience life change.

In the previous topic, we looked at what it means for a disciple to know Christ and his teaching. We talked about the importance of learning God's Word. However, it's not enough to have only head knowledge of Jesus and the Bible. The goal of the spiritual life isn't accumulating Bible knowledge—the goal is experiencing spiritual transformation!

Bible Study

1. Describe someone you know who has grown spiritually. What did that person act like before and after that growth? How has spiritual growth changed your own life?

_____

_____

_____

_____

_____

2. Consider these passages that speak of God's desire to grow us up in the faith, and make us like his Son:

> "And as the Spirit of the Lord works within us, we become more and more like him" (2 Corinthians 3:18, TLB).

> "My dear children, for whom I am again in the pains of childbirth until Christ is formed in you" (The apostle Paul, writing in Galatians 4:19).

> "But the Holy Spirit produces this kind of fruit in our lives: love, joy, peace, patience, kindness, goodness, faithfulness, gentleness, and self-control" (Galatians 5:22–23, NLT).

> "Let your roots grow down into him, and let your lives be built on him. Then your faith will grow strong in the truth you were taught, and you will overflow with thankfulness" (Colossians 2:7, NLT).

What do these verses say about the Lord and his desire for us?

_____

_____

_____

_____

A Definition of *Disciple*

A disciple is a person who follows Jesus—to *know* Jesus and his teaching; to *grow* more like Jesus; and to *go* for Jesus, serving others and making new disciples.

52

3. The apostle Paul writes, "train yourself to be godly" (1 Timothy 4:7; the NASB renders this phrase "discipline yourself for the purpose of godliness"). What do you think Paul means? Why do you think this is hard?

_____

_____

_____

_____

It's worth noting that the present tense verb Paul uses here (translated "train" or "discipline") is the Greek word from which we get our English term "gymnasium." In other words, Paul is insisting that we give our souls a regular workout! Just as we go to the gym to exercise our bodies, we are to engage in spiritual exercises that will strengthen and firm up our souls.

> For more information on spiritual disciplines, see Topics 21–30 in Chapter Five.

Such spiritual practices (or holy habits) are often called spiritual disciplines. They are everything from solitude and silence, Bible reading and prayer, to giving and service. _Any regular activity that we intentionally practice in order to open ourselves up to the Lord's transforming presence can be considered a spiritual discipline._

Just as physical exercise leads to strength and health and fitness, in the same way spiritual exercises, properly understood and utilized, can help us grow to become like Christ.

A wrong view of spiritual disciplines	A right view of spiritual disciplines
Something for monks, nuns, and church leaders	Something for every Christ-follower
Something I am supposed to do for God	A way I can be with God
The goal is doing	The goal is becoming
Performed out of guilt (a "have to")	Practiced out of gladness (a "get to")
An end in themselves	A means to an end—being in God's transforming presence
A sign of spiritual maturity	A means to spiritual maturity

Misconceptions about Growing in God

Transformation Myths	Transformation Truths
Growth is automatic for believers.	Growth has to be pursued.
Maturity is an event or destination.	Maturity is a lifelong process, a journey.
Transformation is entirely up to God.	Transformation ultimately depends on God, but it also requires my participation.
Spiritual progress is mostly about finding and learning the right spiritual information.	Information is one part; "train(ing)" (1 Timothy 4:7), "working out" (Philippians 2:12) and "do(ing)" (James 1:22) are also indispensable. We have to live the truth we know.
Transformation comes from *trying* hard.	Transformation is the result of consistent *training* and constant *trusting* God to empower you.
Following Christ means engaging in a lot of spiritual activities.	The goal of the spiritual life isn't activity; it's intimacy! *Am I learning to love God and love others more and more? Am I taking on the character of Christ?*
God should work in my life exactly the way he's working in another person's life.	Spiritual growth will vary from person to person and from season to season.

4. How is spiritual growth and maturity progressing in your life? Take a few minutes and work through this chart. As you do, consider not just beliefs, but your actions. For example, you may recognize that God's Word is important, but are you reading it?

Tool for Spiritual Growth	Minor factor		Somewhat instrumental				Indispensable to growth			
God's Word	1	2	3	4	5	6	7	8	9	10
The indwelling Spirit of God	1	2	3	4	5	6	7	8	9	10
Relationships/Community	1	2	3	4	5	6	7	8	9	10
Trials and crises	1	2	3	4	5	6	7	8	9	10
Dramatic miracles	1	2	3	4	5	6	7	8	9	10
The passage of time	1	2	3	4	5	6	7	8	9	10
Practicing spiritual disciplines	1	2	3	4	5	6	7	8	9	10
Meeting with a mentor	1	2	3	4	5	6	7	8	9	10
Retreats/Mission trips	1	2	3	4	5	6	7	8	9	10
Prayer	1	2	3	4	5	6	7	8	9	10
Other: _____	1	2	3	4	5	6	7	8	9	10

a. Which of the tools of growth from the chart are you most familiar with? Least familiar with? Did your scoring in any way correspond to how familiar you are with the tool?

_____

_____

_____

_____

_____

_____

b. How does Philippians 1:6, our memory verse for this topic, speak to the whole issue of spiritual growth? What encouragement do you take from it?

_____

_____

_____

_____

_____

_____

c. Referring to the spiritual-growth tools in the chart on page 53, which tool would you like to utilize more in your own spiritual growth? Why? What is one step you can take today toward implementing this tool in your life?

_____

_____

_____

_____

_____

Take-Home Reflections

From Unbelief to Christ-likeness

It's not a cliché. It's a fact: The spiritual life *is* a journey. Coming to Christ and growing to maturity in him is a lifelong process.

At the risk of oversimplifying and over-generalizing, here are some very common, often-observed stages in the spiritual life:

Separated from Christ		New Life in Christ		
unbelief →		**✝ faith** →	**growing pains** →	**effective service**
Skeptic critical, combative	**Seeker** curious, cautious	**New believer** confused, childlike	**Disciple** committed, concerned about kingdom matters	**Disciple-maker** Christ-like catalyst for impacting others
What a person in this stage might say:				
"With so much evil in the world, how can you possibly believe in God?"	"I'm so tired of living this way. There must be more to life."	"Where's that verse about God helping those who help themselves?"	"I am praying for an open door to have a spiritual discussion with my neighbor."	"I want to start a discipleship group with two younger women."
What Jesus says to this person:				
"Come!" (*to* me)	"Repent and believe!" (*in* me)	"Follow (*after* me) and become (*like* me)!		"Go!" (*for* me)
What someone in this stage needs:				
Friendships with authentic believers who model the gospel	A safe place to ask questions about Jesus and his teaching	Relationships with mature believers who demonstrate and explain the basics of the faith	Help in identifying gifts, opportunities to serve with supervision/ feedback	A team of co-laborers, lots of encouragement, freedom to fail

Some people might object to making a distinction between "believers" and "disciples." Our intention is to draw attention to the scores of new believers who have not been trained yet to actually follow Jesus. They haven't been shown how to allow Christ to transform their attitudes, values, actions, habits, relationships, finances, etc. So there are true believers who have yet to begin following him and become disciples in the truest sense of the word.

56

Life Application

An important part of discipleship is learning how to apply God's truths to your life. Below are just a few ways you can start thinking about what you've learned and apply it to your daily life.

1. Memorize our memory verse:

   "Being confident of this, that he who began a good work in you will carry it on to completion until the day of Christ Jesus" (Philippians 1:6).

2. Read Romans 5:3–5. Then spend a few minutes journaling your thoughts about the current problems in your life and how God might be using those to shape you into the image of Christ.

   > "It is the fire of suffering that brings forth the gold of godliness."
   > —Madame Guyon

3. Wrestle with one or two of these questions:

   ▶ What about the idea that "we become like those we spend a lot of time with"? What are the implications of this for a follower of Jesus?

   ▶ The next time trials come, instead of asking the natural, "Why me, God?" question, try asking, "What are you trying to teach me here, Lord?" What kind of difference could this make?

   ▶ In the physical realm, training is easier when you have a trainer and training partners. How do you think this principle might apply to the spiritual realm?

   ▶ Certain things can stunt a person's physical growth. What factors might hinder a person's spiritual growth?

Topic 7: A Disciple Serves

Reaching Out and Serving Like Jesus

"For even the Son of Man did not come to
be served, but to serve, and to give his life
as a ransom for many."

—Mark 10:45

For many believers, faith is like a precious family heirloom. It's ours, and we're thrilled to have it! We know it's extremely valuable. We even mention it from time to time in conversations. But we don't always use it in daily life. Like grandma's china that remains out-of-sight in a large box in the garage, modern faith for many believers can be real, but not exactly relevant.

Contrast that idea of faith with the kind of faith portrayed in the Bible. In the Scriptures, faith isn't something you merely *have*; it's something you *live*. You don't stop with pondering it—you practice it! Biblical faith is less of a noun and more of a verb. The kind of believing Jesus advocated is active and obvious to others.

In other words, we shouldn't expect following Jesus to make for an easy life. Gospel faith is restless and active. It comforts us, but doesn't ever let us get too comfortable. Jesus made it clear there's work to be done. We have a mission to accomplish. Among Christ's final words to his disciples? "Go and make disciples of all nations" (Matthew 28:18–20).

Bible Study

1. Take a few moments to read and carefully consider these Bible passages that call us to action, compel us to go, and challenge us to embrace the same servant lifestyle and disciple-making mission that Jesus embraced:

   ▶ "In the same way, let your good deeds shine out for all to see, so that everyone will praise your heavenly Father" (Jesus, in Matthew 5:16, NLT).

   ▶ "He [Jesus] told them, 'The harvest is plentiful, but the workers are few. Ask the Lord of the harvest, therefore, to send out workers into his harvest field. Go! I am sending you out like lambs among wolves" (Jesus, in Luke 10:2–3).

   ▶ "But you will receive power when the Holy Spirit comes upon you. And you will be my witnesses, telling people about me everywhere—in Jerusalem, throughout Judea, in Samaria, and to the ends of the earth" (Jesus, in Acts 1:8, NLT).

   ▶ "Each of you should use whatever gift you have received to serve others, as faithful stewards of God's grace in its various forms" (1 Peter 4:10).

   What are your thoughts when you read such commands to do good deeds? To go and be a worker in the Lord's harvest field? To be a witness? To serve others?

   _____

   _____

   _____

   _____

   _____

   _____

   _____

2. According to the New Testament, discipleship is the lifelong process of following Jesus in order to become like him. If this is so, we can't just pursue the *character* of Jesus, we also have to take up the *mission* of Jesus and serve others. After all, 1 John 2:6 says, "Whoever claims to live in him must live as Jesus did."

   Read:

   ▶ Matthew 10:40

   ▶ Mark 12:6

   ▶ Luke 4:18

How does Jesus describe himself in each of these passages? What does this mean for followers of Jesus?

_____

_____

_____

_____

_____

_____

_____

3. **Single-minded. Focused. Committed. Intentional.** We could describe Christ's life in all of these ways. So how, practically speaking, can a follower of Jesus today (with a job, bills, school, friends, family, etc.) embrace these same priorities in life?

_____

_____

_____

_____

_____

_____

_____

A healthy approach to discipleship includes both being and doing. It calls for "with-ness" (i.e., being with Jesus) and witness (going for Jesus). Following Jesus is both personal and interpersonal. It encompasses both beliefs and behavior. It results in both internal transformation and external impact. We receive from God and from others, then we share what we have received.

The diagram on the following page illustrates this truth.

"BECOMING A DISCIPLE" is

trusting in Christ alone for salvation and following Jesus in order to *know* Jesus and his teachings; to *grow* more like Jesus; and to *go* for Jesus, serving others and making new disciples. We do this by continually opening up ourselves to God's transforming presence and by getting regular input from other disciples.

PEOPLE WHO INFLUENCE YOU

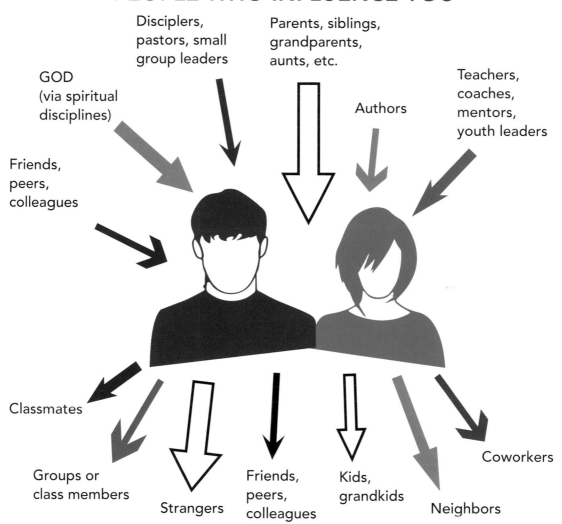

Disciplers, pastors, small group leaders

Parents, siblings, grandparents, aunts, etc.

GOD (via spiritual disciplines)

Authors

Teachers, coaches, mentors, youth leaders

Friends, peers, colleagues

Classmates

Groups or class members

Strangers

Friends, peers, colleagues

Kids, grandkids

Neighbors

Coworkers

PEOPLE WHOM YOU INFLUENCE

"MAKING DISCIPLES" is

leading others to trust in Christ alone for salvation and to orient their lives around the three-fold desire to *know* Jesus and his teaching; to *grow* more like Jesus; and to *go* for Jesus, serving others and making new disciples. We do this by serving, and giving our lives away, as Jesus did. We share with and invest in others the wisdom, truth, experiences, insights, resources, skills, abilities, etc. God has given to us.

Personally embracing Christ's mission to go and make disciples may involve the following:

▶ **Rejecting** the self-centeredness of our culture and embracing the self-less, servant mindset modeled by Jesus (Philippians 2)

▶ **Understanding** you have been saved for a life of good works that match the unique ways God has created or "wired" you (see Ephesians 2:8–10)

▶ **Letting** your light shine out among neighbors, coworkers, friends, etc., by doing those good works in the power of God's Spirit (Matthew 5:16)

▶ **Discovering**, **understanding**, and **utilizing** your God-given abilities to serve and build up the Body of Christ (Romans 12; 1 Corinthians 12, Ephesians 4; 1 Peter 4)

▶ **Getting** equipped to minister to others (Ephesians 4:11–13)

▶ **Taking** the truth, training, and blessings God has given you and turning around and investing that in others (2 Timothy 2:2)

▶ **Learning** how to give a reason "for the hope that is in you," then sharing your own story of how the Good News of Jesus has changed your life (1 Peter 3:15, NASB)

Servanthood Action Scale

Examine each pair of actions or attitudes in the scale below. Where do you see yourself?

Doing occasional acts of service	⇄	Having a servant's heart
Serving in "official" capacities	⇄	Serving in "unofficial" capacities
Helping when asked	⇄	Noticing needs and taking the initiative to help
Focusing on needed tasks	⇄	Focusing on people in need
Serving according to what others need	⇄	Serving according to my gifts and passions
The gift of serving (some believers)	⇄	The command to serve (all believers)
"Out front" visible service	⇄	"Behind-the-scenes" invisible service
Serving within the church	⇄	Serving outside the church

4. Looking at the pairs of actions and attitudes in the scale on page 61, write down where you are now and where you would like to be. What action steps will you take to get where you want to be?

_____

_____

_____

_____

_____

_____

5. Consider your experiences in serving Christ: engaging in ministry, going on mission trips, etc. Describe an experience you felt good about and one you did not feel was successful. What did you learn from these experiences?

_____

_____

_____

_____

_____

_____

_____

_____

_____

_____

_____

_____

_____

Take-Home Reflections

In the gospel of John, Jesus described himself as "sent" by God in multiple passages. These are listed in the box. Look up the verses, read and underline them so you can easily remind yourself who sent Jesus.

Clearly Jesus saw himself as being on a mission from God!

❑ John 3:34	❑ John 8:29
❑ John 4:34	❑ John 8:42
❑ John 5:23–24	❑ John 9:4
❑ John 5:30	❑ John 10:36
❑ John 5:37–38	❑ John 12:44–45
❑ John 6:29	❑ John 12:49
❑ John 6:38–39	❑ John 14:24
❑ John 6:44	❑ John 15:21
❑ John 6:57	❑ John 16:5
❑ John 7:16	❑ John 17:3
❑ John 7:18	❑ John 17:8
❑ John 7:28–29	❑ John 17:18
❑ John 7:33	❑ John 17:21
❑ John 8:16	❑ John 17:23
❑ John 8:18	❑ John 17:25
❑ John 8:26	❑ John 20:21

▶ His single, declared objective was to accomplish the will of his Father in heaven (John 4:34; 5:30; 6:38–39)

▶ He came, he said, not to be served, but to serve and give his life away as a sacrifice (Mark 10:45). His stated purpose was "to seek and save those who are lost" (Luke 19:10, NLT).

▶ To what end? To accomplish his announced intention to "build my church" (Matthew 16:18).

Life Application

An important part of discipleship is learning how to apply God's truths to your life. Below are just a few ways you can start thinking about what you've learned and apply it to your daily life.

1. Memorize our memory verse, Mark 10:45.

2. Work through the personal "Your Inventory of Abilities that Meet Needs" list on pages 65–66. What are some of the unique ways God has gifted you and/or placed desires within you to make an eternal difference? How might your answers serve as clues to the role you can play in serving Christ and making disciples?

3. Wrestle with one or two of these questions:

   ▶ What from the "Your Inventory of Abilities that Meet Needs" list surprises you? What avenue of serving God or making disciples would you like to explore more fully?

   ▶ Who are the people who have poured into your life—and helped you grow spiritually? How exactly did they do that?

   ▶ Do you have people into whom you are intentionally investing? Who? What does that look like?

   ▶ What would you say to the person who said, "I really want to grow in my faith, but I'm honestly not that interested in 'serving others.'" Or "I'm not qualified to 'minister' to someone else"?

   ▶ The New Testament teaches that God gives *each* and *every* believer in Christ *spiritual abilities* for accomplishing His work in the world (Romans 12; 1 Corinthians 12; Ephesians 4; 1 Peter 4). Experience further reveals that we all have *natural talents* and *unique passions* for making a difference. Do you agree that God will get the most glory, and we will feel most fulfilled if we minister, serve, and make disciples in ways that use our strengths and involve our interests? Why or why not?

Your Inventory of Abilities that Meet Needs

I believe God has *gifted* me to *(check all that apply)* . . .

❑ **Invite/recruit:** Reaching out to others to encourage their participation in relationships, groups, or events where they can grow spiritually and serve others

❑ **Meet/greet/host people:** Taking the initiative to show hospitality and make people feel welcomed and accepted

❑ **Pray for others:** The consistent holy habit of interceding for others

❑ **Organize/administrate/plan:** Bringing order to chaos, and handling details to accomplish a task or pull off an event

❑ **Show compassion:** Noticing hurting people and moving into their lives to tangibly demonstrate the love of Christ

❑ **Listen/counsel:** Taking time to hear the hearts and hurts of others and help them process what God is saying to them

❑ **Mentor others:** Coming alongside others so as to share knowledge, model life skills, and/or impart wisdom gleaned from ones' own successes and failures

❑ **Be crafty:** The ability to sew, knit, decorate, etc. to produce beautiful objects for events that bless others

❑ **Shepherd others:** A knack for coming alongside those who are encountering difficulties in life to comfort and guide

❑ **Train others in specific skills:** The ability to pass on the info and skills needed for success in a specific area of life

❑ **Find and distribute important facts:** Making sure people have the information they need to make progress in the faith

❑ **Do construction:** The ability to take basic materials and, using the proper tools, safely build needed items

❏ **Inspire others through artistic endeavors:** The ability to sing, play an instrument, paint, sculpt, write, act, dance, make videos, or take pictures and in that, to communicate God's truth creatively, beautifully and memorably

❏ **Encourage and motivate:** The rare ability to impart new hope and courage to those who have become discouraged

❏ **Share my faith:** The ability to effectively show and tell the good news of Christ's offer to forgive sin and give eternal life

❏ **Help with simple tasks:** The willingness to lend a hand with various projects or random needs that do not require special skills or expertise

❏ **Show mercy:** Demonstrating love, acceptance, and kindness to those who are filled with shame

❏ **Share or give:** Cheerfully donating one's time, energy, effort, resources and/or funds to worthwhile kingdom efforts

❏ **Lead teams/groups/projects:** Guiding people to the successful and satisfying completion of a specific task

❏ **Provide technical and mechanical assistance:** The ability to keep gadgets and gizmos from breaking and/or to fix them when they do stop working

❏ **Lead discussions/teach:** Serving as a catalyst for helping others understand and apply biblical truth

❏ **Cook or bake:** Serving Christ by serving enjoyable meals

CHAPTER 3:

The Basics That Guide a Disciple

Topic 8: The Bible

Understanding God's Living and Active Word

"For the word of God is alive and active.
Sharper than any double-edged sword, it
penetrates even to dividing soul and spirit,
joints and marrow; it judges the thoughts
and attitudes of the heart."

—Hebrews 4:12

Being a disciple means being a student. And being a student means learning. At a minimum, disciples need to know certain things about the Bible, God (Father, Son, and Holy Spirit), and the Church.

What does a devoted follower of Jesus need to understand and believe about the Bible?

The Bible is our primary source for information about God. Another word for receiving information about God is "revelation." Scholars speak of two kinds of revelation: *general* and *special*.

▶ By *general* revelation they mean God's Creation (Romans 1:18–21; Psalm 19); acts where God provides for the needs of all people (Acts 14:17; Psalm 107:9); or the conscience God gave all humans (Romans 2). All of

these point to the existence of God and his power.

▶ *Special* revelation refers, most commonly, to the Bible, God's written word. In the Bible, we see details about God's person and plan, and an explicit record of the teaching and actions of Christ, who is the living Word (John 1:1–18).

We will start with the Bible because it's the foundation of Judeo-Christian faith.

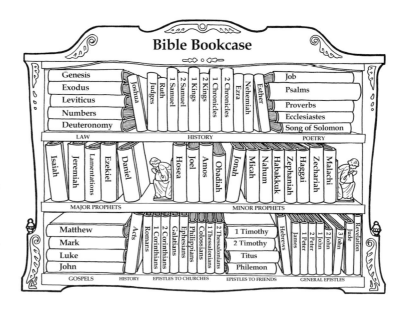

Bible Bookcase

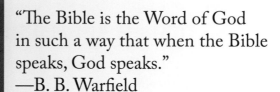

What's so special about the Bible?

In this topic, we'll look at what makes the Bible special: its *influence*, its claims to be of *divine origin*, and its *reliability*. We'll also discuss two additional characteristics of the Bible, that it is *authoritative* and *transformational*.

> "The Bible is the Word of God in such a way that when the Bible speaks, God speaks."
> —B. B. Warfield

From God to Us

Term	Meaning
Revelation	Can mean: (a) God's *act* of unveiling to the world truth about himself and his eternal plan, or (b) The *body of truth* that has been revealed by God. The Bible doesn't reveal *everything* about God to us (Deuteronomy 29:29). But it reveals all we need for life and godliness (1 Peter 1).
Inspiration	The process by which God's Spirit supernaturally guided the human authors of the Bible. Using their own unique personalities and styles, they composed and recorded God's message to mankind.
Inerrancy	The belief that the original writings of Scripture were without error (and to the extent that our modern translations accurately represent the original text, we have a trustworthy Bible).
Canonicity	The divine quality of the Old and New Testament writings given to them through God's inspiration. The leaders of the early church used certain agreed-upon criteria to distinguish "God-breathed," or God-inspired, documents from mere human writings. They then collected those divine writings into one book, our Bible.
Illumination	The special ongoing work of the Holy Spirit to enable God's people to comprehend and apply the written Word of God (Luke 24:44,45; 1 Corinthians 2:11–14). Illumination occurs when we have those "Aha!" moments, when "the light goes on." With God's help, we suddenly "see" the significance of a biblical truth and desire to apply it to our lives.

Bible Study

First, the Bible Is Special Because of Its INFLUENCE.

It's far and away the most published book in the history of the world. Billions of copies have been printed, with millions more distributed annually. Moreover, its values of right behavior, God's love, and forgiveness have positively shaped culture—acting as the driving force behind most humanitarian efforts, much scientific research, art, music, literature, and law—as well as advances in politics, education, treatment of women and children, labor and race relations, etc. However, its influence alone is not reason to trust it.

Second, the Bible Is Special Due to Its Claims To Be of DIVINE ORIGIN.

Some 3,800 times it features the phrases, "God said," or "Thus says the Lord." In other words, the Bible presumes to be the very Word of God! Critics protest that trying to make the case that the Bible is God's Word *by pointing to passages where the Bible claims to be God's Word* is circular reasoning. But consider this: In our courts of law, a person on trial is allowed to testify in his or her own behalf. Such testimony is then weighed in light of all the evidence. Why shouldn't the Bible be afforded this same courtesy?

1. Let's allow the Bible to speak for itself. Perhaps *the* classic statement in the Bible about the Bible is our memory verse for this session. "All Scripture is God-breathed and is useful for teaching, rebuking, correcting and training in righteousness, so that the servant of God may be thoroughly equipped for every good work" (2 Timothy 3:16–17).

    Jot down your initial, overall observations about this verse.

    _____

    _____

    _____

    _____

    ▶ "Scripture" (the Greek word is *graphe*) means "that which is written." In other words, Scripture is the writings of the Old and New Testaments.

    ▶ "God-breathed" expresses the idea of exhalation by God—that the Scripture is the product of the breath of God. God didn't breathe into existing human writings; rather, he inspired the original writings of Scripture to produce works that would reveal his character, works, and will. Sometimes God told the Bible writers the exact words to say (e.g., Jeremiah 1:9). Other times, he used their unique minds, vocabularies, cultures, and experiences—which accounts for the stylistic differences between the Bible books.

2. Another passage that boldly maintains divine authorship of Scripture is 2 Peter 1:16–21. There, Peter addressed the problem of certain false teachers who had come into the church; and charged that the apostles' gospel message was a mere human fable. Peter responded (NLT):

> [16] "For we were not making up clever stories when we told you about the powerful coming of our Lord Jesus Christ. We saw his majestic splendor with our own eyes [17] when he received honor and glory from God the Father. The voice from the majestic glory of God said to him, "This is my dearly loved Son, who brings me great joy." [18] We ourselves heard that voice from heaven when we were with him on the holy mountain.

> [19] "Because of that experience, we have even greater confidence in the message proclaimed by the prophets. You must pay close attention to what they wrote, for their words are like a lamp shining in a dark place—until the Day dawns, and Christ the Morning Star shines in your hearts. [20] Above all, you must realize that no prophecy in Scripture ever came from the prophet's own understanding, [21] or from human initiative. No, those prophets were moved by the Holy Spirit, and they spoke from God."

What do Peter's eyewitness words tell us about Scripture and the way it came to be?

_____

_____

_____

_____

Verses 16–18 describe the Transfiguration (see Mark 9:2–8), the glorious unveiling of Christ, the living revelation of God. Verse 19 then speaks of the written revelation of God and how it illuminates the darkness—our wrong thoughts and actions. Peter says we do well to pay close attention to it (especially in a world filled with so many bogus ideas).

In verse 20, the word "understanding" carries the idea of "unloosing." The idea is that the Scripture is not the result of individuals saying, "Hey, I'd like to 'unloose' a few of my own opinions and ideas." False prophets did that—spouting their own thoughts. But nothing the Biblical prophets wrote is the product of a human's own creativity or opinion.

> "The Bible is alive, it speaks to me; it has feet, it runs after me; it has hands, it lays hold on me."
> —Martin Luther

72

In verse 21, the verb "moved" is interesting. It was also used to describe a ship being driven by a strong wind (Acts 27:15,17). The sailors on board, experienced though they were, could not set the ship's course. They had to let the strong wind take the ship wherever it blew. The chapter portrays the sailors as active and involved, but the wind ultimately determined the destination of the ship.

So it was in the writing of Holy Scripture. Both God and humans were involved in the production of the Bible, but it happened in such a way that God was the ultimate author. He directed the writing and guaranteed the accuracy of it. There was human involvement, but no human agenda.

God-originated, God-breathed, and God-guided . . . *this* is what the Bible claims for itself! Like Jesus of Nazareth claiming to be God in the flesh—if this is true, it changes *everything*!

From these passages, we see that *devoted disciples of Jesus believed the Bible is divine.* It's not just any old book. It's God's Word to the world! It's not a book of rules. As someone has noted, it's a love letter from home! No wonder disciples are drawn to the Bible and want to pay attention to it!

3. Talk about a time when you felt like you'd been pierced by the truth and beauty of God's Word.

_____

_____

_____

Third, the Bible Is Special Because of Its RELIABILITY

Let's consider another factor that makes the Bible special: the overwhelming evidence for its reliability.

Evidence #1: The Trustworthiness of the Biblical Manuscripts

It's important to know that we do not have the original writings of Scripture. We have only

copies. But we have *thousands* of copies—more than 5,000 portions or fragments—and we have copies *close in date to the original writings.* And with all those copies (and thanks to the science of textual criticism) we have:

▶ the knowledge that the Jewish scribes who copied the Scriptures were *obsessed* with accuracy

▶ a very precise sense of the wording of the original documents.

As one would expect, scholars have found variations among some of the copies. Bible scholars are honest about these variations and point them out in study Bible notes. However, Princeton's Bruce Metzger, perhaps the preeminent New Testament scholar of the 20th century, concluded that after 2,000 years of being copied, only 40 of the 20,000 lines of the New Testament are debatable. More importantly, none of these variances affects the basic tenets of the Christian faith. Our modern-day Bibles are *very* credible—far more so than any other historical document of antiquity.

Evidence #2: The Unity of the Scriptures

The Biblical writings were composed by some 40 authors in three languages (Hebrew, Aramaic, and Greek) over a period of 1,500 years. Yet it really is one book with a flowing story and a consistent message.

▶ Throughout its pages, the Bible champions belief in one God in times and regions where polytheism (belief in many gods) was the norm.

▶ The Old Testament foreshadows the New Testament; the New completes the story of the Old.

▶ From start to finish, the Bible calls people to live by faith in God's grace, whereas every other religion depicts humans working to earn God's favor.

Evidence #3: The Preservation of the Scriptures

The Bible has endured through the centuries despite multiple attempts to burn it, ban it, and systematically eliminate it. No other book has survived such hatred and opposition.

> "Truth can and does include approximations, free quotations, language of appearances, and different accounts of the same event so long as they do not contradict."
> —Charles Ryrie

Evidence #4: The Fulfilled Prophecies of the Bible

The Bible contains almost two thousand prophesies: 1,239 prophecies are found in the Old Testament and 578 prophecies are in the New Testament, giving us a total of 1,817. Many of these prophecies are yet to be fulfilled, but hundreds pertaining to Christ's first coming—

many given in excruciating detail—happened exactly as they were foretold! Mathematicians have demonstrated the logical impossibility of that many lucky guesses.

Evidence #5: The Archaeological Record

For most of the modern era, secular scholars have scoffed at many of the Bible's historical and geographical claims. But archaeologists continue to uncover evidence of the Bible's accuracy. At one time, the Hittites were considered an imaginary people found only in the Bible, but in the 1880s archaeological evidence of the Hittites was discovered. Skeptics have also doubted the existence of a real King David, until the Tel Dan inscription was discovered in 1993. Written by the enemies of Israel, this tablet documented the "House of David" as existing long ago.

From this and additional evidence you can research on your own, we see that *the Bible is reliable*. As disciples of Jesus, we can fully trust it—textually, historically, theologically, and spiritually.

> "I would say that the essential difference between the Bible and every other book is that the other books are meant to be read, whereas the Bible is truly meant to read us."—Richard Owens Roberts

Additional Characteristics of the Bible

AUTHORITATIVE

Logically it follows that if the Bible is divine (from God and not humans) and true, we don't have the right to twist it to make it say what we want it to say. We need to be very careful that we've interpreted it correctly. We don't get to explain away teachings that "offend" us. Instead of us sitting in judgment of the Bible, it has the right to judge us.

In other words, the Bible is authoritative, and Jesus' disciples are commanded to submit to its teaching.

This means that for the disciple of Jesus who faces a tough moral choice, the bottom-line issue isn't his or her feelings, what the majority thinks is right according to the latest *Time* or CNN poll, what laws the government has passed, what rulings the Supreme Court has issued, the latest findings of the scientific community, what one's Uncle Louie believes, or what some expert on a talk-show said. The issue is, "What does the word of God say?"

4. Take a few minutes to read and ponder these verses that speak about God's Word. Below each verse, write down what insights you can take away from the passage.

    ▶ "I rejoice in your word like one who discovers a great treasure" (Psalm 119:162, NLT).

_____

_____

▶ "For the word of God is alive and powerful. It is sharper than the sharpest two-edged sword, cutting between soul and spirit, between joint and marrow. It exposes our innermost thoughts and desires." (Hebrews 4:12, NLT)

_____

_____

_____

▶ "So Jesus was saying to those Jews who had believed Him, "If you continue in My word, *then* you are truly disciples of Mine; and you will know the truth, and the truth will make you free." (John 8:31–32, NASB).

_____

_____

_____

TRANSFORMATIONAL

We would be remiss to end this study without talking about the life-changing power of the Scripture. Millions of people over the centuries have pointed to the Bible as the basis for their changed lives!

The story is told of a South Sea islander during World War II who proudly showed his Bible to an American G.I.

"We've outgrown that sort of thing," the soldier smirked.

"It's a good thing *we* haven't," the native replied. "If it weren't for this book I would have killed and eaten you by now."

The Scripture says, and a mountain of evidence and experience shows, that the Bible is alive. Its truth can pierce the hardest heart and heal the most broken soul. No other book can renew our minds and bear supernatural fruit.

Take-Home Reflections

For all these reasons, disciples of Jesus believe:

The Bible is the trustworthy Word of God, the final authority for our beliefs and our behavior.

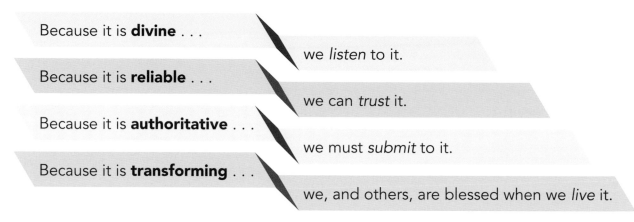

Because it is **divine** . . . we *listen* to it.

Because it is **reliable** . . . we can *trust* it.

Because it is **authoritative** . . . we must *submit* to it.

Because it is **transforming** . . . we, and others, are blessed when we *live* it.

To reject the historic, orthodox Christian teaching about the Word of God is . . .

▶ To see the Bible as a human document on a par with other great human documents—inspiring, but *not* inspired.

▶ To regard the Bible as errant and fallible and *not* worthy of one's full trust.

▶ To consider the Bible as one more option among many sources of potential counsel and wisdom—and *not* one's final authority.

> "Many who claim to believe the Bible from cover to cover have never read it from cover to cover."
> —Rick Warren

Life Application

An important part of discipleship is learning how to apply God's truths to your life. Below are just a few ways you can start thinking about what you've learned and apply it to your daily life.

1. Memorize our memory verse, Hebrews 4:12.

   "For the word of God is alive and active. Sharper than any double-edged sword, it penetrates even to dividing soul and spirit, joints and marrow; it judges the thoughts and attitudes of the heart."

2. Know how to answer the common questions about the Bible's reliability. Get and read the pamphlet called *Why Trust the Bible*. Find it here: www.rose-publishing.com/Why-Trust-the-Bible-pamphlet-P263.aspx

3. Read carefully these words of an unknown writer and on another sheet of paper journal your reaction:

> "This Book is the mind of God, the state of man, the way of salvation, the doom of sinners, and the happiness of believers. Its doctrines are holy, its precepts are binding, its histories are true, and its decisions are immutable.

> "Read it to be wise, believe it to be safe, practice it to be holy. It contains light to direct you, food to support you, and comfort to cheer you. It is the traveler's map, the pilgrim's staff, the pilot's compass, the soldier's sword, and the Christian's character. Here paradise is restored, heaven opened, and the gates of hell disclosed. Christ is its grand subject, our good its design, and the glory of God its end. It should fill the memory, rule the heart, and guide the feet. Read it slowly, frequently, prayerfully. It is a mine of wealth, a paradise of glory, and a river of pleasure. Follow its precepts and it will lead you to Calvary, to the empty tomb, to a resurrected life in Christ—yes, to glory itself, for eternity."

4. Wrestle with one or two of these questions:

   ▶ What criticism do you hear from others about the Bible? What is their reasoning? In two thousand years of church history, Christians have found answers to almost every objective question. You may want to find someone to point you in the right direction to find answers to criticisms you or someone else has about the Bible.

   ▶ What do we know about God from the Scripture that we could not know any other way? What about Jesus' life, death, and ministry?

   ▶ What truth or thought from this study has had the greatest impact on you? Why?

   ▶ Have you ever read the entire Bible? Why or why not? You can read the Bible in a year if you read three chapters a day, Monday through Saturday, and four chapters on Sundays.

   ▶ What's your favorite book or chapter in the Bible? Why? How has it made a difference in your life?

   ▶ What command in the Bible have you been ignoring?

Topic 9: God

Thinking Rightly About the Creator

"Now this is eternal life: that they know
you, the only true God, and Jesus Christ,
whom you have sent."

—John 17:3

A few years ago, a Canadian by the name of Kyle MacDonald conducted an experiment. Inspired by the popular children's game "Bigger and Better," he began with one red paperclip and started swapping. He traded the red paper clip for a fish-shaped pen. Next he exchanged that for something larger and nicer. More swaps followed. After one year and 14 transactions, MacDonald ended up with a two-story house in Saskatchewan. From a red paper clip to a house! It's a true story.

This is a lesson about swapping something far more important than mere objects. Our goal here is to search the Bible and also our hearts. Where we find wrong thoughts and ideas about the one true God, we want to swap them out for accurate beliefs.

Why is this so important?

Perhaps A. W. Tozer, the author of the classic book *The Knowledge of the Holy*, put it best: "What comes into our minds when we think about God is the most important thing about us. . . . We tend by a secret law of the soul to move toward our mental image of God. . . . Were we able to

extract from a man a complete answer to the question, 'What comes into your mind when you think about God?' we might predict with certainty the spiritual future of that man."

> "Without doubt, the mightiest thought the mind can entertain is the thought of God, and the weightiest word in any language is its word for God."—A. W. Tozer

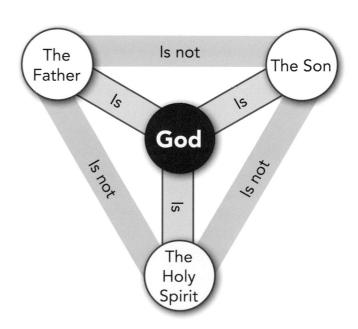

THE BASICS THAT GUIDE A DISCIPLE

What Comes Into Your Mind When You Think About God?

I see God as . . .	Never		Sometimes				Constantly		
An infinite Introvert Aloof, shy, seemingly reluctant to engage me	1 2	3 4	5 6	7 8	9 10				
Loving caring Father Loving, accepting, wise, protective, trustworthy	1 2	3 4	5 6	7 8	9 10				
The CEO of Creation Preoccupied, business-like, busy running the universe	1 2	3 4	5 6	7 8	9 10				
An impersonal Force Vague, mysterious entity/all-encompassing energy	1 2	3 4	5 6	7 8	9 10				
A heavenly genie, Santa Claus, or grandfather Good-natured, generous, winks at my indiscretions	1 2	3 4	5 6	7 8	9 10				
An impossible-to-please coach, referee, or cop Always ready to bust me for my "poor performance"	1 2	3 4	5 6	7 8	9 10				
The angry—perhaps sadistic—judge of the universe Cold, cruel, always glad to zap or smite sinners	1 2	3 4	5 6	7 8	9 10				
Motherly and kind The mother of life and nurturer of all things	1 2	3 4	5 6	7 8	9 10				

Question: If God employed 66 books and 1,139 chapters of the Bible to reveal his character and works, how can we "do justice" to such a monumental topic in one short lesson?

Answer: We *can't!* But hopefully we *can* at least whet our appetite for *theology*—"the study of God."

As we begin this exploration of what a devoted follower of Jesus needs to know about **God**, let's mention a critical theological belief that undergirds the Christian faith—the belief that God is **triune in nature.**

Since the early days of the church, Christians have held to the belief that the one true God exists externally as three persons, Father, Son, and Holy Spirit, and that each person is fully God.

Why Do Christians Believe in the Trinity?

▶ The Bible declares that God is one (Deuteronomy 6:4).

▶ The Bible calls three distinct, divine persons God: The Father (1 Corinthians 1:3), the Son (Hebrews 1:6–8), and the Spirit (Acts 5:3–4).

▶ More than sixty Bible passages mention these three divine persons together.

This diagram is a visual representation of the essential biblical doctrine of the Trinity.

In this lesson we will focus on just the first person of the Trinity, God the Father.

Bible Study

Like a divine photo album, the Scripture includes many great glimpses of God the Father. We could almost close our eyes, open the Bible at random, and point. Whatever page our finger landed upon would reveal something of God's character. But for a vivid snapshot of God in just a few verses, it's hard to beat Psalm 103 (written by David).

Take a few moments right now to read the entire psalm thoughtfully.

1. Now, look at verses 3, 9, 10, 12. What do they say about us and about what God does for his people?

_____

_____

_____

_____

_____

_____

The word "sins" (verse 10) comes from a Hebrew verb that means to "miss the mark." It conveys the idea of moral failure. "Iniquities" (also in verse 10) is from a verb that means to "twist or distort or bend." These are the twisted acts, the wrong behaviors of which we are all guilty.

Verse 12 mentions our "transgressions." This word conveys the idea of "rebellion." This is where we intentionally cross lines we're not supposed to cross. This is willful rejection of God's authority. Such actions result in a fractured relationship. And we did that, not God.

It's not a pretty picture of humanity: moral failure, twisted acts, high-handed rebellion . . . Elsewhere, the Bible makes it clear that what we deserve for our disobedience is death (Romans 6:23). Yet, note the stunning statement in Psalm 103:10, God does *not* treat us as our sins deserve.

In verse 3, David says God *forgives*. This is the idea of "pardon." In verse 12 we see his gracious removal of our sin, "as far as the east is from the west." The idea here is of absolute removal.

In short, we see here the stunning truth that God is **Forgiving**! The *f* in "forgiving" is the first letter in "Father," and helps us form an acrostic in this study.

Human beings are not very forgiving. Often we can't forgive ourselves, but God forgives and he forgives us *completely*.

2. What makes divine forgiveness difficult for your head to believe and your heart to embrace?

_____

_____

_____

_____

3. Now, look again at Psalm 103 verses 4, 8, 11, and 17. What attribute of God is mentioned in each of these verses and how is it described?

_____

_____

_____

_____

David mentions the love of God four times. Much more than mere sentiment, this is God's lavish, loyal, covenant-keeping love. The Hebrew word is *chesed* (kheh'-sed), often translated "lovingkindness." *Chesed* is God's never-ending commitment to be for his people, and pursue them in order to care for and bless them—even when they are in a pitiful state.

We see here that our heavenly father is **Abounding in love.** Perhaps you need to swap out some wrong ideas or beliefs about God—for example, the idea that he abounds in anger, indifference, or cruelty—for this eternal, life-altering truth?

4. Look again at verses 4, 8, and 13. There's an idea that pops up in each of those verses (two times in verse 13). What is it and what does it mean?

_____

_____

_____

_____

In the Old Testament, the word translated "compassion" is almost identical to the Hebrew word for "womb," which leads some Bible scholars to believe that the word is meant to call to mind the depth of feeling that a mother feels for the newborn child who has just come from her womb.

82

David uses that word here of God, calling him a *compassionate father.* This means God's heart goes out to His children who are helpless and vulnerable, in trouble or hurting.

You can probably think of many times in your life when your heart was broken by seeing someone suffer. Maybe your stomach was in knots, or you felt punched in the gut (which is actually the idea behind the New Testament word "compassion"—it's literally a "guts" word). Maybe with a hurting loved one you thought or even said, "I wish it were me suffering instead of you."

5.   Think about and then write down your reaction to this statement: *If we, as imperfect and selfish people, have such tender feelings, how compassionate is our perfect God?*

_____

_____

_____

_____

This snapshot of God in Psalm 103 shows us that our heavenly father is **Tender.**

6.   How does this square with the way you think and feel about God?

_____

_____

_____

_____

Let's review: According to Psalm 103, God is forgiving, abounding in love, tender, and full of compassion. Let's see what else Psalm 103 tells us about God. Re-read verses 8–9, 11, 13, and 17.

7.   Verses 8–9 mention the reality of God's *anger.* And verses 11, 13, and 17 speak of "the fear of the Lord." Why would God be angry? Why should people fear the Lord?

_____

_____

_____

_____

That phrase "fear of the Lord" suggests "jaw-dropping awe" or "breathtaking reverence."

As you read through the Bible, you'll notice that whenever people encounter God, fearful awe is *always* the response. They fall on their faces. They tremble. Their hearts almost stop! Invariably, they speak of God's shattering holiness. Which is exactly what David mentions in verse one: Did you see it? "Praise the LORD, O my soul; all my inmost being, praise his *holy name.*"

In this concise picture of God the Father that is Psalm 103, we see that God is **Holy**.

8. How would you explain the concept of God's holiness to a friend with little or no religious background?

_____

_____

_____

_____

A truth we can extract from these verses is that, God, because he *is* holy, gets angry over sin. Because God is absolute purity and there's no defect in his essential nature, sin is an affront to him.

▶ It wrecks the world he has made.

▶ It damages caring relationships between people, hurting the creatures he loves.

▶ It is a rejection of his kingship over the universe.

Many people speak of God as though he is just a magnified amalgamation of mankind's best features. He's like us, only bigger, more powerful, and definitely more "religious." How might this explain irreverence toward God or a casual attitude about sin?

9. Re-read Psalm 103:14–17. They contrast man and God. How so? What is the psalmist David telling us about God?

_____

_____

_____

_____

We are not long for this world, David says. Not only are we temporary, we live in a world where nothing endures for long:

▶ People and civilizations fade away.

▶ Things and situations constantly change.

▶ Good times don't last.

What a great comfort to remember that our Father in heaven is the One Great Constant:

▶ He doesn't age and lose his physical or mental capacities.

▶ He has always been and he will always be.

▶ God is timeless. He isn't going anywhere.

This gives us security. That's another really comforting truth . . . God is **E**ternal.

10. Look at verses 19–21. How is God pictured there?

_____

_____

_____

_____

_____

Verses 19 says he "established his throne." The verb David uses is a Hebrew word that means "be firm." It conveys the idea of stability. It means to be unshakable. Seated on a throne in heaven, served by angel armies who carry out his perfect will. This implies royal dignity, sovereignty over the universe. In other words, God has dominion. He is in charge. And if he reigns over the universe, then surely he reigns over our lives.

That's the last detail we can take away from this brief look at Psalm 103, one scriptural snapshot of God. He is **R**uling the universe.

David points out much truth about God in this psalm. He notes that God is:

▶ **F**orgiving

▶ **A**bounding in love

▶ **T**ender

▶ **H**oly

▶ **E**ternal

▶ **R**uling the universe.

Look down that list and notice what those things reveal about God. Do you see it? God is a F-A-T-H-E-R. He's our perfect heavenly Father!

Here's the bottom-line: Psalm 103 is about swapping. When life is confusing and/or hard, when we're not sure what to think, David reminds us that we have a choice. We can settle for murky, subjective feelings about God or we can swap all that for what God has clearly revealed about himself.

David would urge us to make the swap. "Instead of choosing to doubt or despair . . . because of *what* is happening (or might happen) in your life, choose to focus on the one *who* has you. Focus on your heavenly Father."

In a nutshell, disciples of Jesus believe:

God is the Creator and Judge of all—and He's the loving Father of those who put their faith in Christ.

Why does the thought of God as a heavenly *Father* leave so many people cold?

All earthly fathers are imperfect. And sadly, some are downright evil or sadistic. Many people have a tendency to think of God as a kind of heavenly version of their own earthly dad. So, for example, if your father was or is distant and stern, you may subconsciously assume God is like that. This is a natural tendency—for us to project the qualities of our human fathers onto God.

Others are put off by the term "Father" because they see it as chauvinistic to refer to God in masculine terms only. But does the term "Father" necessarily mean that God is exclusively masculine in his nature or that all things feminine are somehow second-rate? Not at all!

Genesis 1 tells us that God created *both* male and female humans "in His image." Furthermore, in several places in Scripture, God is portrayed in terms that we might typically regard as feminine. For instance, he is described as having given birth to Israel (Deuteronomy 32:18). And he is likened to a mother showing compassion to a nursing child (Isaiah 49:15) and to a mother comforting a child (Isaiah 66:13). Jesus even used the image of a mother hen gathering its chicks to express his affection for the people of Jerusalem.

Yet, even given all that, it's important to recognize that Jesus, endowed with divine wisdom and a comprehensive human vocabulary said, "Pray like this: 'Our *Father* in heaven . . .'"

Take-Home Reflections

God's Attributes at-a-Glance

Developing a deeper understanding of God begins with learning about his attributes—the essential qualities that make up his nature. The Bible overtly mentions or describes all sorts of things that are true of God. This is not an exhaustive list. For example, it doesn't mention that God is: Spirit, merciful, gracious, patient, faithful, or jealous. But it will at least start you thinking about who God is and what he is like.

God is . . .	Scripture	Definition	Implication for your life
Eternal	Gen. 21:33 Ps. 90:2 Rev. 1:8	God is outside of and unbounded by time.	
Good	Ex. 33:19 Ps. 145:9	God is perfectly benevolent, merciful and gracious to his creatures.	
Holy	1 Peter 1:16 1 John 1:5	God is perfect—wholly set apart and separate from all sin and evil.	
Immutable	Ps. 102:27 Mal. 3:6 James 1:17	God is unchanging and unchangeable in his being.	
Infinite	1 Kings 8:27 Ps. 145:3 Acts 17:24	God is without ends or limits.	
Just	Acts 10:34–35; 17:31 Rom. 2:11	God is absolutely fair. He does not show partiality. He maintains perfect moral standards	
Loving and forgiving	Ps. 103:17 Eph. 2:4–5 1 John 4:8, 10	God seeks the highest good of his creatures at his own infinite cost.	
Omnipotent	Matt. 19:26 Rev. 19:6	God is all-powerful. Nothing can or will thwart his will.	
Omnipresent	Ps. 139:7–12 Jer. 23:23–24	God is present everywhere.	
Omniscient	Ps. 139:1–4; 147:4–5	God knows all things (actual and possible).	
One	Deut. 6:4 1 Cor. 8:6	God is unique. He alone is God. He is indivisible in his essence.	
Sovereign	Eph. 1:4–14, 21	God is the supreme ruler of the universe, independent of any authority outside himself.	

God is . . .	Scripture	Definition	Implication for your life
Transcendent	Ps. 13:1 Isa. 8:17	God is separate from and beyond the universe. He is above our intelligence and understanding.	
Triune	Eph. 4:4–6 Heb. 1:6–8 Acts 5:3–4	God eternally exists as, Father, Son, and Holy Spirit, and each person is fully God.	
True	John 14:6; 17:3	God advances and confirms that which is true; his Word is trustworthy.	

Life Application

An important part of discipleship is learning how to apply God's truths to your life. Below are just a few ways you can start thinking about what you've learned and apply it to your daily life.

1. Memorize our memory verse, John 17:3.

2. Read carefully these words of J. I. Packer, author of *Knowing God,* and on another sheet of paper journal your reaction:

    "The stress of the [New Testament] is not on the difficulty and danger of drawing near to the holy God, but on the boldness and confidence with which believers may approach Him. . . . To those who are Christ's, the holy God is a loving Father; they belong to his family; they may approach Him without fear, and always be sure of His fatherly concern and care. This is the heart of the New Testament message."

3. Wrestle with one or two of these questions:

    ▶ What attribute(s) of God do you find most difficult to comprehend? Why do you think you have difficulty with these descriptions of God?

    ▶ The Scriptures portray God variously as a: loving Father, righteous Judge, strong Tower/Fortress/Refuge/Rock, reigning King, merciful Helper, faithful Shepherd. Thinking about your life lately, which of these images of God resonates most deeply with you? Why do you think that is so?

    ▶ When in your life have you felt closest to God? What were the circumstances of your life at the time?

    ▶ In Mark 14:36, Jesus called God "Abba, Father". *Abba* is an Aramaic word for "father" that suggests extreme intimacy (Romans 8:15 and Galatians 4:6). It is like our English word "Daddy." How does this square with your experience with God?

Topic 10: Jesus

The Essential Truth About Christ

"For in Christ all the fullness of the Deity
lives in bodily form."

—Colossians 2:9

We are exploring what it means to be a disciple (or follower) of Jesus Christ. A disciple is a person who follows Jesus—to *know* Jesus and his teaching; to *grow* more like Jesus; and to *go* for Jesus, serving others and making new disciples.

Discipleship isn't a short course; it's a lifelong journey. It involves three aspects:

▶ a "learning" part—knowing and believing certain truths

▶ a "character" aspect—undergoing genuine transformation from the inside out

▶ a "serving" component—serving God and others

Thinking about *what disciples believe*, let's turn our focus to Jesus.

Who is he? Is Jesus truly God's son? Why do hundreds of millions of people worldwide claim allegiance to him? What do we know about him, really? More importantly, what do we *need* to know and believe about him, in order to follow him?

Let's look first at the *nature* of Jesus. Then, during our Bible Study, we'll examine the *life* of Jesus.

The Nature of Jesus Christ

For two millennia, people have argued and puzzled over Jesus. Was he merely human? Was he divine? Could he really have been the Creator walking among his creation? Here's what the Bible says: Jesus was both God and Man.

The Humanity of Jesus	The Deity of Jesus
He was a direct descendant of King David Matthew 1:1	**Isaiah prophesied the Messianic child to be born would be "mighty God"** Isaiah 9:6
Mary, a human woman, was his mother Matthew 1:18; Galatians 4:4	**He himself claimed a unique relationship with God the Father** Matthew 11:27
He felt hunger Mark 11:12	**He claimed the authority to forgive sins** Mark 2:5-7
He got tired John 4:6	**The apostle John, Jesus' most intimate earthly friend, called him God** John 1:1
He experienced stress Matthew 26:38	**He claimed and demonstrated authority over death** John 2:19
He had a fleshly, touchable human body John 1:14; Luke 7:38; cf. 1 John 1:1	**He claimed to be from heaven and sent by God** John 3:13; 6:38, 13:3; 17:8
He felt human grief John 11:35	**He called God his father, making himself equal with God** John 5:18
He ate and drank Luke 7:34	**He called himself by the name God used to reveal himself to Moses** John 8:58
He slept Mark 4:38	**He claimed his death was his choice, not the result of a human plot** John 10:17
He sweat Luke 22:44	**He claimed oneness with the Father a statement the Jews regarded as blasphemous and tantamount to making himself out to be God.** John 10:30
He experienced thirst John 19:28	**He claimed that those who saw him, had essentially seen God the Father** John 14:9
He bled John 19:34	**He claimed ownership of all that God owns** John 16:15
He died 1 Corinthians 15:3	**He accepted Thomas referring to him as "My God"** John 20:28
The apostle Paul, who encountered Jesus, referred to him as a man 1 Timothy 2:5	**The apostle Paul referred to him as God, "in very nature" as the "image of the invisible God" and said that he possessed "all the fullness of God … fullness of Deity"** Philippians 2:5-11; Colossians 1:15-17, 19
The writer of Hebrews described Jesus as "fully human in every way" Hebrews 2:17	**The writer of Hebrews called Jesus "the radiance of God's glory and the exact representation of his being" and described him as unchanging** Hebrews 1:3, 13:8
He faced all common human temptations Hebrews 4:15	

A disciple reads these Scripture verses and concludes that Jesus was and is *God incarnate*—God in the flesh, God embodied, the unique God-Man. This is *not* to say he is two persons or two identities or two wills in one body. Jesus is *not* a hybrid being, half God and half man.

Historic, orthodox Christianity teaches that Jesus is one person with two distinct natures—a one-hundred percent divine nature and a one-hundred percent human nature. Theologians refer to this as the "hypostatic union":

Jesus Christ is fully God (the Son of God) and fully man (the son of Mary), inseparably united in one person forever.

How could this be? Theologian Charles Ryrie explains: "The virgin birth was [the] special miracle performed by the Third Person of the Trinity, the Holy Spirit, whereby the Second Person of the Trinity, the eternal Son of God, took to Himself a genuine, though sinless, human nature and was born as a man, without surrendering in any aspect, His deity."

So, incarnation means the Second Person of the triune Godhead stepped out of eternity into time, he "became flesh and made his dwelling among us" (John 1:14). The Creator entered his creation. Or, as one man quipped, "God moved into the neighborhood." This is a big deal! Theologian John Walvoord, in his book, *Jesus Christ Our Lord,* says, "The incarnation of the Lord Jesus Christ is the central fact of Christianity. Upon it the whole superstructure of Christian theology depends."

Because such an idea is supra-logical—beyond human ability to understand—and because some people are unable to live with not knowing, attempts have been made to "solve" this theological riddle of Christ's nature—leading to errors and heresies. Some of these attempts are shown in the diagram below. If you are curious, you can use the Internet to look up information about each of these "isms."

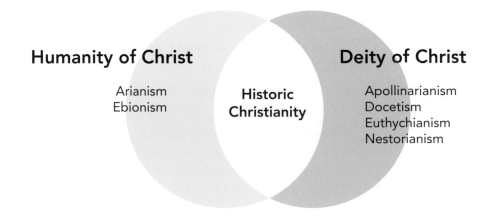

Humanity of Christ

Arianism
Ebionism

Historic Christianity

Deity of Christ

Apollinarianism
Docetism
Euthychianism
Nestorianism

Bible Study

Jesus asks us the most important question ever:

"Who Do You Say that I Am?"

And beliefs and opinions about him run the gamut.

- Legend or myth
- Archangel become man (Jehovah's Witness)
- Avatar or way-shower (New Age)
- Ethical teacher (Humanism)
- Miracle worker or healer
- Peasant revolutionary
- Spiritual mystic
- Prophet (Islam)
- Bringer of knowledge (Gnosticism)
- Controversial rabbi
- Man upon whom the divine Christ-spirit descended
- Manifestation of God (Bahai)
- Political martyr
- Victim of a religious perfect storm
- Populist preacher
- Hebrew shaman
- Religious reformer
- Freedom fighter for social justice
- Reincarnation of Horus—the son of the god Osiris
- Nazarene carpenter
- God-man
- Jewish messiah
- Son of God
- Savior of the world

1. What beliefs have you heard others express about Jesus?

_____

_____

_____

_____

2. What are your biggest questions about Jesus?

_____

_____

_____

_____

The Life of Jesus Christ

Almost everything we know of Christ's birth is eyebrow raising. We know his mother was a young, unwed mom who had pledged herself to marry a poor, Jewish carpenter from Nazareth (Matthew 13:55). There are claims of angelic visits, a miraculous conception, and feed trough for a baby crib.

On the big night, there was a surprise visit by a group of wild-eyed shepherds. Beyond that, Luke makes it clear that Jesus' birth did *not* generate much fanfare beyond a couple of elderly folks at the temple making a few startling statements about him a week or so later (Luke 2:25–38).

In his gospel, Matthew focuses on a delegation of foreign dignitaries who showed up at a later date (Matthew 2:1–12). They brought expensive gifts to Jesus because they viewed him as special, even royalty. Their arrival greatly disturbed the paranoid King Herod. Those sketchy details from Matthew and Luke are the extent of what we know about Jesus' entrance into the world.

We know even less about his childhood and youth, except that he was precocious (Luke 2:47), and that at some point he entered his stepfather's carpentry trade (Mark 6:3).

Most of what we know about Jesus happened *after* he began his public ministry. In his early thirties, the carpenter hung up his hammer and became a transient teacher within the Jewish faith community. He assembled some followers—disciples or students. He made claims of being the long-awaited Messiah—veiled at first, but over time his claims were more overt. His teachings were wild and provocative, revolutionary, and even life-altering.

If you've never read the gospels, it is strongly suggested that you do so. Reading the gospels leads to five conclusions about Jesus' life. Let's explore those conclusions.

Conclusion 1

Consider what Jesus said and did in the following situations:

> ▶ ***When a small group brought their paralyzed friend to him . . .***

"And Jesus seeing their faith said to the paralytic, 'Son, your sins are forgiven.'

"But some of the scribes were sitting there and reasoning in their hearts, 'Why does this man speak that way? He is blaspheming; who can forgive sins but God alone?'" (Mark 2:5–7, NASB)

3. Why were Jesus' listeners so shocked by his words here?

_____

_____

The story continues . . . .

"'But so that you may know that the Son of Man has authority on earth to forgive sins'—He said to the paralytic, 'I say to you, get up, pick up your pallet and go home.'

"And he got up and immediately picked up the pallet and went out in the sight of everyone, so that they were all amazed and were glorifying God, saying, 'We have never seen anything like this.'" (Mark 2:10–12, NASB)

4. What would have been your reaction had you witnessed this event in person?

_____

_____

_____

▶ *When he suddenly found himself in the middle of a sudden storm on the Sea of Galilee . . .*

"And there arose a fierce gale of wind, and the waves were breaking over the boat so much that the boat was already filling up. Jesus Himself was in the stern, asleep on the cushion; and they woke Him and said to Him, 'Teacher, do You not care that we are perishing?'

"And He got up and rebuked the wind and said to the sea, 'Hush, be still.' And the wind died down and it became perfectly calm." (Mark 4:37–39, NASB)

5. If you were one of the men on the ship with Jesus, how would you explain the experience to others?

_____

_____

_____

_____

▶ *When he happened upon a funeral procession . . .*

"Now as He approached the gate of the city, a dead man was being carried out, the only son of his mother, and she was a widow; and a sizeable crowd from the city was with her.

"When the Lord saw her, He felt compassion for her, and said to her, 'Do not weep.'

"And He came up and touched the coffin; and the bearers came to a halt. And He said, 'Young man, I say to you, arise!'

"The dead man sat up and began to speak. And *Jesus* gave him back to his mother." (Luke 7:12–15, NASB)

6. What do you make of such words and deeds? Journal your impressions here:

_____

_____

_____

Conclusion 1: Jesus lived an extraordinary life!

Conclusion 2

Now, consider these biblical statements by and about Jesus:

▶ "Can any of you prove me guilty of sin?" (John 8:46).

▶ "God made him who had no sin to be sin for us, so that in him we might become the righteousness of God" (2 Corinthians 5:21).

▶ "For we do not have a high priest who is unable to empathize with our weaknesses, but we have one who has been tempted in every way, just as we are—yet he did not sin" (Hebrews 4:15).

▶ "He committed no sin, and no deceit was found in his mouth" (1 Peter 2:22).

▶ "But you know that he appeared so that he might take away our sins. And in him is no sin" (1 John 3:5).

7. From these verses, what do you know about the nature and character of Jesus?

_____

_____

_____

_____

Conclusion 2: Jesus lived a sinless life!

Conclusion 3

For three years Jesus said unbelievable things. He did undeniable miracles. His words and works thrilled the masses . . . and infuriated the religious establishment. The Jewish scribes, Pharisees, and Sadducees saw Jesus as a problem at best, a heretic at worst. Working with the hated Roman authorities, they arrested and tried Jesus, and got him sentenced to death. On a Friday, in the spring of AD 33, Jesus was crucified. His followers were terrified. The "Jesus movement" appeared to be over.

Take a few minutes to read and ponder these verses that speak of Jesus' death:

"But he was pierced for our rebellion, crushed for our sins. He was beaten so we could be whole. He was whipped so we could be healed. All of us, like sheep, have strayed away. We have left God's paths to follow our own. Yet the LORD laid on him the sins of us all." (Isaiah 53:5–6, NLT)

"As Jesus was going up to Jerusalem, he took the twelve disciples aside privately and told them what was going to happen to him. 'Listen,' he said, 'we're going up to Jerusalem, where the Son of Man will be betrayed to the leading priests and the teachers of religious law. They will sentence him to die. Then they will hand him over to the Romans to be mocked, flogged with a whip, and crucified. But on the third day he will be raised from the dead.'" (Matthew 20:17–20, NLT)

> "I am trying here to prevent anyone saying the really foolish thing that people often say about Him: 'I'm ready to accept Jesus as a great moral teacher, but I don't accept his claim to be God.' That is the one thing we must not say. A man who was merely a man and said the sort of things Jesus said would not be a great moral teacher. He would either be a lunatic—on the level with the man who says he is a poached egg—or else he would be the Devil of Hell. You must make your choice. Either this man was, and is, the Son of God, or else a madman or something worse. You can shut him up for a fool, you can spit at him and kill him as a demon or you can fall at his feet and call him Lord and God, but let us not come with any patronizing nonsense about his being a great human teacher. He has not left that open to us. He did not intend to."—C. S. Lewis, *Mere Christianity*

▶ "Then some [the chief priests and the whole Sanhedrin] began to spit at him; they blindfolded him, struck him with their fists, and said, 'Prophesy!' And the guards took him and beat him." (Mark 14:65)

▶ "Those passing by were hurling abuse at Him, wagging their heads, and saying, 'Ha! You who *are going to* destroy the temple and rebuild it in three days, save Yourself, and come down from the cross!'" (Mark 15:29–30, NASB)

▶ "He was handed over to die because of our sins" (Romans 4:25, NLT)

▶ "Christ suffered for our sins once for all time. . . . He suffered physical death." (1 Peter 3:18, NLT)

▶ "Jesus Christ laid down his life for us." (1 John 3:16)

8. What details do these assorted passages reveal about the death of Christ?

_____

_____

_____

_____

Conclusion 3: Jesus died a gruesome death—for us!

Conclusion 4

Now read these two passages, describing what happened *after* Christ's crucifixion:

▶ "But very early on Sunday morning the women went to the tomb, taking the spices they had prepared. They found that the stone had been rolled away from the entrance. So they went in, but they didn't find the body of the Lord Jesus. As they stood there puzzled, two men suddenly appeared to them, clothed in dazzling robes.

"The women were terrified and bowed with their faces to the ground. Then the men asked, 'Why are you looking among the dead for someone who is alive? He isn't here! He is risen from the dead! Remember what he told you back in Galilee, that the Son of Man must be betrayed into the hands of sinful men and be crucified, and that he would rise again on the third day.'" Luke 24:1–7, NLT)

▶ "For I delivered to you as of first importance what I also received: that Christ died for our sins in accordance with the Scriptures, that he was buried, that he was raised on the third day in accordance with the Scriptures, and that he appeared to Cephas, then to the twelve. Then he appeared to more than five hundred brothers at one time, most of whom are still alive, though some have fallen asleep. Then he appeared to James, then to all the apostles. Last of all, as to one untimely born, he appeared also to me." (The apostle Paul writing in 1 Corinthians 15:3–8, ESV)

Just days after Jesus' gruesome death, a wild rumor began to sweep through Jerusalem. The followers of Jesus were suddenly, excitedly, and boldly claiming *Jesus of Nazareth had risen from the dead.* Sure enough, no one could find his body. Over the next month or so, more than 500 people claimed encounters with the risen Christ.

Despite threats to stop broadcasting this news and spreading the message of Christ—or else—the disciples of Jesus didn't stop. A new faith community, called the Church, sprang up. Flowing out of the ancient Jewish faith, this new way of knowing, serving, and loving God became known as "the way" of Jesus (Acts 9:2, 19:9, 23; 24:14, 22).

Conclusion 4: Jesus experienced a glorious resurrection!

Conclusion 5

9. In your heart and mind, which of the following is the most compelling evidence that Jesus rose from the dead?

    A. The empty tomb—in spite of its being guarded by Roman soldiers

    B. The number of eyewitnesses (including some who were hostile or skeptical—and others who were still alive when Paul wrote 1 Corinthians)

    C. The changed lives of the eyewitnesses

    D. The fact that the first Jewish believers changed their day of worship from the Sabbath (Saturday) to the first day of the week (Sunday)

    Why?

    _____

    _____

    _____

    _____

10. Lastly, consider these statements by and about Christ regarding the future:

    ▶ "So you also must be ready, because the Son of Man will come at an hour when you do not expect him." (Matthew 24:44)

    ▶ "And if I go and prepare a place for you, I will come again and will take you to myself, that where I am you may be also." (John 14:3, ESV)

    ▶ "Christ was sacrificed once to take away the sins of many; and he will appear a second time, not to bear sin, but to bring salvation to those who are waiting for him." (Hebrews 9:28)

    ▶ "For the Lord himself will come down from heaven, with a loud command, with the voice of the archangel and with the trumpet call of God, and the dead in Christ will rise first. (1 Thessalonians 4:16)

    ▶ "Look, I am coming soon, bringing my reward with me to repay all people

98

according to their deeds. I am the Alpha and the Omega, the First and the Last, the Beginning and the End." (Revelation 22:12, NLT)

Based on these passages, what are some of the reasons Jesus will return to earth? And what should be our mindset in this time of waiting?

_____

_____

_____

_____

Conclusion 5: Jesus is coming again some day!

Take-Home Reflections

30 Reasons Jesus Came to Earth

1. To fulfill the law	Matthew 5:17
2. To call sinners to repentance	Matthew 9:13; Mark 2:17; Luke 5:32
3. To seek the lost	Luke 19:10
4. To save the lost	Luke 19:10; 1 Timothy 1:15
5. To preach the gospel	Mark 1:38
6. To "explain" God, to reveal him to the world	John 1:18; 14:9
7. To bring judgment	John 9:39
8. To serve	Matthew 20:28; Mark 10:45
9. To give his life as a ransom for sin	Matthew 20:28; Mark 10:45
10. To save the world, not judge it	John 3:17; 12:47
11. To bring light, to enlighten people	John 1:9; 12:46
12. To give abundant life to the world	John 6:33, 50; 10:10
13. To do the will of the Father	John 6:38; Hebrews 10:9
14. Because he was sent by the Father	John 3:16; 6:39; 7:28; 8:42; 9:4; 16:28
15. To testify to the truth	John 18:37
16. To be a king	John 18:37
17. To suffer and die	John 12:27
18. To bring blessing to the world by turning people from sin to God.	Acts 3:26
19. To bestow power for new creatures to live new lives, as God intended	Romans 8:3–4
20. To confirm the ancient promises of God	Romans 15:8
21. To redeem sinners from the curse of the law and adopt them into God's family	Galatians 4:4–5
22. To be a merciful and faithful high priest for sinners	Hebrews 2:17
23. To atone for our sins	Hebrews 9:28; 1 Peter 2:24; 1 John 4:10
24. To give us an example to follow	1 Peter 2:21
25. To destroy the works of the devil	1 John 3:8
26. To break the power of the devil and cast him out	Hebrews 2:14; John 12:31
27. To proclaim good news to the poor	Luke 4:18
28. To set prisoners and the oppressed free	Luke 4:18
29. To give sight to the blind	Luke 4:18
30. To proclaim the year of the Lord's favor	Luke 4:18

For all these reasons, a disciple believes this about Jesus Christ:

Fully God and fully human, Jesus is the Lord of the universe and the Savior of all who trust in Him.

▶ He lived an extraordinary—and sinless—life!

▶ He died a gruesome death—for sinners!

▶ He experienced a glorious resurrection!

▶ He is coming again one day!

Life Application

An important part of discipleship is learning how to apply God's truths to your life. Below are just a few ways you can start thinking about what you've learned and apply it to your daily life.

1. Memorize our memory verse, Colossians 2:9:

    "For in Christ all the fullness of the Deity lives in bodily form."

2. Talk with a non-believing friend about this study of Christ. Decide together to have an honest dialogue, not a heated debate. Ask a lot of questions and listen. See what his or her objections are to the gospel—the good news of Jesus. Ask if you may share what you are learning. Do so in a humble, non-preachy way. Remember, it is not up to you to "save" anyone or change hearts and minds. That's the Holy Spirit's work (we'll talk about him in the next session). Make sure you pray for your friend before and after your discussion.

3. Wrestle with one or two of these questions:

    ▶ If you could choose to have been an eyewitness at any event in Christ's life here on Earth, which event would you choose? Why?

    ▶ Why do you think the religious leaders in Jesus' day got so angry with him, and the irreligious people were so attracted to him?

    ▶ Why is Jesus' sinlessness so crucial?

    ▶ After the resurrection, the disciples seemed to be galvanized and strengthened in their faith. Why do you think this is? How can we make the resurrection more real in our experience?

    ▶ What's one question that still bugs you about Jesus?

    ▶ When have you felt closest to Christ in your life? What were the circumstances?

THE BASICS THAT GUIDE A DISCIPLE

Topic 11: The Holy Spirit

Your Indwelling Counselor and Guide

"But the Advocate, the Holy Spirit, whom
the Father will send in my name, will
teach you all things and will remind you of
everything I have said to you."

—John 14:26

No doubt you've heard people speak of the "Holy Ghost." Maybe you were confused. If so, you're not alone. The "Holy Ghost" is another name for the "Holy Spirit." And if that isn't confusing enough, even among those who love Jesus and are seeking to follow him, there are questions and uncertainty about the person and work of the Holy Spirit.

Since a disciple of Jesus Christ needs a proper understanding of the Holy Spirit, let's turn our attention to the third person of the trinity.

> "You have a glorious helper—the Holy Ghost—and by his power you may accomplish miracles of holiness."—Charles Spurgeon

And since a disciple of Jesus needs to be able to use God's Word (2 Timothy 2:15), let's have you look up a number of Bible passages that reveal important truths about the nature and activity of the Holy Spirit.

Our prayer is that when we're done, you'll have less confusion and more understanding about the one, apart from whom, there can be no spiritual life and no spiritual growth.

Bible Study

The Deity of the Holy Spirit: God . . . or something less?

Look up the following passages and jot down in the central column what they teach about God's Holy Spirit. Then, in the right hand column, write down a personal application or implication of this truth.

Scripture reference	What the Bible says about the Spirit	What this means to us
Acts 5:3-4		
2 Corinthians 3:18		
Hebrews 9:14		
1 Corinthians 2:10		

The Personality of the Holy Spirit: Is the Spirit a "person" or not?

By saying that the Holy Spirit is a "person," we don't mean that he has a human body, but that he has the characteristics of personhood: intelligence, a moral code, rationality, a sense of self, emotions, and so on. Some say that the Holy Spirit is not a person at all, but instead a force or power—a "thing." Read the passages below and decide for yourself.

Scripture reference	What the Bible says about the Spirit	What this means to us
John 16:13-14		
Ephesians 4:30		
1 Corinthians 12:11		
Romans 8:26		

Further evidence of the personhood of the Holy Spirit is that the Bible tells us:

▶ the Holy Spirit possesses intelligence (Isaiah 11:2).

▶ the Holy Spirit is distinguishable from mere power (Acts 10:38; 1 Corinthians 2:4).

▶ the Holy Spirit loves (Romans 15:30).

▶ the Holy Spirit is included in the Trinitarian formula with the two persons of the "Father" and the "Son."

The Names of the Holy Spirit: What do they reveal?

This is not, by any means, a complete list, but consider what these names and titles tell us about the Holy Spirit.

Scripture reference	What the Bible says about the Spirit	What this means to us
Hebrews 10:29		
John 14:16, 26		
Romans 8:15		
1 Peter 1:10–11		

In the Upper Room (see John 13–17) on the night before his crucifixion, Jesus spoke important last words to his disciples and prayed for them. Among the reassurances he gave them was a promise to send "another Helper" (John 14:16, 26 NASB, ESV). The Greek word is *paraklete*, which literally means "one called alongside." The King James Version renders this word "Comforter"; the New International Version and the New Living Translation translate it "Advocate."

"Every time we say we believe in the Holy Spirit, we mean we believe that there is a living God able and willing to enter human personality and change it."—John Owen

1. What has been your understanding and experience of the Holy Spirit up until now?

_____

_____

_____

104

The Works of the Holy Spirit: What exactly does the Spirit do?

Here we want to get a broad, but accurate sense of the many ministries of the Holy Spirit. Look up the passages listed, and jot down what you discover about his work.

Scripture reference	What the Bible says the Spirit does	What this means to me
Genesis 1:1–3		
2 Peter 1:21		
Luke 1:35		
John 16:8		
Titus 3:5		
Ephesians 1:13–14		
Ephesians 2:18		
1 Corinthians 6:19		
1 Corinthians 12:13		
Romans 8:14		
Romans 8:16		
Romans 8:26–27		
Romans 15:16		
John 16:12–14		
1 Corinthians 12:7–11		
Acts 13:4		
Ephesians 5:18		
Galatians 5:16–17		
Galatians 5:22–23		
Philippians 3:3		

We see from this brief survey, that in the eternal plan of God, the Holy Spirit is instrumental to our salvation. He is the one who regenerates—gives new life to—those who are spiritually dead (John 3:3–7; Titus 3:5). He then moves into the lives of believers (1 Corinthians 6:19), giving us the power to live as we should. He seals us, guaranteeing us heaven (Ephesians 1:13) after this life. What's more he unites us permanently with Christ and his body (1 Corinthians 12:13).

The Spirit does so much more: leading, reassuring, convicting of sin, empowering, making us holy, praying for us. And in a confusing world, he serves as our ever-present teacher and guide. Look at what John 16:13–14 says:

"The Spirit of truth . . . will guide you into all truth. He will not speak on his own; he will speak only what he hears, and he will tell you what is yet to come. He will bring glory to me by taking from what is mine and making it known to you."

How amazing! We have not only been given the Bible—a treasure chest full of infinite Truth, but God has also given us a divine tutor to guide us in our study of God's Word. It is only as we diligently and humbly search the Word, under the leadership of the Spirit, that we find ourselves being directed and led in healthy, God-honoring ways.

> "I firmly believe that the moment our hearts are emptied of selfishness and ambition and self-seeking and everything that is contrary to God's law, the Holy Spirit will come and fill every corner of our hearts.
>
> "But if we are full of pride and conceit, ambition and self-seeking, pleasure and the world, there is no room for the Spirit of God. I also believe that many a man is praying to God to fill him, when he is full already with something else.
>
> "Before we pray that God would fill us, I believe we ought to pray that He would empty us. There must be an emptying before there can be a filling; and when the heart is turned upside down, and everything that is contrary to God is turned out, then the Spirit will come."
> —Dwight L. Moody

2. Followers of Jesus are called to "follow the Spirit's leading" in every part of life (Galatians 5:25, NLT). What does that process look like in your life?

_____

_____

_____

_____

3. What's the most surprising or most encouraging takeaway for you from this study of the Holy Spirit?

_____

_____

_____

_____

_____

_____

In a nutshell, disciples of Jesus believe:

The Holy Spirit is the third Person of the Trinity who initiates and superintends spiritual life and growth in those who trust Christ and follow him.

Take-Home Reflections

Examine the chart below which shows characteristics that each person in the Trinity share.

Divine Attributes	Father	Son	Holy Spirit
Eternal	Romans 16:26–27	Revelation 1:12–17	Hebrews 9:14
Creator of all things	Psalm 100:3	Colossians 1:15–16	Psalm 104:30
Omnipresent (capable of being all places at once)	Jeremiah 23:24	Ephesians 1:20–23	Psalm 139:7
Omnisicient (knows all things)	1 John 3:20	John 21:17	1 Corinthians 2:10
Wills and acts supernaturally	Ephesians 1:3–5	Matthew 8:3	1 Corinthians 12:7–11
Gives life	Genesis 1:11–31; see also John 5:21	John 1:4; see also John 5:21	Romans 8:10–11
Strengthens believers	Psalm 138:3	Philippians 4:13	Ephesians 3:16
Savior, salvation	Psalm 62:1	Acts 4:12	Titus 3:3-5

Life Application

An important part of discipleship is learning how to apply God's truths to your life. Below are just a few ways you can start thinking about what you've learned and apply it to your daily life.

1. Memorize our memory verse, John 14:26.

    "But the Advocate, the Holy Spirit, whom the Father will send in my name, will teach you all things and will remind you of everything I have said to you."

2. Read Ephesians 5:15–21 for an intriguing look at what a "Spirit-filled" Christian looks like. Jot down some of your impressions here:

    _____

    _____

    _____

    _____

    _____

    _____

    _____

3. Wrestle with one or two of these questions:

    ▶ What are some difficult decisions you are facing now? How can you rely on the Word of Truth (Colossians 1:5) and the Spirit of Truth (John 16:13) to find the guidance you need?

    ▶ What do these verses mean and how do we obey them? "Do not stifle the Holy Spirit" (1 Thessalonians 5:19, NLT), "and do not bring sorrow to God's Holy Spirit by the way you live" (Ephesians 4:30, NLT).

    ▶ What are some ways you sense the Spirit of God "convicting" you lately—trying to get your attention, seeking to get you to adjust your thinking or actions?

Topic 12: The Church

Realizing Your Need for Community

"I will build my church, and the gates of
Hades will not overcome it."

—Matthew 16:18

The late great Dorothy Sayers once said that God has suffered three great humiliations:

1. the incarnation—wherein the Infinite became finite

2. the cross—where Jesus took all the sin and shame of the world upon himself

3. the church— In an awesome act of self-denial, God entrusted his reputation to ordinary people

This last one was probably intended as a joke. But for those who've had bad experiences with organized religion, mentions of church aren't humorous.

There is something appealing about a privatized spirituality, an individual faith. And yet Jesus and his original followers said much about church. What's more, the gospels show that a disciple is one who follows Jesus by faith and *in community*. And let's not forget the exhortation given in Hebrews 10:25: "Not giving up meeting together, as some are in the habit of doing, but encouraging one another—and all the more as you see the Day approaching."

Let's look at it: What is this spiritual community called "the church" and why is it indispensable?

Bible Study

God's Revelation: *What Does the Bible Say About the Church?*

The first occurrence of the word "church" in the Bible is found in Matthew 16:18. Jesus is talking there with his disciples about the various opinions people have about him. Let's listen in on the conversation:

> He said to them, "But who do you say that I am?"
>
> Simon Peter answered, "You are the Christ, the Son of the living God."
>
> And Jesus said to him, "Blessed are you, Simon Barjona, because flesh and blood did not reveal *this* to you, but My Father who is in heaven.
>
> "I also say to you that you are Peter, and upon this rock I will build My church; and the gates of Hades will not overpower it." (Matthew 16:15–18, NASB)

You are probably aware there's been much debate throughout church history about how to understand this exchange.

▶ Roman Catholics believe this was Peter's installation as the first Pope.

▶ Protestants think Jesus was simply affirming Peter's faith and saying such strong belief in him is the foundation of the church.

Greek scholars note that Christ's literal words are, "You are *Petros* (the Greek word for "small rock" or "stone") and upon this *petra* (the Greek word that means "bedrock") I will build my church.

> "Healthy spiritual growth requires the presence of the other—the brother, the sister, the pastor, the teacher. A private, proudly isolated life cannot grow. The two or three who gather together in Christ's name keep each other sane. Spiritual growth cannot take place in isolation. It is not a private thing."—Eugene Peterson

1. What do you think this statement by Christ means?

_____

_____

_____

_____

Whatever one's view, 1 Corinthians 3:11 says "No man can lay a foundation other than the one which is laid, which is Jesus Christ." Clearly, Jesus Christ is the church's true and ultimate foundation—their *bedrock*.

Now, what about the word "church"? The Greek word is *ekklesia*—a compound word made up of the preposition that means "out from" and the verb that means "to call." So ekklesia means "to call out from." The word was used even in non-biblical literature to refer to a gathering or assembly of people.

In the New Testament it primarily refers to one of two things:

▶ A *local* assembly of Christians living in a particular locale—1 Corinthians 1:2; 1 Thessalonians 1:1; Revelation 1:11. We might think of this as the church— little "c."

▶ The *universal* body of believers—all Christ-followers everywhere, even in heaven (Matthew 16:18; Ephesians 1:22–23; Colossians 1:18; Hebrews 12:23). We could refer to this as the Church—big "C."

This simple chart illustrates the difference between the two:

The *Local* church	The *Universal* Church
Physical and visible, even if very small and informal—even two or three people gathered in his name, according to Matthew 18:20.	Spiritual and invisible
Attendees include believers and unbelievers	Only believers are members
Only the living	All those in Christ whether dead or alive
Many expressions	One entity
Assorted denominations	Transcends denominations
A portion of the body of Christ	The entire body of Christ
Assorted types of government	Jesus Christ is the true and only head

When did Jesus begin his "church building" project? Most Protestant Christians believe the Church officially began at Pentecost (Acts 2), when God poured out his Spirit on the disciples gathered in Jerusalem.

2. Take a few moments to read Acts 2. Note especially verses 42–47. What were the practices of this first group of Spirit-filled followers of Jesus?

This fast-growing assembly of Christ-followers was initially local, centered in Jerusalem, and almost completely Jewish. But as the disciples obeyed the command of Acts 1:8, they moved out into Gentile (non-Jewish) regions. Over time the church became a fascinating mix of people from different nations, races, religious backgrounds, and ethnicities.

The epistles of the New Testament give us little peeks into church organization and practice during the first century. But nowhere do we find even one verse that gives us a concise *definition* of "church."

Instead what we find in the New Testament are descriptive analogies. Writer Philip Yancey has pointed out that Judaism had always been simple to grasp. It was a distinct race of people, linked by blood ties and cultural tradition. But this new entity called *the church* was radically different. This explains all the metaphors in Scripture for the growing, worldwide assembly of people following the way of Jesus.

New Testament Metaphors of the Church

Church compared to	Scripture
An inheritance	"His glorious inheritance in his holy people" (Ephesians 1:18)
A new humanity	"His purpose was to create in himself one new humanity" (Ephesians 2:15)
God's household	"Consequently, you are no longer foreigners and strangers, but fellow citizens with God's people and also members of his household." (Eph. 2:19)
A building/temple	"Built on the foundation of the apostles and prophets, with Christ Jesus himself as the chief cornerstone. In him the whole building is joined together and rises to become a holy temple in the Lord." (Eph. 2:20–21)
A body (with Christ as head)	"And he is the head of the body, the church" (Colossians 1:18)
A living house	"You also, like living stones, are being built into a spiritual house" (1 Peter 2:5)
A chosen people	"But you are a chosen people" (1 Peter 2:9)
A holy, royal priesthood	"To be a holy priesthood . . . .a royal priesthood" (1 Peter 2:5, 9)
A nation set apart for God	"But you are . . . a holy nation, God's special possession" (1 Peter 2:9)
A flock	"Be shepherds of God's flock that is under your care" (1 Peter 5:2)
A pure bride	"Come, I will show you the bride, the wife of the Lamb." (Revelation 21:9; see also 2 Corinthians 11:2)

The Church is often referred to as a body. In 1 Corinthians 12, Paul develops this metaphor, saying, "The human body has many parts, but the many parts make up one whole body. So it is with the body of Christ. . . . Yes, there are many parts, but only one body. . . . some parts of the body that seem weakest and least important are actually the most necessary . . . if one part suffers, all the parts suffer with it, and if one part is honored, all the parts are glad (vss. 12, 20, 22, 26, NLT).

3. What strikes you about the image of the church as a "body"?

_____

_____

_____

_____

_____

4. In what ways is this a difficult metaphor for people in our culture[1] to embrace?

_____

_____

_____

_____

_____

5. Read Ephesians 2:20–21. What's the Church picture or comparison here and what does it suggest?

_____

_____

_____

_____

_____

---

1   A culture that ranks the worth of people and also champions the idea of doing one's own thing, going one's own way, blazing one's own trail, remaining first and foremost "an individual."

According to the apostle Paul, the Church is God's epic building project. Picture one of those great and gorgeous European cathedrals that, in some cases, took craftsmen centuries to assemble, stone by stone.

That's the idea here, only with the Church, God is the builder (and occupant!) and we believers are *living* stones (1 Peter 2). As we saw in the previous lesson about the Holy Spirit, God lives inside each of his children—dwelling in each individual part of his temple. But the world gets the clearest and best picture of God's love and beauty in the overall structure, which is the Church.

6. Read Ephesians 5:22–33. What does this analogy teach you about the Church?

_____

_____

_____

_____

_____

_____

We have all been to weddings. We've all seen a beautiful bride, making her grand appearance at the start of a lavish ceremony. We gasp! She is stunning! She's never looked this good in all her life!

Ah, but if you had seen her late the night before or earlier that morning—*before* the make-up and hair care crew arrived, and before she put on that exquisite dress—it would have been a different story.

That's a great picture of the destiny of the Church. The bride we see right now is—ahem—"not quite together." We are not as beautiful as we will be one day. Just you wait!

Our Response: *So what should we do in light of these truths?*

We need to THINK rightly about the Church.

Look carefully at the following chart:

What Church Is Not . . . and What It Is

The church is not	The church is
A physical building or a place	A living body and a people
A man-made organization	A divinely built organism
A group of people who "have it all together" and look down their noses at those who aren't as "together"	A group of broken but redeemed people who are full of love and concern and who don't play favorites and/or assign rank or worth to others
A self-serving enterprise	A God-serving and world-serving entity
A calendar of activities	A community devoted to ministry
A religious resort or club	A spiritual emergency room
Meant to be internally focused	Meant to be eternally and externally focused
Where I go to see how well others meet my needs	Where I go to see about serving others, trusting that my needs will get met in the process
A disposable option for Christians	The beloved bride of Christ

7. Based on those biblical observations, what mistake in thinking is present in each of the following situations?

    ▶ Saying, "I love Jesus, but I can't stand church!"

_____

_____

_____

▶ Driving past the building where you worship on Sunday and saying, "That's my church!"

_____

_____

_____

_____

_____

▶ Looking for a perfect church or picking a church solely on the services it offers.

_____

_____

_____

_____

▶ The children's rhyme that uses fingers and hands to say, "Here's the church and here's the steeple. Open the doors and see all the people."

_____

_____

_____

_____

▶ Saying, "I'm going to church."

_____

_____

_____

_____

Take-Home Reflections

We need to LIVE rightly as the church.

To summarize, disciples of Jesus believe the following about the Church:

The Church is the community of Christ-followers through which the triune God is carrying out his will on earth today.

Here's a quick list of some of the ways the Bible commands us, as members of Christ's body, to engage with our brothers and sisters in Christ individually, and with the people of God corporately. How well are *you* living out your calling? Check the appropriate box for each example.

Command	Consistently	Occasionally	Infrequently
Showing sacrificial love to fellow Christians John 13:34			
Honoring brothers and sisters in Christ Romans 12:10			
Living in harmony with fellow believers Romans 12:16			
Refusing to judge other Christians Romans 14:13			
Accepting other believers as Christ accepted me Romans 15:7			
Showing warmth to fellow disciples Romans 16:16			
Making the effort to be agreeable 1 Corinthians 1:10			
Encouraging other Christ followers 2 Corinthians 13:11			
Serving fellow believers Galatians 5:13			
Being patient and forgiving toward other believers Ephesians 4:2			
Working to preserve unity with other believers Ephesians 4:3			
Doing the work God has appointed for me Ephesians 2:10; 4:16			
Being truthful in my interactions with others Ephesians 4:25			
Trying to build others up Ephesians 4:29			

Command	Consistently	Occasionally	Infrequently
Demonstrating kindness and compassion Ephesians 4:32			
Submitting to others Ephesians 5:21			
Being humble and servant-hearted Philippians 2:5–8			
Forgiving Christians who sin against me Colossians 3:13			
Warning other believers who are straying Colossians 3:16			
Inspiring other believers to do good Hebrews 10:24			
Meeting together regularly with other Christians Hebrews 10:25			
Resisting the urge to talk ill of other believers James 4:11			
Refusing to grumble and complain against others James 5:9			
Practicing hospitality toward fellow Christians 1 Peter 4:9			
Giving gladly to the needs of other believers 2 Corinthians 9:7, 12			
Seeking to grow up in my salvation 1 Peter 2:2; 2 Peter 3:18			
Using your gifts to grace others 1 Peter 4:10			
Worshiping with other believers Acts 13:2			
Following the leadership of pastors and elders Hebrews 13:17			

8. What about the above exercise surprises, encourages, or concerns you?

_____

_____

_____

_____

Life Application

An important part of discipleship is learning how to apply God's truths to your life. Below are just a few ways you can start thinking about what you've learned and apply it to your daily life.

1. Memorize our memory verse, Matthew 16:18.

    "I will build my church, and the gates of Hades will not overcome it."

2. Ponder the statements under "Wise Words About Church Community." These quotes are from an assortment of Christian leaders about why it's so vital for each of us to be deeply involved in a local church community.

3. Wrestle with one or two of these questions:

    ▶ Respond to this statement: "Because we are 'the body of Christ,' Christians are eternally connected, permanently attached, linked together with Jesus Christ and with one another. Our future and our fortunes are tied together. We are different, but we're interdependent. We desperately need each other to function healthily in this world." Do you agree? Why or why not?

    "Healthy spiritual growth requires the presence of the other—the brother, the sister, the pastor, the teacher. A private, proudly isolated life cannot grow. The two or three who gather together in Christ's name keep each other sane. Spiritual growth cannot take place in isolation. It is not a private thing."—Eugene Peterson

    ▶ Jean Vanier has said: "There is no ideal community. Community is made up of people with all their richness, but also with their weakness and poverty, of people who accept and forgive each other, who are vulnerable with each other. Humility and trust are more at the foundation of community than perfection." Do you agree? Why is this so hard to develop?

    ▶ Someone has observed that in more than twenty centuries of church history, it's only been in the last century that believers have stopped saying, "I *belong* to such-and-such a church" or "I'm a *member* of _____ church" and started saying "I *go to* _____" or "I *attend* _____ church." Do you see any problems with this change of vernacular? What does it say about how people relate to their church?

    ▶ Do you have a church family? A faith community to which you belong, people to whom you are committed and accountable? If not, what holds you back?

Wise Words About Church Community

"Let him who is not in community beware of being alone. Into the community you were called—the call was not meant for you alone; in the community of the called you bear your cross, you struggle, you pray. You are not alone even in death, and on the Last Day you will be only one of the great congregation of Jesus Christ.
—Dietrich Bonhoeffer, *Life Together*

"Communion is strength; solitude is weakness. Alone, the free old beech yields to the blast and lies prone on the meadow. In the forest, supporting each other, the trees laugh at the hurricane. The sheep of Jesus flock together. The social element is the genius of Christianity."
—Charles Spurgeon

"Many Christians have been infected with the most virulent virus of modern American life, what sociologist Robert Bellah calls 'radical individualism.' They concentrate on personal obedience to Christ as if all that matters is 'Jesus and me,' but in doing so miss the point altogether. For Christianity is not a solitary belief system. Any genuine resurgence of Christianity, as history demonstrates, depends on a reawakening and renewal of that which is the essence of the faith—that is, the people of God, the new society, the body of Christ, which is made manifest in the world—the church."
—Chuck Colson, *The Body*

"You can sit in a sanctuary and listen to a sermon, and have the best intentions in the world about doing something about it, but if you don't have somebody who can say next week, 'Did you act on that?' you can bet you will fail to do it."
—Roberta Hestenes

"I'm convinced that spiritual growth happens best in an environment of intimacy. And intimacy is not going to happen in the congregation, where people look at the back of one another's heads. The Bible shines best when its truth is being pressed up against the wall of real-life scenarios and situations. You can't get that very often in the sanctuary."
—Gordon MacDonald

"When people are in small groups where someone knows them—where they can ask the threatening, embarrassing, naïve questions, and share where they are—then they can take giant steps in their faith. That just doesn't happen in a church service of 200 or 500 people."
—Howard Hendricks

"Can I be a Christian without joining other Christians in the church? Yes, it is something like: being a soldier without an army, a seaman without a ship, a business man without a business, a tuba player without an orchestra, a football player without a team or a bee without a hive."
—Mrs. William P. Janzen

"It is the lone member of the congregation, who holds himself aloof from a more intimate Christian fellowship, who is likely to stunt or damage his spiritual progress."
—John R. W. Stott

"The virtuous soul that is alone . . . is like the burning coal that is alone. It will grow colder rather than hotter."
—St. John of the Cross

CHAPTER 4:

Twelve Things That Mark a Disciple (The Fruit of the Spirit and a few more)

Topic 13: Love

The Hallmark of a Follower of Jesus

"A new command I give you: Love one another.
As I have loved you, so you must love one
another. By this everyone will know that you
are my disciples, if you love one another."

—John 13:34–35

What's the best way to show people you follow Jesus? Wear a cross around your neck? Get a religious tattoo—maybe a Bible verse—in Greek or Hebrew? What about Christian T-shirts or one of those "Jesus fishes" on your vehicle with a catchy bumper sticker just below it?

None of that is wrong. If you feel led to do such things, great. But Jesus indicated his followers should be marked by something much deeper, higher, and more compelling.

Christ called his disciples to love one another—just check out the memory verse for this lesson. Notice what else he said: Loving as *he* loved is what singles us out as his followers. Love is our calling card. Loving others well—even our enemies—is the best case we could *ever* make for the truth of the gospel.

In Mark 1, Jesus said, "Follow me, and I will *make you become* fishers of men." Bottom-line, he was saying, "Let me change you." In other words, discipleship is more than learning certain truths and participating in various "Christian" activities. Discipleship means becoming like Jesus. It means seeing his character begin to form in our own lives. That character begins and ends with love.

"Love" in the Bible

> "Let all that you do be done in love."—1 Corinthians 16:14, NASB

The primary Old Testament Hebrew words translated "love" are *ahab* and *chesed*.

Ahab, typically means "to desire, delight in, or breathe after" someone or something (as in longing for something). When describing male-female, husband-wife relationships the word may have sexual connotations. However, it is also used to describe:

▶ Parent-child relationships (Genesis 22:2)

▶ In-law relationships (Ruth 4:15)

122

▶ A servant's love for his master (Exodus 21:5)

▶ The affection between intimate friends (2 Samuel 1:26)

▶ God's love for us (Exodus 20:6; Deuteronomy 7:13)

The other word, *chesed,* is often translated "loving kindness" or "steadfast love" when referring to God's faithful, covenant love for his people—his commitment to show them goodness and favor (Psalm 17:7; 63:3). When used of people, *chesed* is often translated "kindness" or "loyalty" (Genesis 24:49; 2 Samuel 2:5).

In the New Testament, the Greek words *agape* and *phileo* are used to speak of both human and divine love. Some have tried to distinguish sharply between the two, saying that *agape* refers to God's perfect love for us; and *phileo* refers to mere human, brotherly love or friendly affection. But such distinctions oversimplify. In Scripture, there is much overlap. For example, God is said to *phileo* humans (Revelation 3:19). And humans are also encouraged to love (*phileo*) God (1 Corinthians 16:22).

There is much we could say about love, and in this study, we'll be talking about what the Bible says about love.

Bible Study

Biblical Truths About Love

Love originates in God because he is love.

1. Read carefully these verses from 1 John:

   > Dear friends, let us continue to love one another, for love comes from God. Anyone who loves is a child of God and knows God. But anyone who does not love does not know God, for God is love.

   > God showed how much he loved us by sending his one and only Son into the world so that we might have eternal life through him. This is real love—not that we loved God, but that he loved us and sent his Son as a sacrifice to take away our sins.

   > Dear friends, since God loved us that much, we surely ought to love each other. (1 John 4:7–11, NLT)

   a. John tells us here God is the essence of love. Given that this is his *nature*, how does John describe God's *actions*?

   _____

   _____

   _____

   _____

   _____

   b. According to John, what are the expected actions of a child of God?

   _____

   _____

   _____

   _____

   _____

The spiritual life can be boiled down to one word: love.

2. Check out this key passage from Mark's gospel:

> One of the teachers of the law came and heard them debating. Noticing that Jesus had given them a good answer, he asked him, "Of all the commandments, which is the most important?"

> "The most important one," answered Jesus, "is this: 'Hear, O Israel: The Lord our God, the Lord is one. Love the Lord your God with all your heart and with all your soul and with all your mind and with all your strength.' The second is this: 'Love your neighbor as yourself.' There is no commandment greater than these."
> (Mark 12:28–31)

It's worth noting that in the time of Christ, the leaders of Jewish religious culture had dissected the Mosaic Law into 613 individual commandments[1]—365 "don'ts" (one for each day of the year!) and 248 "do's." They argued incessantly over which ones were the most important. And they put in time and effort to make sure they were good Jews: Obeying requirements for food, worship, idols, clothing, work, money, marriage, farming, sex, hairstyles, legal, lending, health, parent-child and employer-employee/slave relationships, mourning, proper sacrifices, priest's duties, and more.

a. Do the people of today's church still argue about rules that should be followed? What rules have you heard others say are important?

_____

_____

_____

b. Jesus reduced 613 rules to one principle, with two parts: *Love God* and *love people*. When life gets complex, and we want to know what rule to follow, Jesus tells us to rely on this guiding principle. Why do we so often find this simplified, straightforward command so difficult to live out?

_____

_____

_____

_____

1 "613 Commandments," *Wikipedia*: https://en.wikipedia.org/wiki/613_commandments (accessed August 8, 2016)

Loving God and loving people are a package deal.

3. Let's look again at 1 John 4:

> If someone says, "I love God," but hates a fellow believer, that person is a liar; for if we don't love people we can see, how can we love God, whom we cannot see? And he has given us this command: Those who love God must also love their fellow believers." (1 John 4:20–21, NLT)

a. These are sobering words! What would you say if someone responded to this verse and said, "Yeah, but my boss—if you knew him, you'd know why I despise him!"?

_____

_____

_____

_____

Even the Ten Commandments illustrate this basic "Love God, Love People" principle. The first four commandments are about loving God, and the final six commandments have to do with relating in love to others. We've seen Jesus highlight this connection in talking about the Great Commandment; John echoes it in his epistle. God doesn't want us to miss this: *We can't separate loving him from loving others!*

> "Do not waste time bothering whether you 'love' your neighbor; act as if you did."—C. S. Lewis

Love is more an action than an emotion.

4. "Dear children, let us not love with words or speech but with actions and in truth" (1 John 3:18). Why is it dangerous to speak of love as a feeling—as something that we fall into or fall out of? Why aren't warm feelings enough?

_____

_____

_____

_____

God's love is sacrificial and unconditional.

5. Read John 3:16 if you are not able to quote it from memory.

a. What was the result of God's great love for the world? Is there such a thing as a love that doesn't cost anything? Why or why not?

_____

_____

_____

_____

b. Read Romans 8:31–39. List all the things that the apostle Paul says can separate a child of God from God's love. What actions disqualify us from receiving his affection?

_____

_____

_____

c. What does this tell us about the way we are to love others?

_____

_____

_____

God's love extends even to "enemies."

6. Consider these words of Jesus:

"You have heard that it was said, 'Love your neighbor and hate your enemy.' But I tell you, love your enemies and pray for those who persecute you, that you may be children of your Father in heaven. He causes his sun to rise on the evil and the good, and sends rain on the righteous and the unrighteous. If you love those who love you, what reward

"What does love look like? It has the hands to help others. It has the feet to hasten to the poor and needy. It has eyes to see misery and want. It has the ears to hear the sighs and sorrows of men. That is what love looks like."—Augustine

will you get? Are not even the tax collectors doing that? And if you greet only your own people, what are you doing more than others? Do not even pagans do that? Be perfect, therefore, as your heavenly Father is perfect." (Matthew 5:43–48)

a. Practically speaking, what does it look like to love an enemy? In day-to-day life? On social media? When talking with friends and the enemy isn't around?

_____

_____

_____

_____

b. Read Jesus' famous Parable of the Good Samaritan in Luke 10:25–37. As you do, remember that the Jews and Samaritans in Jesus' day couldn't stand each other—for historical, racial, and cultural reasons. Where in your own experience have you seen this kind of "risky, unexpected" love?

_____

_____

_____

_____

God's love is jaw-droppingly beautiful!

7. Take a few minutes to slowly read 1 Corinthians 13—often called the "Love Chapter" of the Bible.

> "Love slays what we have been that we may be what we were not."
> —Augustine

a. Why would Paul suggest that spiritual abilities, theological knowledge, or religious actions can actually get in the way of genuine love?

_____

_____

_____

_____

b. Now, read 1 Corinthians 13 a second time, inserting your own name every time you see the word "love." How would your life and relationships be different if you loved like that?

_____

_____

_____

_____

c. What's the most amazing display of love you've ever seen by another person?

_____

_____

_____

_____

Love makes room for those who are different.

Read Romans 14. In this chapter, Paul talks about a common problem of the church. Many followers of Jesus have different convictions about some behaviors not expressly forbidden by God. For first-century believers in Rome, it was the issue of eating meat that had been part of pagan rituals. For modern believers it might be an issue like drinking a beer or a glass of wine.

8. How does love make a difference when Christians have different scruples or standards on issues like these?

_____

_____

_____

_____

_____

Our love can become displaced.

9. Ponder this verse: "Do not love the world nor the things in the world. If anyone loves the world, the love of the Father is not in him" (1 John 2:15, NASB). What does it mean to "love the world"? Why is this a problem? How can a person tell if he or she is in love with "the world"?

_____

_____

_____

_____

We can't love rightly apart from God's enabling Spirit.

In Galatians 5:19–21, Paul talks in depressing detail about all the selfish and wrong ways we act when left to ourselves. Then he writes the phrase, "But the fruit of the Spirit is love" (Galatians 5:22). Here he offers a supernatural possibility—letting God's Spirit reign and rule in us, bringing forth a harvest of love.

What's distinctive about a follower of Jesus? The same virtue that marked our Savior—love. In the strength and security, the wonder and power of Christ's sacrificial, unconditional love for us, we are free to love others. Because we are loved eternally, and perfectly by the Perfect One, we have nothing to fear. We can move toward others to give and serve and bless—just as he did.

We love because he first loved us.

Take-Home Reflections

To Love or Not to Love

Look at this chart to see in what direction a follower of Jesus can direct his or her love.

Things the Bible calls us to love:	Things the Bible warns us NOT to love:
Our neighbor Leviticus 19:18	**Violence** Psalms 11:5
The strangers and foreigners who reside in our midst Leviticus 19:34; Deuteronomy 10:19	**Cursing others** Psalms 109:17
The Lord our God Deuteronomy 6:5; 10:12	**Being simple-minded** Proverbs 1:22
God's salvation Psalms 18:1–2	**Transgression** Proverbs 17:19
Justice Psalms 99:4	**Sleep** Proverbs 20:13
God's law and commandments Psalms 119:47, 97, 113, 127, 140, 167	**Pleasure** Proverbs 21:17
The name of God Psalms 119:132	**Wine** Proverbs 21:17
Wisdom Proverbs 4:5–6	**Money** Ecclesiastes 5:10; 1 Timothy 3:3; 6:10; Hebrews 13:5
Discipline Proverbs 12:1	**Evil** Amos 5:15
Those who reprove or correct us Proverbs 15:12	**Perjury** Zechariah 8:17
Good Amos 5:15	**The approval of others more than the approval of God** John 12:43
Kindness Micah 6:8	**This present world** 2 Timothy 4:10; 1 John 2:15
Our enemies Matthew 5:44	
Fellow disciples John 13:34	
All God's people Ephesians 1:15	
(To husbands) **Your wife** Ephesians 5:25; Colossians 3:19	
The Lord Jesus Christ Ephesians 6:24	
Our brothers and sisters in Christ 1 Thessalonians 4:9; Hebrews 13:1; 1 Peter 1:22	
The imminent appearing or second coming of Christ 2 Timothy 4:8	
(To young wives and mothers) **Your husband and children** Titus 2:4	

Life Application

An important part of discipleship is learning how to apply God's truths to your life. Below are just a few ways you can start thinking about what you've learned and apply it to your daily life.

1. Memorize our verse, John 13:34–35.

2. Review this lesson. On a separate sheet of paper, journal your response to this truth: *We will never know how to love until we first know that we are loved.*

3. Practice loving others. We will only become loving people by doing loving acts. Like any skill, getting good at love requires practice and repetition! Pick a couple of the loving acts listed in "Show Your Love" on the next page, or invent your own and try them out this week.

4. Wrestle with one or two of the following:

   ▶ Do you have to *like* somebody in order to *love* them in the way that Christ commands? Why or why not?

   ▶ Is there someone you've treated with cruelty, hatred or violence? If love is a hallmark of Christians, how can you react the next time you're in a similar situation? How can you make things right with the person you've wronged?

   ▶ Do you have an "enemy"? A bully at school, disrespectful boss, mean neighbor, manipulative person, critic on social media, political candidate, or arrogant relative? How can you pray for them and for yourself?

Show Your Love

- Secretly serve a roommate, classmate, teacher, coworker or friend. Identify a need and meet it, without revealing what you have done or taking credit.

- Give a loved one a hug for no reason.

- Do a dreaded chore for a family member—one that he or she really struggles to complete.

- Clear the table—without anyone prompting you.

- Wash the dishes or put them in the dishwasher without being asked.

- Change that diaper the moment you realize it's dirty and/or wet. Don't wait for someone else to "catch a whiff"!

- Offer to run errands for a friend who is frazzled.

- Do something sweet for your wife or mother—choose a day other than Mother's Day!

- Practice a not-so random act of kindness for a neighbor.

- Sneak into someone else's room one morning and make the bed.

- Give someone your undivided attention. Ask them questions and really listen for one hour.

- Notice a friend's needs. Then meet them before being asked.

- Take twenty minutes to sit down and write a letter of encouragement to someone who has marked your life.

- Say a prayer for someone you don't get along with or just don't like. Ask God to help you love this person the way that he does.

- Identify something that needs to be done that nobody else seems to notice. Go through the proper channels and do it!

- Donate your expertise to someone who really needs it.

- Take your kids with you to help a friend or family member.

- Tithe your waking, non-working, and non-school moments for one week. If that comes to five hours, then that's 300 minutes a day. Agree to spend thirty minutes daily serving someone different for the next seven days.

- Gather your small group or discipleship group and secretly go help someone in need.

- Pile your family in the car, drive around until you see an elderly person doing yard work. Tell him or her you have two free hours and ask, "How can you use us?"

- Offer to babysit for three hours for a harried homemaker.

- Clean your dad's vehicle.

- Double your portions as you prepare supper and invite a neighborhood family to join you. Or take a meal to an elderly neighbor.

- Tutor a kid who's having trouble in school.

Topic 14: Joy & Peace

Life as God Meant for It to Be

"May the God of hope fill you with all joy
and peace as you trust in him, so that you
may overflow with hope by the power of
the Holy Spirit."

—Romans 15:13

When we think about the *qualities* that mark a follower of Jesus, two rare and beautiful virtues that come to mind are *joy* and *peace*.

▶ Bob is a guy who goes to church regularly. He would quickly tell you about his faith in Christ. But if you watched him for very long, you'd soon see he doesn't have a ton of joy in his life. Most days he's tense and fretful—not free and full of peace. There's a heaviness about him that, frankly, is painful to be around.

▶ Tricia on the other hand has a serene and lighthearted quality about her. She doesn't just smile, she's radiant. You know that old hymn "It Is Well with My Soul"? Tricia could be a walking advertisement for that idea. Just being with her is a delight and a comfort.

"Joy is the mark of a true Christian."
—William Wilberforce

© Bristol Works, Inc. www.rose-publishing.com

Bible Study

Joy: What Is Joy?

The Old Testament Hebrew word *simha* and the New Testament Greek word *chara* convey a deep internal gladness that both comes from and culminates in external expression. In other words, joy is both a condition or quality and an action. We practice it (rejoicing) in order to possess it (joyfulness). True joy inevitably leads to heartfelt rejoicing, and vice versa. Expressions of joy can be individual or corporate, private or public, reserved or exuberant, quiet or noisy. As such, feasting, singing, shouting, dancing, bowing, praying, laughing are all valid expressions of joy.

Where Does Joy Come From?

1. Take a moment and read Nehemiah 8:10; John 15:11 and 1 Thessalonians 1:6. What strikes you about these verses?

_____

_____

_____

_____

Phrases like "the joy of the Lord" (Nehemiah 8:10), verses where Christ refers to his joy (Luke 10:21; John 15:11; 17:13), and references to the joy of the Holy Spirit (1 Thessalonians 1:6) remind us that *our Triune God is joyful.* When we list his attributes, we are quick to mention how he is holy, just, gracious, omnipotent, loving, sovereign, etc. Not many of us think often about the truth that "God is *joyful*!" But in addition to the verses above, consider Zephaniah 3:17, "The LORD your God is in your midst, A victorious warrior. He will exult over you with joy, He will be quiet in His love, He will rejoice over you with shouts of joy**."**

"Joy is the serious business of heaven."—C. S. Lewis

Ultimately just as the Lord is the source of all true love (see "Topic 13: The Hallmark of a Follower of Jesus"), so he is the source of all authentic joy. And because he lives within us by his Spirit, infinite joy is readily available to us even in the midst of hard times. "You have made known to me the path of life; you will fill me with joy in your presence, with eternal pleasures at your right hand." (Psalm 16:11).

How Do We Cultivate Joy?

The fact that we are told, "Always be joyful" lets us know that joy is not exclusively a feeling (1 Thessalonians 5:16, NLT). Rather than being an emotion that comes and goes, joy is a quality that we can cultivate. It is something we can kindle, fan into flame—or, to switch metaphors, harvest: "But the fruit of the Spirit is . . . joy" (Galatians 5:22, NASB).

In the Bible, gladness is always tied to God (see Psalm 32:11; 64:10; 104:34; 126:3; Joel 2:23). At least forty verses connect the *act of rejoicing* with *the state of gladness*. In other words, joy comes from looking beyond temporary circumstances to the unchanging person and promises of God.

In the Bible, we see joy when people:

- ▶ Receive an invitation from Jesus (Luke 19:6)

- ▶ Hear the news of God's salvation in Christ (Luke 2:10–11)

- ▶ Discover the kingdom of heaven (Matthew 13:44)

- ▶ Encounter the truth of the empty tomb—Christ's resurrection (Matthew 28:8)

- ▶ Hear the teaching of Jesus (John 15:11)

- ▶ Experience answers to prayer (John 16:24)

- ▶ Spend time with the people of God (Acts 2:46)

- ▶ Understand and believe the gospel of Jesus (Acts 8:39)

- ▶ Get to be part of spreading the truth of God (Acts 13:38–42)

- ▶ Write about and remember their experience with Jesus (1 John 1:4).

Happiness or Joy? What's the Difference?

The Bible doesn't draw a sharp distinction between happiness and joy. In fact, it seems at times to use the words synonymously. But what our culture calls happiness and what the Bible describes as happiness are indeed two different things. Read Psalm 13 (it's short) and then study this chart:

Worldly Happiness	Heavenly Joy
More of an emotion	More of a virtue or character quality
A fickle feeling of giddiness	A settled stance of gladness
Determined by human circumstances	Determined by Godly realities
Gathered from worldly events	Given ultimately by God
Destroyed by difficulties	Shaken but not destroyed by difficulties
Found on the surface of life	Stems from the depths of the heart
Comes and goes	Resides within the hearts of disciples
Something people hope to find	Something people can cultivate

2. How does Psalm 13 illustrate the real possibility of joy despite tough circumstances?

_____

_____

_____

_____

3. What would you say about joy to a friend who battles with ongoing depression?

_____

_____

_____

_____

It's worth noting that a number of the psalms are—well, not the sorts of upbeat, peppy "songs" you'd hear in many church services. These raw and honest expressions speak about painful realities and disturbing situations. They *don't* deny the truth that life is often hard; they *do* represent an attempt to remember that in the hard times God is always good and in control.

> "Joy is a continuous, 'defiant Nevertheless'"—Karl Barth

By holding this tension, the psalms show that joy isn't the result of fickle feelings, but from the choice to put hope in eternal certainties. The psalms teach us that while we don't rejoice *because of* tragedy, we can still be glad *in the midst of it*. How? By trusting that we are held by a God who is with us, who one day will dry every tear.

Rejoicing (the action) is an expression of this faith; it's an exercise in hopeful surrender to God and a refusal to treat temporal circumstances as the final word.

Because of all this, we can experience a kind of quiet confidence—even when life is unpleasant. We don't have to go through life despairing, full of gloom and doom. It seems impossible, but we can grieve current hurts even as we rejoice in future hopes.

As we better understand God's purposes and more willingly embrace them, we can learn and practice gratitude instead of grumbling (James 1:2). Instead of ranting at the world, we can rest and rejoice in God's sovereign care.

31 Simple Ideas for Cultivating Gladness

This weekend declare that it is "Celebration Saturday." Then . . .

1. Loudly say "Amen!" in church.

2. Reflect on God's character—who he is.

3. Review God's works—what he's done.

4. Remember God's promises—what he pledges he will do.[2]

5. Celebrate "little" things: "Madison hit a home run!" "Josh made his bed."

6. Celebrate "big" things—birthdays, anniversaries, promotions, etc.

7. This week, buy or bake a dessert for *no* reason or for *any* and *every* reason.

8. Throw confetti.

9. Celebrate in small groups.

10. Have a festival: a barbecue, potluck, neighborhood block party, etc.

11. Cheer more often for the little blessings of life.

12. Notice God's creation. Shake your head in wonder. Stop and marvel.

13. Don't be so serious! Lighten up! Be silly!

14. Joke around more. Let your playful side come out and play.

15. Smile more often.

16. Find and hang out with joyful people.

17. Look back at family pictures and old videos.

18. Become a better laugher. Chuckle. Giggle. Laugh. *Belly* laugh. Guffaw. Cackle. Hoot. Snort. Roll on the floor.

19. Give high fives and fist bumps.

20. Cry tears of joy at God's goodness.

21. Lead others in giving three cheers.

22. Throw spontaneous dance parties.

23. Play the thankful game.

24. Pray for a cheerful attitude.

25. Ask God's Spirit to grow the virtue of "joy" in your life (Galatians 5:22)—then work with him to harvest it.

26. With an accountability partner, remove the habit of grumbling from your life (see Philippians 2:14).

27. Embark on a mission to stop being pessimistic and focus on the positive.

28. Buy or borrow some praise CDs.

29. Sing. Sing loudly. Sing like you mean it.

30. Think about the words you're singing when singing worship songs.

31. If you're a hugger, hug someone.

2 "God's Bible Promises," *Bibleinfo.com*: http://www.bibleinfo.com/en/topics/bible-promises (accessed August 8, 2016).

4. Which of these things do you do? Not do? Which ones will you choose to do this week?

_____

_____

_____

_____

Peace: What Is Peace?

5. Take a moment to ponder this verse:

"You will keep in perfect peace all who trust in you, all whose thoughts are fixed on you!" (Isaiah 26:3, NLT)

a. What's the promise here?

_____

_____

_____

_____

The most common term for peace in the Old Testament is the well-known Hebrew word *shalom*. It is used more than 350 times, and it is an unbelievably rich word, with a wide range of connotations.

Depending on the context *shalom* can refer to **wholeness** and **intactness, health** and **well-being,** or **security** and **prosperity.** Shalom speaks of **blessing** and **joy, vitality** and **fruitfulness, community** and **harmony.** And if all that weren't enough, it's **neighborliness,** deep **satisfaction** and **rest.**

Look at those words in the definition of *shalom*. Ponder them. *Shalom*, God's peace, means so much more than "things are okay."

Real peace, God's peace, isn't just the *absence* of visible tension and conflict, it is the *presence* of deep wholeness and joy. Shalom is "life to the full" (John 10:10). Shalom is what we get when we experience life rooted in a right relationship with a good and holy, all-powerful, all-wise God.

b. Where is your life marked by God's *shalom*? Where is it not?

_____

_____

_____

The reason God's offer of peace is so beautiful is because we live in world that is shattered by sin, not permeated with *shalom*. The good news, the gospel, tells us that Jesus, "the Prince of Peace," came to bring *shalom*! Let's look briefly at three kinds of peace we can enjoy as followers of Jesus:

Eternal Peace

6. Read Luke 2:14. What was the angelic announcement to the shepherds about the birth of Christ?

_____

_____

Many Christmas cards render this verse "peace on earth, good will toward men," but the most literal translation of the angelic announcement is "peace to men on whom his favor (grace) rests." In other words, peace with God. A right relationship with God. Acceptance. Forgiveness. Salvation, by grace alone, through faith in Christ alone (Ephesians 2:8–9).

Someone has said that in the birth of Christ, God offered the world a peace treaty. And in his death at the cross, Christ signed that treaty in his own blood.

Do you feel a need for such peace? The assurance that you are right with God? If so, review "Topic 4: Assurance of Salvation."

Interpersonal Peace

7. Consider the meaning of this verse: "If it is possible, as far as it depends on you, live at peace with everyone" (Romans 12:18).

a. How would you explain this verse to a child?

_____

_____

_____

b. When is it not possible to have peace with others?

_____

_____

_____

Because God has taken the initiative to make peace with us, we can follow in the footsteps of Jesus—and take the initiative to move toward our "enemies" and seek peace.

8. How are things going in your life with having peace with others? Look at the scale below and plot your key relationships right now—with a spouse (if married), parents, children, coworkers, neighbors, friends, fellow church members, etc.

A Relational Peace Scale

war		enmity		conflict		mistrust		tension		neutrality		civility		cordiality		harmony		trust		love
-10	-9	-8	-7	-6	-5	-4	-3	-2	-1	0	1	2	3	4	5	6	7	8	9	10

a. Which of your personal relationships need work? And what specifically does that "work" call for on your part?

_____

_____

_____

_____

Internal Peace

9. Read Philippians 4:6–7. What do these verses tell us about how to experience internal peace; the peace *of* God within our own hearts and souls?

_____

_____

_____

Because God is the source of true joy and real peace, followers of Jesus can experience these realities, and see them grow in our lives. We can be different when we work with the One who works in us!

Take-Home Reflections

Trouble-ometer Indicate how much difficulty you are experiencing right now in the following categories—the lower the number, the greater the trouble.	Things are hopeless!	Continual crisis	I'm paralyzed by fear.	Constant high stress	Significant problems	Moderate unease	Bumps in the road	Minor heartburn	No real complaints	Total peace and joy!
My relationship with my parents	1	2	3	4	5	6	7	8	9	10
My marriage	1	2	3	4	5	6	7	8	9	10
The welfare of my children	1	2	3	4	5	6	7	8	9	10
My job/career situation	1	2	3	4	5	6	7	8	9	10
My financial condition	1	2	3	4	5	6	7	8	9	10
My physical health	1	2	3	4	5	6	7	8	9	10
My closest friends	1	2	3	4	5	6	7	8	9	10
My neighbors	1	2	3	4	5	6	7	8	9	10
My teachers/administrators	1	2	3	4	5	6	7	8	9	10
My coworkers	1	2	3	4	5	6	7	8	9	10
My academic situation	1	2	3	4	5	6	7	8	9	10
My overall emotional state	1	2	3	4	5	6	7	8	9	10
My connection with God	1	2	3	4	5	6	7	8	9	10
My overall feeling about my life (where I'm headed, etc.)	1	2	3	4	5	6	7	8	9	10

Life Application

An important part of discipleship is learning how to apply God's truths to your life. Below are just a few ways you can start thinking about what you've learned and apply it to your daily life.

1. Memorize our verse, Romans 15:13.

   "May the God of hope fill you with all joy and peace as you trust in him, so that you may overflow with hope by the power of the Holy Spirit."

2. Using a concordance, survey all the Bible verses that contain the words *joy* and *peace*. What additional insights does this quick study give you into these virtues?

3. Do you have conflict with another person that you can set aside and "agree to disagree" in order to have peace?

4. Wrestle with one or both of the following:

   ▶ Look at the chart on page 141. What can you do to experience God's peace and joy despite your current difficulties?

   ▶ Read and ponder 1 Thessalonians 2:19–20; 3:9 and Psalm 16:3. How do other believers contribute to our joy? How have you seen this in your life?

Topic 15: Patience, Kindness, & Goodness

Enjoying Radical Relationships

"The fruit of the Spirit is love, joy, peace, forbearance, kindness, goodness, faithfulness, gentleness and self-control. Against such things there is no law."

—Galatians 5:22–23, NASB

It was former heavyweight champion Mike Tyson who famously said, "Everybody has a plan until they get punched in the face." That wry observation isn't just true of boxing. We could also apply it to our relationships.

> "This is the whole of Christianity. There is nothing else. . . . It is easy to think that the Church has a lot of different objects—education, building, missions, holding services. . . . The Church exists for nothing else but to draw men into Christ, to make them little Christs. If [we] are not doing that, all the cathedrals, clergy, missions, sermons, even the Bible itself, are simply a waste of time. God became man for no other purpose."—C. S. Lewis, *Mere Christianity*

How *easy* it is for disciples of Christ to study and discuss great biblical concepts like love. How *hard* it is to be loving when we step into the arena of marriage or work! According to Galatians 5:22–23, our lives—and our interactions with others—can and should be marked by supernatural patience, kindness, and goodness. How does this happen? What's involved in receiving such graces from God, cultivating them, and then sharing them with others around us?

We're examining the qualities that mark a follower of Jesus.

It's worth repeating: discipleship isn't just studying the Bible and engaging in religious activities. Rather, it involves a slow, steady transformation into Christ-likeness. In other words, it isn't simply knowing and doing new things; it's becoming the new people God created us to be.

Before we look at how the Bible describes patience, kindness, and goodness, take a shot at defining them yourself.

Patience:

_____

Kindness:

_____

Goodness:

_____

In our study today, we'll examine how the Bible uses these terms.

Bible Study

Patience

The most common Old Testament Hebrew word translated "patience" comes from a verb that means "to be long." The idea is that one with this virtue takes a long time to get riled up. In other words, he or she is "slow to anger."

In the New Testament two primary Greek words convey the idea of patience. The first, _hypomené_, means to "remain under"—to remain steady during tests and trials. It is often translated "endure" or "persevere" without grumbling or complaining.

The other word, _makrothumia_, refers to patience as the ability to bear, tolerate, or put up with others without becoming provoked. The word suggests restraint, being slow to speak and slow to become angry (James 1:19).

1. Check out Nehemiah 9:17. This verse discusses divine patience:

   "They [the ancient people of Israel] refused to listen, and did not remember Your wondrous deeds which You had performed among them; so they became stubborn and appointed a leader to return to their slavery in Egypt. But You are a God of forgiveness, gracious and compassionate, slow to anger and abounding in lovingkindness; and You did not forsake them." (Nehemiah 9:17, NASB)

   What stands out to you most about this description of God?

   _____

   _____

   _____

The Bible tells us that "God is love" (1 John 4:8) and that "Love is patient" (1 Corinthians 13:4). Logically, it follows then that *God is patient.*

The apostle Paul wrote: "But God had mercy on me so that Christ Jesus could use me as a prime example of his great patience with even the worst sinners. Then others will realize that they, too, can believe in him and receive eternal life" (1 Timothy 1:16, NLT).

It wasn't just Paul. God is infinitely patient with all of us! He does not treat us as our sins deserve (Psalm 103:10). He is restrained, slow to become angry. He waits and delays judgment because he is merciful (2 Peter 3:9).

Can you believe such good news? Because God is essentially patient, he is always patient *with us.* Not only this, but because the perfectly patient One now *indwells us by his Spirit*— we have what it takes to be patient with others. Look at what God's Spirit inspired the apostle Paul to command:

> "Therefore, as God's chosen people, holy and dearly loved, clothe yourselves with compassion, kindness, humility, gentleness and patience. Bear with each other and forgive one another if any of you has a grievance against someone. Forgive as the Lord forgave you." (Colossians 3:12–13)

2. How would you rate yourself 1–5 in the area of patience?

> ▷ 1 = I can't help expressing disgust when things don't go right. I get angry, yell at people and threaten their job.

> ▷ 2 = I don't express disgust openly but I think incompetent people are worthless.

> ▷ 3 = I accept that there are delays, misunderstandings, malfunctions, and situations in life that go wrong. I can tolerate some problems.

> ▷ 4 = I realize there may be reasons for problems that aren't evident and accept that most people are doing the best they can.

> ▷ 5 = I do my best to keep a positive attitude and keep going. I don't lose my temper. I know God has a purpose for delays, frustrations, and problems.

Why would you rate yourself that way?

_____

_____

_____

Patience is a wonderful virtue. We admire it when we see it in others. We'd all agree it's a behavior we'd like to exhibit more often. So we study it, and ask God to help us have it. And do our best to have patience the next time life punches us in the face!

Kindness

In the New Testament, a number of Greek words express the idea of kindness.

▶ One New Testament Greek word translated "kindness" is the word *philanthropia* from which we get our English word philanthropy. It means "love for mankind" and suggests providing generously to others. This is the word found in Acts 28:2.

▶ Another word is the word *philadelphia*, which refers to "brotherly affection that results in acts of kindness" (Romans 12:10; 2 Peter 1:7).

▶ A third is the Greek word translated simply "kindness" in Galatians 5:22, *chrestotes* (see also Ephesians 2:7), which can also be translated "good" (as in Romans 3:12).

▶ In "Topic 13: Love," we saw one of the words translated "love" is also translated "kindness." This word, *chesed*, is often translated "loving kindness" or "steadfast love" when referring to God's faithful, covenant love for his people (Psalm 17:7; 63:3). When used of people, *chesed* is often translated "kindness" or "loyalty" (Genesis 24:49; 2 Samuel 2:5).

Put all this together and the idea behind the concept of biblical kindness is a kind of benevolent friendliness and sympathy that gets richly expressed in words and deeds. In other words, kindness isn't just a warm feeling, it is action on behalf of another.

Look at this verse that speaks of an unusually kind woman: "Now in Joppa there was a disciple named Tabitha (which translated in Greek is called Dorcas); this woman was abounding with deeds of kindness and charity which she continually did" (Acts 9:36, NASB).

3. Who in your life would you say "abounds in kindness"?

_____

_____

_____

As with patience, kindness finds its ultimate expression in God's actions toward us:

▶ "Or do you show contempt for the riches of his kindness, forbearance and patience, not realizing that God's kindness is intended to lead you to repentance?" (Romans 2:4).

▶ "But God is so rich in mercy, and he loved us so much, that even though we were dead because of our sins, he gave us life when he raised Christ from the dead. (It is only by God's grace that you have been saved!) For he raised us from the dead along with Christ and seated us with him in the heavenly realms because we are united with Christ Jesus. So God can point to us in all future ages as examples of the incredible wealth of his grace and kindness toward us, as shown in all he has done for us who are united with Christ Jesus" (Ephesians 2:4–7, NLT).

4. List some of the specific ways God has shown kindness to you.

_____

_____

_____

_____

_____

Given God's immense kindness to us (Colossians 1–2), Paul discusses how followers of Jesus ought to respond (Colossians 3–4). In Colossians 3:12–13, he writes:

"Therefore, as God's chosen people, holy and dearly loved, clothe yourselves with compassion, kindness, humility, gentleness and patience. Bear with each other and forgive one another if any of you has a grievance against someone. Forgive as the Lord forgave you."

> "Be kind. Everyone you meet is fighting a hard battle."—Author unknown (variously attributed to Plato, Philo of Alexandria, Ian Maclaren, John Watson)

5. What does to "clothe yourself with . . . kindness" mean to you?

_____

_____

_____

_____

Goodness

Consider the following passages that discuss *goodness*:

▶ "The LORD is good to everyone. He showers compassion on all his creation" (Psalm 145:9, NLT).

▶ "And concerning you, my brethren, I myself also am convinced that you yourselves are full of goodness, filled with all knowledge and able also to admonish one another" (Romans 15:14, NASB).

▶ "So then, while we have opportunity, let us do good to all people, and especially to those who are of the household of the faith" (Galatians 6:10, NASB).

▶ "So we keep on praying for you, asking our God to enable you to live a life worthy of his call. May he give you the power to accomplish all the good things your faith prompts you to do" (2 Thessalonians 1:11, NLT).

▶ "In the same way, let your light shine before others, that they may see your good deeds and glorify your Father in heaven" (Matthew 5:16).

6. What do these verses say about the Lord's character, the way he relates to people, and the new nature of a child of God?

_____

_____

_____

_____

_____

As we follow Jesus and experience his patience with us and his kindness and goodness toward us, we learn to treat others in those same ways. As we become more and more secure in his love and confident that our lives are in his gentle, wise hands, we experience great and greater freedom in our dealings with people. We aren't "needy" when we rub shoulders with others. This liberates us to be generous, to help, and to bless. Suddenly we can overlook faults and let go of slights—both real and perceived. We can put up with the quirks and flaws of others. Rather than seeking to get even, we can resolve to bless.

> The fruit of the Spirit aren't just graces to receive or virtues to study, but qualities to practice.

Such relationships are possible only as we allow the Holy Spirit to control us (Galatians 5:22–23). Apart from such power, they are impossible.

Take-Home Reflections

Relational Role Play

Good intentions aren't enough in hard situations. *Planning* to be patient, kind, and good in your dealings with others is fine. But when others are harsh and situations are tense, the best plans can disappear like your breath on a cold morning. Don't just plan—practice. By yourself or with a friend, think through, talk through, or better yet, role play how you could respond in a Christ-like way in each of the everyday scenarios below.

Real-life Situation	My instinctive, natural reaction	A better response
A family member is about to make you late for an event that's very important to you.		
A coworker, obviously upset about something else, is taking it out on you.		
One rainy day after work, you see your supervisor—not a nice person—in the parking lot with the hood of his car up.		
You find out your "ex" made a really nasty comment about you on Facebook.		
You are still sitting and waiting in the doctor's lobby an hour and a half past your appointment time.		
A single mom has asked if you would watch her children for a couple of hours—but you really don't enjoy kids.		
The neighbors blare loud music all hours of the night, even after you politely asked them to tone it down due to your new baby.		

Life Application

An important part of discipleship is learning how to apply God's truths to your life. Below are just a few ways you can start thinking about what you've learned and apply it to your daily life.

1. Memorize our memory verse Galatians 5:22–23, NASB.

   "The fruit of the Spirit is love, joy, peace, forbearance, kindness, goodness, faithfulness, gentleness and self-control. Against such things there is no law."

2. Wrestle with one or two of these questions:

   ▶ It's been suggested that in the same way we only get better at a thing—running, weight lifting, etc.—by training to do that thing, the only way we'll ever get better at patience is by purposely putting ourselves in situations that will force us to slow down and/or deal with frustrating people. Advocates of this approach suggest picking the longest line at the bank drive-thru window, or resisting the urge to avoid that annoying person at work. What are the pros and cons of taking such a direct approach to learning patience?

   ▶ Two common proverbs champion the idea of patience: "Good things take time" and "Good things come to those who wait." When have you seen these proverbs prove to be true in your own life?

   ▶ This week, what's a specific act of kindness you could show to someone in your life who maybe doesn't "deserve" it? Write it down in the space below.

Topic 16: Faithfulness & Gentleness

Becoming God's Humble Servant

"Take my yoke upon you and learn from
me, for I am gentle and humble in heart,
and you will find rest for your souls."

—Matthew 11:29

We become like those with whom we associate.

This is one of the great truisms of life. Friends tend to pick up each other's speech habits. Roommates mimic one another's mannerisms. Couples begin to think alike and sometimes even to look alike!

In other words, it's not just adolescents who battle peer pressure. All of us are susceptible to the influence of others. This is why the Bible warns us to avoid bad company (1 Corinthians 15:33) and to "walk with the wise" (Proverbs 13:20). This does not mean that we avoid unbelievers (many are good citizens), but we avoid people who get us into trouble.

For followers of Christ, this truism is fantastic news. It means by spending time *with* Jesus, we really can become *like* Jesus. In Galatians 5:22–23 we are given a snapshot of the heart of Jesus, an example of the way he lived.

In this lesson, we want to examine the virtues of *faithfulness* and *gentleness*. What are these qualities, and what do they look like in a disciple's life?

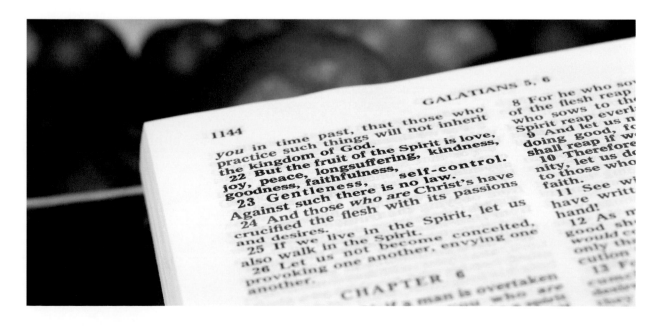

Bible Study

Faithfulness

One of the traits that Paul says marks Spirit-filled followers of Christ is faithfulness. The Greek word is *pistis*, which is almost always translated "faith," though it can be rendered "faithfulness." It conveys confidence, certainty, or trust. To have faith is to have those things; to be faithful is to inspire such things in others.

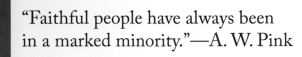

"Faithful people have always been in a marked minority."—A. W. Pink

Ponder these verses that highlight the faithfulness of our God:

▶ "Because of the LORD's great love we are not consumed, for his compassions never fail. They are new every morning; great is your faithfulness" (Lamentations 3:22–24).

▶ "But Christ is faithful as the Son over God's house. And we are his house, if indeed we hold firmly to our confidence and the hope in which we glory" (Hebrews 3:6).

▶ "If we are faithless, [Jesus] remains faithful—for he cannot deny himself" (2 Timothy 2:13, ESV).

1. Having pondered these verses, how would you describe faithfulness?

_____

_____

_____

In everyday terms, to be faithful means to be dependable. It means to be trustworthy, loyal, and consistent. A faithful person is reliable. You can count on him or her. If you are faithful, it means you will be there. You'll show up. You'll do what you said. You'll keep your promises—even when you're tired, or don't feel like it.

2. Describe a time in your life when you were blessed by God's faithfulness.

_____

_____

_____

The Difference Faithfulness Makes

When a person is faithful—literally "full of faith"—it leads to a radically different life!

Expressions of Faith	→	Faithful Actions
"I was made by God—for his glory."	→	"I refuse to live today as if life is all about me."
"I am called and sent by God."	→	"I will seek my place in God's kingdom."
"I am uniquely blessed and gifted by God."	→	"I will use all that God has given me to serve and to bless others."
"God has promised to meet all of my needs in Christ Jesus."	→	"This frees me up to move toward others and meet their needs."
"Jesus has called me to be his disciple—to follow him and become like him."	→	"I will serve others, pouring out my life as Jesus served and poured out his life."
"Jesus is Lord of heaven and Earth—I will stand before him one day and give an account for how I have lived."	→	"I will live this day, with that day in view."

Gentleness

3. How would you define the word "gentleness"? What words or images come to mind when you think of someone who is gentle?

_____

_____

_____

The Greek word for "gentleness" is *prautes*. It was used in ancient times to refer to a *tame* beast, a *pleasant* person, or a *lenient* punishment. When this word gets translated as "meek," it is wrongly understood by some to suggest weakness or wimpiness—being soft or a pushover or a doormat. This is *not* the biblical idea.

> "Jesus made this absolutely plain. The chief characteristic of Christian leaders . . . is humility not authority, and gentleness not power."
> —John Stott

A tamed circus elephant is enormously powerful, but its strength is under control as it gently goes through its paces. Biblical gentleness is the same way. Instead of "powering up" in tense situations and "going off" on people when they do irresponsible things, gentle people allow the Spirit of God to pervade their lives. They are calm, humble, non-threatening—the very opposite of harsh or irritated. Instead of the power of pride and anger, a gentle disciple of Jesus opts for the power of humility. And as Proverbs 15:1 indicates, anger is no match for gentleness and humility!

Consider how the prophet Isaiah described God's Servant, the Messiah—Jesus—who would one day come: "A bruised reed he will not break, and a smoldering wick he will not snuff out. In faithfulness he will bring forth justice" (Isaiah 42:3).

4. When in your life have you been most touched by the gentleness of Christ? What were the circumstances? What happened?

_____

_____

_____

_____

For a great snapshot of faithfulness and gentleness in action, we need look no further than the actions of Christ on the night he was betrayed.

- ▶ He gathered together with his disciples—despite knowing that before the night was through, they would all betray, deny and/or desert him. Nevertheless, he was faithful to them and gentle with them. He tenderly washed their feet. He earnestly taught them important truths. He passionately prayed for them.

- ▶ And he wasn't only faithful to his followers. In his prayer he mentioned his utter faithfulness to the task God had given him to do (John 17:4).

- ▶ Later, in the Garden of Gethsemane, even when he was grieved by the terrible reality of what awaited him, he reiterated his desire to be faithful to the Father's will (Luke 22:42).

- ▶ Then, when violence broke out and one of those who had come to arrest him suffered a wound, Jesus gently touched the man and healed him (Luke 22:51).

What humility! What a servant! No one ever faced greater pressure or stress than Christ did on that night. And yet, he responded to every situation and every person with absolute faithfulness and gentleness.

What's your takeaway from this session? On a separate sheet of paper, journal your thoughts, perhaps even a prayer.

Take-Home Reflections

The following time-tested practice is called by different names. Bill Bright, the founder of Campus Crusade for Christ (now Cru) called it "spiritual breathing."

Essentially, it is taking a few moments to get alone in God's presence. If you find your heart and mind don't want to calm down, ask the Lord for internal peace.

▶ Breathe deeply. Recognize that God is with you and in you. Remember that he is gracious and kind. Through Christ, God is your heavenly father who cares for you. Trust his love.

▶ Ask him to show you any attitudes or actions that are inconsistent with a life lived in God. So, for example, as God points out your worry over a situation beyond your control—your fear over finances or health, a critical spirit toward someone, harshness toward your children—release these things into God's grace and care.

▶ Don't be in a rush. Linger in God's presence. Don't self-diagnose. Let God reveal. When he identifies things that are making your soul sick, respond in humility. Don't resist. Agree with God, and accept his forgiveness. This is really what "confession" is (see 1 John 1:9).

▶ Express your desire to be rid of everything toxic, to live in freedom, and to repent—to change your thinking and behavior about unhealthy things. Then ask to receive the blessings that God wants to give you.

Life Application

An important part of discipleship is learning how to apply God's truths to your life. Below are just a few ways you can start thinking about what you've learned and apply it to your daily life.

1. Memorize our verse, Matthew 11:29.

2. In one sitting, read John 13–21. Put yourself in the narrative. Pretend you are there with the twelve disciples. Watch Jesus. Pay close attention to his words. Notice his humility—how he serves faithfully and gently.

3. Wrestle with one or two of the following:

   ▶ Can you think of some ways in which you think, talk, act, look, and dress like other people with whom you spend a lot of time? What other characteristics might you be picking up from them?

   ▶ Who are some of the people in your life you'd classify as "gentle"? What specifically do they do or not do to warrant this description?

   ▶ What are some specific areas of your life in which you could stand to be more faithful—either from God's point of view or toward other people?

   ▶ We all have "pet peeves"—things that tend to get under our skin, and cause us to react strongly instead of gently and humbly. What are some of your pet peeves? How do you handle them?

Topic 17: Self-Control

Keeping It All in Check

"Like a city whose walls are broken
through is a person who lacks self-control."

—Proverbs 25:28

How Much Self-Control Do You Have?

Let's start with a quick personal assessment. For each of the following situations, on a typical day, what are the chances that you would respond in a God-honoring, people-blessing, soul-enhancing way? Place an X underneath the appropriate percentage.

Situation	0%	25%	50%	75%	100%
You're trying to lose weight, but a friend is serving her famous "Death by Chocolate" dessert. You want to resist, but it is the most delicious thing you ever put in your mouth.					
You've been wanting to get up thirty minutes earlier so you can start the habit of reading the Bible before work. But now the alarm is going off . . . and it's so early . . . and ten more minutes of sleep would be awesome.					
On the way home from work, an accident on the expressway causes a delay. As you creep along the guy behind you lays on his horn and gestures wildly at you when you let someone merge over in front of you.					
As you're bringing bags and bags of expensive groceries into the kitchen, your surly, ungrateful teenager complains that you forgot to get a new box of Choco-Carb Clusters cereal.					
On Facebook, someone posts a completely ridiculous video of the political candidate you can't stand, and the candidate is saying something totally outrageous.					
In the most crucial moment of the most important game of the season, the umpire makes a terrible call against your child.					
You walk into the living room to discover that your toddler has "finger-painted" the sofa with the contents of his diaper.					

Situation	0%	25%	50%	75%	100%
The hotel you're staying in (alone) has complimentary premium channels. The movie line-up features several NC-17 films.					
You discover that back-stabbing coworker who is always throwing people under the bus has made a huge mistake and is blaming you.					
It's 4:42 in the afternoon and while prepping for that important business meeting at 8:00 the next morning, you realize the report contains the wrong numbers. And even if you could correct it, the copy machine is on the fritz.					

According to the New Testament, a Christian disciple is a person who follows Jesus for three reasons:

▶ To *know* Jesus and his teaching

▶ To *grow* more like Jesus

▶ To *go* for Jesus, serving and making new disciples.

Bible Study

Disciples who grow to be more like Jesus take on his character. One important aspect of Christ-likeness is having and demonstrating *self-control*.

1. How would you define and describe the quality or attribute of self-control?

_____

_____

_____

_____

This virtue is listed as one of the nine "fruit of the Spirit" in Galatians 5:22–23. The Greek word translated "self-control" there is *enkrateia*. It speaks of corralling one's emotional impulses, bridling ones' appetites or passions, and resisting temptation. The result is a person who is purposeful and in harmony with the will of God.

A self-controlled man is wisely restrained, not wildly reactive. A self-controlled woman is intentional not impulsive. When we are self-controlled we refrain from indulging our momentary selfish whims. Instead we choose actions that will result in long-term joy.

2. Read the following passage from the Bible:

"When [Jesus' accusers] hurled their insults at him, he did not retaliate; when he suffered, he made no threats. Instead, he entrusted himself to him who judges justly" (1 Peter 2:23).

How did Jesus demonstrate self-control? What might he have done instead?

_____

_____

_____

_____

_____

3. Read the following passage from the Bible:

"Do you not know that those who run in a race all run, but only one receives the prize? Run in such a way that you may win. Everyone who competes in the games exercises self-control in all things. They then do it to receive a perishable wreath, but we an imperishable. Therefore I run in such a way, as not without aim; I box in such a way, as not beating the air; but I discipline my body and make it my slave, so that, after I have preached to others, I myself will not be disqualified." (1 Corinthians 9:24–27, NASB)

a. Paul refers to runners and athletes. What can they teach us about self-control?

_____

_____

_____

_____

b. What would you say if someone said, "Self-control is just another word for willpower"?

_____

_____

_____

_____

The teaching of the New Testament is that we have more "will-weakness" than willpower. The gospel shows us that self-control doesn't come from a hardened resolve. It comes from a humbled heart. Rather than steeling our wills . . . we need to surrender them. Instead of grabbing the steering wheel of our lives, we give the wheel to another—to the Holy Spirit.

No book of the Bible illustrates this better than the Apostle Paul's letter to the church at Ephesus, the book of Ephesians. These six short chapters are a masterpiece of theological writing, a beautiful summary of the Christian life.

> ▶ In chapters 1–3, Paul doesn't tell Christians to *do* anything; instead, he gushes about all the amazing things God has done for us in Christ.

> ▶ In chapters 4–6 Paul shows how all those spiritual blessings make a difference in the way we live from day-to-day. He rattles off thirty-five specific commands for how we should be interacting in the home, in the church, and in the world.

> Ironically, we find self-control only when we relinquish control of ourselves to another.

Reading this divine "to do" list for Christians in Ephesians 4–6 can be intimidating—unless and until you pay close attention to Ephesians 5:18. That verse commands, "Don't be drunk with wine, because that will ruin your life. Instead, be filled with the Holy Spirit" (NLT).

4. Why do you think Paul compared and contrasted life in the Spirit with drunkenness?

_____

_____

_____

_____

Anyone who's ever had too much to drink knows the controlling power of alcohol. It takes over a person's personality—the inhibited person becomes outgoing, the frustrated person wants to pick a fight, the stoic person becomes sentimental. Though it's always wrong to *drive* under the influence of alcohol, it's always right to *live* under the influence of the Spirit (Galatians 5:16–18)!

It's worth noting that this command is in the present tense. That means it's to be an ongoing, never-ending reality. Being filled with or under the influence of God's Spirit is to be the moment-by-moment way of life for a disciple.

Also, the verb Paul uses in Ephesians 5:18 is passive. In other words, being filled with the Holy Spirit isn't something we make happen; it is something that happens *to us*. God does it—but only when we desire his control and open ourselves up to his guiding, transforming presence.

Important Points to Remember

▶ If you're a Christian, God's Spirit lives in you (Romans 8:9)—whether you "feel" him or not. As someone once quipped, "He's *resident* in you—even if you're not allowing Him to be *president* of you." This means Christians don't need to "receive the Spirit"—we need to unleash the Spirit.

▶ We can't be *filled* with the Spirit when we are *grieving* the Spirit (Ephesians 4:30) or *quenching* the Spirit (1 Thessalonians 5:19). Being filled with the Spirit is a way of saying we are surrendering to his control and allowing him to lead us (Romans 8:14).

▶ There's no secret prayer for "being filled with God's Spirit." It requires acknowledging and confessing any wrong attitudes or actions so that you will be a clean vessel, useful to the Lord (see 1 John 1:9; 2 Timothy 2:21). Jesus said the Spirit would be like a river within us (John 7:38–39). Not letting the Spirit fill us is like damming up that "holy river." However, when we confess known sin we "blow up the dam." After confession comes expression, telling God about our desire to have his Spirit rule in our hearts and minds and lives.

Every day—and all through each day—we must choose:

▶ Will I yield control of my life to the indwelling Spirit of God?

▶ Or will I try to power through situations in my own strength?

Those who have tried human willpower know the futility of such an approach. You may be able to resist temptation for a time, but wrong impulses and fleshly desires are like the waves at the beach. They keep coming at you relentlessly.

> "Self-control is not control by oneself through one's own willpower but rather control of oneself through the power of the Holy Spirit."—Jerry Bridges

The disciple realizes *Though I cannot truly control my behavior, I can control who controls my behavior.* Biblical self-control is choosing to say "no!" to the flesh, our old fallen human nature, and surrendering control instead to the Holy Spirit.

A disciple of Jesus allows the Spirit of God to fill him or her. This means listening to his promptings, soliciting his guidance, relying on his power. The fruit of such a life is divine strength—being able to resist sin, confess when we fail, get up again, and carry out God's will.

Verbal Self-Control

Consider these insights from the book of Proverbs, written by Solomon. Each one reinforces our need for spiritual power in restraining our tongue.

▶ "Where there are many words, transgression is unavoidable, but he who restrains his lips is wise" (10:19).

▶ "The lips of the righteous bring forth what is acceptable, but the mouth of the wicked what is perverted" (10:32).

▶ "With *his* mouth the godless man destroys his neighbor" (11:9).

▶ "Reckless words pierce like a sword, but the tongue of the wise brings healing" (12:18).

▶ "The LORD detests lying lips, but he delights in men who are truthful" (12:22).

▶ "The one who guards his mouth preserves his life; the one who opens wide his lips comes to ruin" (13:3).

▶ "The heart of the wise instructs his mouth and adds persuasiveness to his lips" (16:23).

▶ "Pleasant words are a honeycomb, sweet to the soul and healing to the bones" (16:24).

▶ "Even a fool, when he keeps silent, is considered wise; when he closes his lips, he is considered prudent" (17:28).

▶ "He who guards his mouth and his tongue, guards his soul from troubles" (21:23).

▶ "A lying tongue hates those it crushes, and a flattering mouth works ruin" (26:28).

▶ "Do you see a man who is hasty in his words? There is more hope for a fool than for him" (29:2).

Take-Home Reflections

Consider Your Speech Habits

Take some time to prayerfully, honestly consider the content of your recent conversations, your verbal interactions and writings (Facebook posts, Tweets, etc.). What do you find? On which side of the table do you find yourself most of the time? What do you need to do?

Sinful Speech Habits	or	Holy Speech Habits?
False teaching—advocating unbiblical ideas	—	Declaring God's truth with holy fear and trembling
Grumbling and complaining	—	Expressing gratitude and appreciation
Criticizing, critiquing, or fault-finding	—	Praying: "Show me the log in my eye." (Matthew 7:5)
Bragging, boasting, or taunting	—	Humility in speech
Flattery or insincere speech	—	Speaking the truth in love
Avoiding hard but necessary conversations	—	Confronting with tenderness and genuine concern
Slander, gossip, or backstabbing	—	Talking to others, rather than about them
Exaggerating or misrepresenting	—	Speaking accurately and with integrity
Lying—including shading the truth; telling half-truths, lies of omission, etc.	—	Truth-telling—no misleading, no matter what
Enticing or inciting others to evil	—	Exhorting others to holiness
Blaming others	—	Naming, owning, admitting, and confessing all of my faults
Blasphemy	—	Praising God in words, hymns, and songs
Snide, rude, or insensitive comments	—	Verbal kindness, honor, courtesy, and respect
Belittling, insulting, or cutting remarks	—	Speech that encourages, builds-up, strengthens
Verbal abuse	—	Choosing and using words that bring healing and give life
Idle, careless, silly, or worldly speech	—	Sharing the gospel; discussing eternal realities
Cursing or profanity	—	Talking about what is good, beautiful, and noble

Sinful Speech Habits	or	Holy Speech Habits?
Negativity or pessimism	—	Expressing faith and hope in God's goodness and power
Arguing, bickering, or accusing	—	Seeking peace and pursuing conflict resolution
Expressing bitterness or rehashing old resentments against others	—	Extending and requesting forgiveness
Shaming or "guilting" others with words	—	Blessing others with words of grace and mercy
Heated conversations about God with skeptics and unbelievers	—	Gently giving a reason for the hope within you; using loving words
Talking incessantly	—	Silence

Life Application

An important part of discipleship is learning how to apply God's truths to your life. Below are just a few ways you can start thinking about what you've learned and apply it to your daily life.

1. Memorize our memory verse, Proverbs 25:28.

   "Like a city whose walls are broken through is a person who lacks self-control."

2. Read the Book of Ephesians in one sitting—from a translation you don't typically use.

3. Wrestle with one or two of these questions:

   ▶ What does our memory verse mean? Why the picture of a wall-less city?

   ▶ How would you respond to someone saying, "How can you say Jesus had self-control? He went through the temple with a whip, driving out the moneychangers, and turning over tables!"?

   ▶ What's the hardest thing about giving up control of your life?

   ▶ In the world of sports, we often hear about the importance of players or teams "buying in" to a coach's system, philosophy, or training regimen. In what ways is being filled with the Spirit like "buying in" to his leadership?

   ▶ If we rarely see the fruit of the Spirit in our lives (Galatians 5:22–23), is that a sure sign we are not allowing ourselves to be filled with the Spirit (Ephesians 5:18)?

Topic 18: Forgiveness

Being a Conduit of God's Mercy and Grace

"Bear with each other and forgive one another
if any of you has a grievance against someone.
Forgive as the Lord forgave you."

—Colossians 3:13

We live in a fallen, broken world. There's no way to avoid getting hurt—or hurting others. We collect scars even as we cause them. How then, is it possible for things like the following three examples to happen?

▶ Only days after a man opens fire in a church Bible study, killing nine innocent people, relatives of the victims attend a legal hearing to address the gunman. The teary first words of the very first speaker are, "I forgive you."

▶ A POW, who was sadistically abused while in captivity during World War II, longs to meet with the evilest of his guards, not to exact revenge, but to extend forgiveness.

▶ A mother befriends the young gang member who murdered her son and, when he finishes his prison sentence, unofficially adopts him.

Since, on any given day, we are both victims and perpetrators, we need to become experts at *forgiveness*.

Two things are true about a devoted follower of Jesus:

▶ He or she understands being *forgiven*.

▶ He or she understands being *forgiving*.

Bible Study

To learn about the concept of forgiveness, we could go to multiple places in the Bible. But perhaps one of the best passages is a story Jesus told. Take a moment to read the parable of the unmerciful servant from Matthew 18:21–35:

Then Peter came to Jesus and asked, "Lord, how many times shall I forgive my brother or sister who sins against me? Up to seven times?"

Jesus answered, "I tell you, not seven times, but seventy-seven times.

"Therefore, the kingdom of heaven is like a king who wanted to settle accounts with his servants. As he began the settlement, a man who owed him ten thousand bags of gold was brought to him. Since he was not able to pay, the master ordered that he and his wife and his children and all that he had be sold to repay the debt.

"At this the servant fell on his knees before him. 'Be patient with me,' he begged, 'and I will pay back everything.' The servant's master took pity on him, canceled the debt and let him go.

"But when that servant went out, he found one of his fellow servants who owed him a hundred silver coins. He grabbed him and began to choke him. 'Pay back what you owe me!' he demanded.

"His fellow servant fell to his knees and begged him, 'Be patient with me, and I will pay it back.' "But he refused. Instead, he went off and had the man thrown into prison until he could pay the debt. When the other servants saw what had happened, they were outraged and went and told their master everything that had happened.

"Then the master called the servant in. 'You wicked servant,' he said, 'I canceled all that debt of yours because you begged me to. Shouldn't you have had mercy on your fellow servant just as I had on you?' In anger his master handed him over to the jailers to be tortured, until he should pay back all he owed.

"This is how my heavenly Father will treat each of you unless you forgive your brother or sister from your heart."

1. Jesus told this story when Peter asked a question about *forgiveness*.

   a. How would you explain forgiveness to a child?

   _____

   _____

   _____

166

The Meaning of Forgiveness

The Greek word, *aphesis*, translated "to forgive" means to pardon, or to remove guilt. This gracious act doesn't erase the wrong act itself or take away the consequences of hurtful words and bad behaviors; however, it does effectively remove the wrongdoer's *guilt* and our own need to *get revenge*.

The other primary New Testament verb translated "forgive" (Luke 7:42–43; Ephesians 4:32) is *charizomai*. It means to graciously and generously cancel a debt.

The Mechanics of Forgiveness

Consider Matthew 6:15, "If you do not forgive others their sins, your Father will not forgive your sins."

To understand this verse and the concept of forgiveness more fully, let's dig into one of Jesus' parables. Take the time to read it now, Matthew 18:21-35.

In this parable Jesus is teaching us about sin and forgiveness. It is not difficult to tell who the characters are intended to represent. The king or master is representative of God. The servant, represents an average person.

b. In the parable, what was the plea of the man heavily in debt (vs. 26)?

_____

_____

_____

The man's proposal is both ridiculous and sad. One scholar claims that a single silver talent represented 6,000 days' worth of wages for an average Palestinian worker (that's twenty-seven years of work!). So, ten thousand talents would be the equivalent of sixty million days wages (working for 164,383.5 years). And that's if we're talking about talents of *silver*. It would be far more if Jesus meant talents of *gold*!

c. What's Jesus point? What debt do we owe God because of our failure to properly love and honor him?

_____

_____

_____

We are either naïve, ignorant, or prideful to think *we* can somehow erase the debt we owe God. Spiritually speaking, the truth is that we keep dishonoring God *and adding to our debt!* Jesus' point is that our debt to God is far greater than we could ever pay back or even comprehend.

d. Read verse 27 again. What does the master or the king do for the man?

_____

_____

_____

_____

e. Read Colossians 2:13–14. How—not in the parable, but in the real world—is God able to cancel the enormous spiritual debts of sinful people?

_____

_____

_____

_____

The man in the parable asked for time. "Be patient!" he cried. He got infinitely more than that. He got the slate wiped clean, a big, thick ledger book full of bills—all cancelled! The king purged the books, expunged the records. Can you imagine?

Just before he died on the cross, Jesus cried out, *tetellesthai,* or "It is finished!" This word was found on first-century invoices or accounting ledgers. It's meaning? *Paid in full.*

PAID IN FULL

f. Summarize the rest of the story. What did the forgiven man do next?

_____

_____

_____

_____

g. How did the king respond when he heard about what the forgiven man had done?

_____

_____

_____

2. Read Matthew 18:34–35 and James 2:13. What's the warning for those who have experienced God's forgiveness but are unwilling to extend such mercy to others?

_____

_____

_____

The "Messiness" of Forgiveness

All this talk about forgiveness raises a number of questions. Let's look at a few of them.

How are we supposed to forgive the "unforgiveable"?

3. How would you counsel a friend who has been the victim of a great betrayal, horrific abuse, or a criminal act resulting in tragic loss? What can we possibly say that doesn't seem glib, trite, or like a cliché?

_____

_____

_____

The word "resentment" comes from two Latin words *re* meaning "again" and *sentire* meaning "to feel." Resenting someone is to relive over and over again the pain or hurt they caused. In a real sense it is to be tortured by the pain of bitterness and unforgiveness.

What about vengeance? Isn't forgiveness unfair?

4. Read Hebrews 10:30 and Romans 12:19. What do these verses say about divine justice?

_____

_____

_____

What if I have lingering negative feelings?

For instance, sometimes I think about the person who hurt me and I start to feel angry or weird all over again. Does that mean I haven't forgiven?

5. Read three passages from Philippians: 1:6; 2:12–13; 3:12–16. How do these verses suggest that forgiveness might be

> All too often we lose sight of how lavishly God has forgiven our wrongs, and we focus instead on how others have violated our rights.

a. A decision:

_____

_____

_____

b. An event:

_____

_____

_____

c. And an ongoing process?

_____

_____

_____

What about the person who continues to cause me harm?

6. Read 1 Corinthians 5, NLT. What does this passage say about putting up boundaries? Note the reference to abusive people in verse 11.

_____

_____

_____

Loving and forgiving our enemies means seeing them as fellow human beings who are loved by God and in need of his mercy and grace. The Bible *never* suggests that forgiving others—especially those who continue to act in hurtful ways—means tolerating abuse or subjecting yourself to ongoing physical or emotional danger. That isn't love; it's a kind of masochism. It isn't helpful or honorable; it's dysfunctional.

What about reconciliation and restoration?

7. Read 1 Thessalonians 5:11 and Romans 12:10. What do these verses suggest about restoring relationships after one or both parties have engaged in hurtful actions?

_____

_____

_____

_____

Forgiveness is not the same thing as reconciliation. Forgiveness means to pardon others, to no longer demand payment for their sins. Reconciliation is "restoration to harmony in relationship." With God, such restoration is always possible; but with humans it's tricky. Forgiveness is required, but the person who is forgiven may not change or become more trustworthy. In some instances, one person may not want to remain bitter, but he or she also may not wish to resume a relationship like before.

We can take the initiative to release people from their moral debts and still not enjoy reconciliation and restoration. Those blessings require repentance, confession on the part of the offender, and sometimes, restitution.

Take-Home Reflections

From Jesus' parable of the unforgiving servant, we see that

To be unwilling to forgive is to . . .	To forgive is to . . .
Disobey God's command (Colossians 3:13)	**L**earn what it means to trust God deeply
Ignore the infinite mercy God has shown us	**I**ncarnate the Gospel
Experience the tortuous effects of bitterness	**V**anquish the power of evil (Romans 12:21)
	Experience freedom and peace
Refusing to forgive is lethal!	**Choosing to forgive is life-giving!**

Forgiveness is the only path to the abundant life Jesus offers. The unwillingness to forgive is a kind of living death. Disciples of Jesus are marked by a forgiving spirit.

Life Application

An important part of discipleship is learning how to apply God's truths to your life. Below are just a few ways you can start thinking about what you've learned and apply it to your daily life.

1. Memorize our verse, Colossians 3:13.

2. Read one or two of the stories in the chart "Bible Stories of Forgiveness."

3. Wrestle with one or two of the following:

   ▶ Is it possible to "forgive and *forget*?" Is it necessary to forget?

   ▶ When we've wronged another, is it enough to simply ask God's forgiveness?

   ▶ Is there anyone you can think of from whom you need to ask forgiveness?

   ▶ What person or people in your life do you need to forgive?

Bible Stories of Forgiveness

Story Title	Reference(s)
Jacob and Esau	Genesis 25, 27, 32, 33
Joseph Forgives His Brothers	Genesis 37—50
David and Mephibosheth	2 Samuel 9
Prodigal Son	Luke 15
Casting the First Stone	John 8

Topic 19: Overcoming

The Ongoing Battle with Sin and Temptation

"Fight the good fight of the faith. Take hold
of the eternal life to which you were called
when you made your good confession in
the presence of many witnesses."

—1 Timothy 6:12

In his book *Learning from the Giants*, John C. Maxwell observed that "Disappointment comes when reality falls short of our expectations." For example, you finally make reservations at that chic new bistro that everyone has been *raving* about. You're primed for stellar service and amazing French food—but for some reason, the chef and staff at Le Veau D'or have an off night. You leave majorly bummed out. Why?

Here's the truth, at one time or another, every Christian ends up *disappointed*. This is because we often get it in our heads that following Jesus is going to lead to a certain outcome . . . but then life, reality and/or God don't cooperate.

Let's examine this idea of spiritual disappointment—the common phenomenon of spiritual reality not living up to our spiritual expectations. And the struggle we all experience as a result of this disappointment.

Great Expectations

Put a check mark in the box for any of the following spiritual expectations you've had.

- ☐ If I humbly ask God to forgive my sins, he will.

- ☐ Turning to Jesus is the quickest, surest way to fix my problems—marital, financial, occupational, academic, social, medical, etc.

- ☐ God will always be with me, always love me, always approve of what I do.

- ☐ If I pray hard enough God might "zap me" and take away sinful desires or bad habits.

- ☐ If I tack the expression "in Jesus' name, amen" to the end of my prayers, God is obligated to give me whatever I've asked for.

- ☐ I should always expect to "sense" or "feel" God's presence in my life.

❑ A devoted Christian should never and will never get depressed.

❑ If I follow certain principles or parenting techniques my kids will never turn away from God.

❑ If I have enough faith I can enjoy a life of continual physical health and financial prosperity.

❑ The gospel and followers of Christ will always be honored in our culture.

❑ Here and now, I can have the experience of heaven—flawless people, including myself; perfect situations; everything and everyone unaffected by sin; etc.

❑ There are certain sins that I would *never* commit.

❑ In many aspects, following Jesus will actually make my life harder and more complicated.

❑ I can mature in my faith, in this life, to the point that I will no longer be tempted by certain sins.

❑ It's possible to arrive at a place in this life where I have constant peace, unending bliss, and unshakeable faith all day, every day.

❑ I can be wholeheartedly devoted to Christ and be liked and admired and accepted by everyone.

❑ The spiritual life is going to be an exhausting race and a brutal battle.

For each box you checked, ask yourself these questions:

▶ Why do I expect this to be true in my experience?

▶ What passage(s) in the Bible tells me I should expect this?

▶ Has this expectation always been true in my experience?

Bible Study

Listen to the confessions of three very different Christians:

▶ "My upbringing was totally dysfunctional. I was the only child of a single mom with drug and alcohol issues. By the time I graduated high school, my mom had been married four times to three different guys! In between, she had five or six live-in boyfriends. We moved about every six months. It was constant drama. So when I heard the gospel as a teenager, all that talk of "new life" and "being saved," I jumped at it. For sure, my life changed. But if I'm honest, there's still a lot of drama in my life, and it's not even my mom now. I look at some of the ways I act and think *I am so screwed up! Shouldn't I be different?*"—Savannah, 23, grad student

▶ "For as long as I can remember, two things have been true. One, I have always loved God and tried to follow Christ. And, two, I've been attracted to guys. I never consciously chose that. It just is. Over the last 20 years, I bet I've prayed 10,000 times, 'God, if I'm not supposed to have these urges, would you please . . . *please* . . . take them away?' He hasn't. You tell me: Why wouldn't God answer that prayer?"—Karl, 33, accountant

▶ "For the first six or seven years after divinity school, being a pastor was really gratifying. Then it slowly became grueling. I felt like all around me people were drowning, and meanwhile I was barely keeping my own head above the waterline. I never thought serving God and serving people would be so hard."—Walter, 49, ex-minister

1. What words or phrases would you use to describe what these three are feeling?

_____

_____

_____

_____

_____

2. In what ways do you relate to their disappointment or disillusionment?

_____

_____

_____

_____

_____

3. What are the biggest disappointments you've experienced so far with God, the spiritual life, or following Christ?

_____

_____

_____

_____

_____

_____

Spiritual Reality According to the Bible

Take a few minutes to read, ponder, and write a response to these nine Scripture passages that discuss and/or describe the experience of being a follower of Christ. The first one has been filled out as an example.

The passage	What it reveals about struggle	My reality
"Let us not become weary in doing good, for at the proper time we will reap a harvest if we do not give up." (Galatians 6:9)	*Doing good can wear you out and make you feel like giving up, but there's a reward if we hang in there!*	*Volunteering in kids' ministry is tough. I feel like quitting some weeks, but I know it's worth it!*
"Let us not become weary in doing good, for at the proper time we will reap a harvest if we do not give up." (Galatians 6:9)		
"For I do not do the good I want to do, but the evil I do not want to do—this I keep on doing." (Romans 7:19)		
"Not only that, but we rejoice in our sufferings, knowing that suffering produces endurance, and endurance produces character, and character produces hope." (Romans 5:3–4, ESV)		
"Indeed, all who desire to live a godly life in Christ Jesus will be persecuted." (2 Timothy 3:12, ESV)		
"The temptations in your life are no different from what others experience. And God is faithful. He will not allow the temptation to be more than you can stand. When you are tempted, he will show you a way out so that you can endure." (1 Corinthians 10:13, NLT)		
"For our struggle is not against flesh and blood, but against the rulers, against the authorities, against the powers of this dark world and against the spiritual forces of evil in the heavenly realms." (Ephesians 6:12)		

The passage	What it reveals about struggle	My reality
"Be of sober spirit, be on the alert. Your adversary, the devil, prowls around like a roaring lion, seeking someone to devour." (1 Peter 5:8, NASB)		
"Here on earth you will have many trials and sorrows. But take heart, because I have overcome the world." (John 16:33, NLT)		
"Dear friends, I urge you, as foreigners and exiles, to abstain from sinful desires, which wage war against your soul." (1 Peter 2:11)		

4. What are your big takeaways from this exercise? How do these verses describe the spiritual reality of a follower of Jesus?

_____

_____

_____

We speak often of becoming *disillusioned*—and we say that like it's a bad thing. But consider for a moment what that word really means. The prefix *dis*—means "apart, away, or without," so to be *disillusioned* is literally to be "without illusions." It means to be pulled away from what we only *thought* was real and true! Disillusionment is actually *the process of coming back to reality*. That may not be fun. But it's vital and good.

What's the reality of the spiritual life, of following Jesus?

When we read the Scripture, we often spin it by

▶ Forcing the Bible to say things it doesn't say

▶ Ignoring its clear but dark truths

However, if we *don't* spin Scripture, we would likely come to the following conclusions:

▶ Life is hard. And faith in Christ doesn't promise to make things easy. In fact, following Jesus means we can expect the world to hate us, the enemy of our souls to assault us, and our unredeemed human nature to fiercely resist God's transforming work within us. We can and should expect an epic struggle because the spiritual life is a fight. We live in a world at war.

We can expect to grow spiritually, but never arrive at perfection this side of heaven. We will face powerful temptations up until the day we die. We will resist them sometimes, and we will cave in lots of other times. Not even our worst failures will alter God's love for us.

Even though we are God's beloved children, we should expect to face trials—lots of little ones and others that are big and terrifying. No Christian gets a pass from suffering. The Scripture doesn't guarantee anyone a disease-free or accident-free life. On the contrary, the Bible says life will have its bitter moments and its glorious ones too. And the history of God's people shows this to be true. When the pain doesn't take our breath

> "How often we look upon God as our last and feeblest resource. We go to him because we have nowhere else to go. And then we learn that the storms of life have driven us, not upon the rocks, but into the desired haven."—George MacDonald

away, the beauty just might. We will cry a lot. And we will do our share of laughing too.

> "Your life is not going to be easy, and it should not be easy. It ought to be hard. It ought to be radical; it ought to be restless; it ought to lead you to places you'd rather not go."
> —Henri Nouwen

We could go on and on:

▶ How we won't understand many things.

▶ How many of our prayers won't be answered in ways we'd like.

▶ How serving others will be exhausting, and how some will never acknowledge our sacrifice, and others will actually grumble at our efforts.

We will want to quit again and again, which is why we need to follow Jesus with others alongside to encourage us.

Understanding these things is how we become healthily disillusioned about the spiritual life. These are the realities we should expect.

How we imagine the spiritual life . . .

smooth • predictable
• always inspiring
• full of clarity

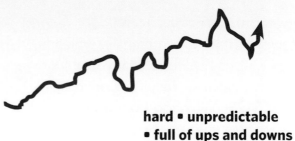

What the spiritual life is really like . . .

hard • unpredictable
• full of ups and downs
• full of ambiguity

Take-Home Reflections

C. S. Lewis' ingenious book, *The Screwtape Letters* tells the tale of a crafty, mid-level devil giving advice to a less wily apprentice. Screwtape, the older demon, discusses the way God often gives new converts obvious reminders of his presence, warm spiritual feelings, and even a strong desire to turn away from temptation.

"But," Screwtape continues, "He never allows this state of affairs to last long. Sooner or later He withdraws, if not in fact, at least from their conscious experience, all those supports and incentives. He leaves the creature to stand up on its own legs—to carry out from the will alone duties which have lost all relish. It is during such trough periods, much more than during the peak periods, that it is growing into the sort of creature He wants it to be."

In other words, God allows his children to struggle. Struggle is a normal part of the spiritual life. Struggle is how we grow and make progress in the faith. If you are struggling in the faith, it's not a sign of failure. It's a sign you are on the path that all disciples are called to walk.

So keep walking. *And make sure you walk with other believers.* Discipleship is a hard battle and a holy journey, but we were never meant to fight or journey alone (Ecclesiastes 4:12).

If we don't give up, we will be able to say what the apostle Paul said just before his death, "I have fought the good fight, I have finished the race, I have kept the faith" (2 Timothy 4:7).

Life Application

An important part of discipleship is learning how to apply God's truths to your life. Below are just a few ways you can start thinking about what you've learned and apply it to your daily life.

1. Memorize our verse, 1 Timothy 6:12.

2. Read the sections from Paul's second letter to the Corinthians in which he describes his life as a devoted follower and servant of Jesus (2 Corinthians 6:4–10; 11:23–28). Why and how do you think Paul was able to endure such struggle?

3. Wrestle with one or two of the following:

   ▶ What were your expectations of God and of the spiritual life when you first came to faith?

   ▶ Have any of those expectations changed as you've grown spiritually?

   ▶ What has this lesson helped you see differently about following Jesus?

   ▶ What specific spiritual battles are most fierce in your life right now—fighting envy, lust, or doubt; trying to develop healthy spiritual habits, etc.?

Topic 20: Perseverance

Dealing with Doubts, Trials, and Fears

"Blessed is the one who perseveres under trial
because, having stood the test, that person
will receive the crown of life that the Lord has
promised to those who love him."

—James 1:12

It's tough to keep hanging in there when you're feeling doubts and facing problems, isn't it?

Maybe you're:

▶ A person with a lofty dream that is going to require grueling years of schooling—and even then you'll have no guarantees of success.

▶ Someone whose spouse is bitter and impossible to please.

▶ Caring for an aging parent with Alzheimer's or a child who requires around-the-clock care.

▶ A cancer patient who's facing another round of chemo with another drug because the last one was ineffective— just like the first two.

▶ The friendly kid at a new school who constantly gets teased, shunned and thinks, *What's the use? Why even try?*

▶ A laid-off worker who has sent out one hundred resumes without a single request for a follow-up interview.

Because life is tough—and sometimes brutal—lots of people quit things every day. They quit a job or walk away from a friendship. They give up on a dream or pull the plug on a marriage.

For anyone who is trying to follow Jesus, life's painful and persistent hardships can foster serious doubt. If you're struggling, you may even be asking questions like:

▶ Is God real?

▶ Why isn't this "faith in Christ thing" working?

▶ I thought Jesus came to make my life better and more blessed?

In this lesson, we want to look at the rare and wonderful quality of perseverance. Disciples have this trait because Jesus, the one they follow, had it. Why should you keep trusting the Father in heaven and walking with him, when doing so doesn't seem to make your life easier or better? In truth, in many places of the world, being a Christian makes your life exponentially *harder*. Is it really possible to "keep the faith" in a world filled with trouble?

Let's study perseverance and see how we can cultivate this noble virtue in our lives.

Bible Study

Perseverance: What Does It Mean?

In the New Testament, there are two primary Greek words that get translated "perseverance." One is *proskartere*. It means "to adhere" or "to cling" or "to be devoted." Some of our English Bibles translate it "to continue (in something)," "to be steadfast," or "to be constant."

Get this: In Mark 3:9, this word has been used of a boat that has been made ready for Jesus, devoted for his use, and sits waiting nearby. In Acts 10:7, it describes a faithful personal attendant. In short, the idea of perseverance is persisting, staying, waiting, not leaving—and doing all that when it's hard or boring, when you're being opposed, or whether or not you *feel* like it.

The other word is *hupomone*. It conveys the same ideas of endurance, patience, being steadfast, having to wait. Again, the implication is that you are weary of your hard circumstances, and tired of waiting for things to change. You want to throw in the towel. But the voice of perseverance urges, "Don't quit. Hang in there. Cling. Remain faithful despite the opposition and the tantalizing promises of life elsewhere."

In what specific ways are followers of Christ supposed to persevere?

Take a look at these verses that urge followers of Jesus to *persevere* in some aspect of the life of faith:

▶ "Be joyful in hope, patient in affliction, faithful in prayer" (Romans 12:12).

▶ "Let us not become weary in doing good, for at the proper time we will reap a harvest if we do not give up" (Galatians 6:9).

▶ "But you must remain faithful to the things you have been taught. You know they are true, for you know you can trust those who taught you" (2 Timothy 3:14, NLT).

▶ "Therefore, since we are surrounded by such a great cloud of witnesses, let us throw off everything that hinders and the sin that so easily entangles. And let us run with perseverance the race marked out for us" (Hebrews 12:1).

▶ "Be on guard. Stand firm in the faith. Be courageous. Be strong" (1 Corinthians 16:13, NLT).

▶ "Devote yourselves to prayer, being watchful and thankful" (Colossians 4:2).

▶ "And pray in the Spirit on all occasions with all kinds of prayers and requests. With this in mind, be alert and always keep on praying for all the Lord's people" (Ephesians 6:18).

▶ "So then, brothers and sisters, stand firm and hold fast to the teachings we passed on to you, whether by word of mouth or by letter" (2 Thessalonians 2:15).

1. This, of course, is only a partial listing of verses that call Christians to persevere, but what specific areas do you see mentioned?

_____

_____

_____

2. How would you rate yourself when it comes to persevering in the areas just mentioned?

_____

_____

_____

3. Read Hebrews 6:1–8 and 10:26–31. The New Testament includes a lot of warnings like these about falling away from faith. Here are a few other examples:

▶ "You will be hated by all because of My name, but it is the one who has endured to the end who will be saved." (Jesus, speaking in Matthew 10:22, NASB)

▶ "As God's coworkers we urge you not to receive God's grace in vain." (2 Cor. 6:1)

▶ "See to it, brothers and sisters, that none of you has a sinful, unbelieving heart that turns away from the living God." (Hebrews 3:12)

What do you make of these verses? What are they saying?

_____

_____

_____

4. How would you describe the difference between a true believer who still sins and a "make believer" who never really had true faith and still sins?

_____

_____

_____

5. Check out these verses that speak of what God does to help disciples to persevere and remain faithful:

 ▶ "I give them eternal life, and they shall never perish; no one will snatch them out of my hand. My Father, who has given them to me, is greater than all; no one can snatch them out of my Father's hand" (Jesus, speaking in John 10:28–29).

 ▶ "God's gifts and his call are irrevocable" (Romans 11:29).

 ▶ "For I am confident of this very thing, that He who began a good work in you will perfect it until the day of Christ Jesus" (Philippians 1:6, NASB).

 ▶ "All praise to God, the Father of our Lord Jesus Christ. It is by his great mercy that we have been born again, because God raised Jesus Christ from the dead. Now we live with great expectation, and we have a priceless inheritance—an inheritance that is kept in heaven for you, pure and undefiled, beyond the reach of change and decay. And through your faith, God is protecting you by his power until you receive this salvation, which is ready to be revealed on the last day for all to see" (1 Peter 1:3–5, NLT).

What's That About?

I heard some Christians arguing about "the perseverance of the saints." They were wrestling with the question, "Can a believer lose his or her salvation?" or "Is it possible to have true faith and then turn away from it?" This is a hotly debated issue, but most Christians would agree with these statements:

- Some who claim to be believers are not truly born again due to misunderstanding of the gospel, insincerity, or misplaced trust, etc.

- God alone knows the truth about a person's heart and spiritual condition.

- Even redeemed people will continue to sin.

God is faithful to bring his children home. Those who have exercised genuine, saving faith—they've been made alive spiritually and declared righteous by virtue of Christ's death and resurrection on their behalf—cannot be un-adopted by God. Despite failure and sin, we cannot invalidate God's grace. He will faithfully see to it that we "persevere" and enter into everlasting life.

According to these verses, why—if we have faith in Christ—do we not have to fear?

_____

_____

_____

6. Writing to Christians who were facing a lot of hard things in life, the apostle James said:

"Consider it pure joy, my brothers and sisters, whenever you face trials of many kinds, because you know that the testing of your faith produces perseverance. Let perseverance finish its work so that you may be mature and complete, not lacking anything" (James 1:2–4).

Does that seem ridiculous to you? How is it possible to be joyful in hard times?

_____

_____

_____

Notice a couple of things. First, the passage says "whenever" and not "if by chance." In other words, trials are a fact of life. Disciples of Jesus don't get a pass from the troubles of this world. (You can study more about this truth in "Topic 19: Overcoming.")

Trials are never fun. But if we faithfully persevere, God brings good things out of our bad situations.

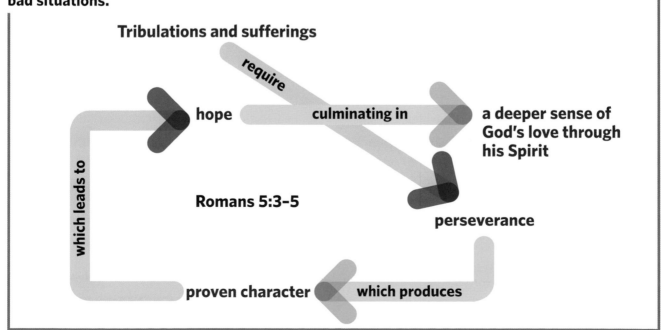

Notice also that James says difficulties come our way not to ruin us, but to develop us and strengthen us. Trials are the God-ordained/God-orchestrated "laboratory" wherein we can develop perseverance. All that waiting, trusting, and clinging is how we come to know firsthand that we are tougher than we imagined, that we can endure more than we thought. And why? Because our God is more faithful than we ever dreamed.

What can we do to cultivate perseverance in our lives?

The Lord has given his children four great resources for the hard times of life:

1. **His Word.** "All Scripture is God-breathed and is useful for teaching, rebuking, correcting and training in righteousness, so that the servant of God may be thoroughly equipped for every good work" (2 Timothy 3:16–17).

   The trustworthy promises of the Bible can shore up our flagging faith.

2. **His Spirit.** "But the Advocate, the Holy Spirit, whom the Father will send in my name, will teach you all things and will remind you of everything I have said to you. Peace I leave with you; my peace I give you. I do not give to you as the world gives. Do not let your hearts be troubled and do not be afraid" (John 14:26–27).

   The indwelling Spirit can give us the power to continue to cling.

3. **His People.** "I thank my God every time I remember you. In all my prayers for all of you, I always pray with joy because of your partnership in the gospel from the first day until now" (Paul writing to the Philippians, from prison, 1:3–5).

   The body of Christ can surround us and provide encouragement to keep going.

4. **His Mission**. "But thanks be to God! He gives us the victory through our Lord Jesus Christ. Therefore, my dear brothers and sisters, stand firm. Let nothing move you. Always give yourselves fully to the work of the Lord, because you know that your labor in the Lord is not in vain" (1 Corinthians 15:57–58).

   Participation in an eternally worthy task can keep us focused on what matters.

What is perseverance? It is continuing to follow Jesus, even when he leads us to and through harrowing chapters of life. It is hanging on to and cultivating your faith through life's difficult times.

> "Perseverance is . . . a call to faithfulness, but it is also an affirmation that somehow, in spite of our failures, God will bring His committed people through the difficulties and concerns of life to their promised destiny in Christ."
> —Gerald L. Borchert

Ultimately, we are able to cling to God because he holds us firmly in his hands.

Take-Home Reflections

A Perseverance Self-Check

Check all the actions of perseverance you intend to live out.

By God's grace, secure in the love of Christ, and in the power of the Spirit:

☐ I will consistently open and read the Scripture, setting my hope on the things God says are true, and seeking to be a doer of the Word.

☐ I will be honest and authentic in prayer.

☐ I will, when I do, think, or say, wrong things, turn quickly to Jesus, who has forgiven me and who loves me unconditionally.

☐ I will honor my commitments—even when I don't feel like it.

☐ I will, by God's grace, step out in faith to do something that I feel is God's will but that makes me uncomfortable.

☐ I will seek to be faithful, not for the rest of my life, but in this moment.

☐ I will humble myself—confessing my sin, and asking forgiveness from those whom I have hurt.

☐ I will value and practice the disciplines of biblical community and spiritual friendship.

☐ I will initiate a much-needed conversation with a family member, friend, or coworker.

☐ I will cling desperately to God in my current trials—like a drowning person clinging to a lifeline.

Life Application

An important part of discipleship is learning how to apply God's truths to your life. Below are just a few ways you can start thinking about what you've learned and apply it to your daily life.

1. Memorize our memory verse, James 1:12.

   "Blessed is the one who perseveres under trial because, having stood the test, that person will receive the crown of life that the Lord has promised to those who love him."

2. Talk over the results of your Perseverance Self-Check with a trusted, confidential friend.

3. Share with the same friend or another, one of the current struggles in your life. Ask for prayer and encouragement as many struggles don't have easy answers, and some cannot be solved in this lifetime.

CHAPTER 5:

Ten Spiritual Disciplines That Shape a Disciple

Topic 21: Worship

Bringing God Glory in All You Do

"So whether you eat or drink or whatever
you do, do it all for the glory of God."

—1 Corinthians 10:31

Ask a few people what the word "worship" means to them, and you're likely to get a wide variety of answers. And each of these can be an important *part* of a person's worship of God.

What Does Worship Mean?

Common Responses	What That Means
"It's what we call the gathering at our church on Sunday mornings."	Worship is a meeting on a certain day at a certain place at a certain time.
"It's what we do at church between the welcome and announcements and the sermon."	Worship is spiritual music—it's singing songs with other Christians.
"Worship is spiritual music—it's singing songs with other Christians."	Worship is a certain body posture or an outward act of enthusiasm.
"It's turning away from secular stuff and focusing on spiritual truth."	Worship is a retreat from earthly realities.

"Every man is bound somewhere, somehow, to a throne, to a government, to an authority, to something that is supreme, to something to which he offers sacrifice, and burns incense, and bends the knee."
—G. Campbell Morgan

As has been stated before, a disciple is a person who follows Jesus—to *know* Jesus and his teaching; to *grow* more like Jesus; and to *go* for Jesus, serving others and making new disciples.

In other words, discipleship involves learning new insights, taking on a new character, and engaging in new behaviors. Some of these new behaviors are referred to as spiritual disciplines or practices.

When we think of the practices that shape a disciple, it's good to start with *worship*.

1. What words, images, etc. come to mind when you think of the word "worship"?

_____

_____

_____

First, we'll look at the meaning of that word.

Worship Defined and Described

Read these verses, one from the Old Testament, and one from the New Testament:

▶ "Come, let us worship and bow down, let us kneel before the LORD our Maker." (Psalm 95:6, NASB)

▶ "But the hour is coming, and is now here, when the true worshipers will worship the Father in spirit and truth, for the Father is seeking such people to worship him. God is spirit, and those who worship him must worship in spirit and truth." (John 4:23–24, ESV)

The Hebrew word translated *worship* in Psalm 95:6 is *shachah*. It means literally "to bow down." The idea is bending low or prostrating oneself as a way of giving honor or paying homage or expressing devotion.

The Greek word translated worship in John 4 is *proskyne*. It also conveys this same idea of bowing with respect and devotion (see Matthew 2:11, 4:9, and 28:9).

What about our English word "worship"? It is derived from the Old English term "worthship"—literally, having worth or value.

Put all those meanings together and in the most basic sense:

> "It is not a thing which a man can decide, whether he will be a worshiper or not, a worshiper he must be, the only question is what will he worship? Every man worships—is a born worshiper."
> —Frederick Robertson

> Worship is assigning worth and value to someone (or something), and then—out of respect, gratitude, affection, devotion, or fear— bowing one's life before that someone (or something).

Bible Study

Based on our definition and description of worship, there are two important implications:

1. Everyone worships someone or something.

2. A disciple seeks to worship God and God alone.

Everyone Worships Someone or Something.

If worship is about ascribing value, then every person does that. Everybody has things—people or goals or dreams—he or she considers valuable—and usually one "something" viewed as having supreme worth. So it's never a question of "*Will* we worship?" but rather, "*Who* or *what* will we worship?"

Think of all the "created" things to which people can and do assign worth or ascribe value:

▶ Family

▶ Marriage

▶ Educational credentials

▶ Children

▶ Grandchildren

▶ A boyfriend or girlfriend

▶ Friendships

▶ A job, career, work

▶ A financial portfolio

▶ A dream (retirement, having your own business, vacation home, etc.)

▶ A political ideology

▶ The success of a sports team

▶ Health

▶ Fitness

▶ Physical appearance

▶ Acclaim

▶ The approval of others

▶ Sexual gratification

▶ Accomplishments

▶ Winning (being the best at everything)

▶ Popularity

▶ A reputation or image

"He who has not learned to worship will find God and this world wearisome. If you've trusted in Christ as your Savior, but you've really not learned to worship God, chances are you have found the Christian life disappointing."
—Ravi Zacharias

Many of these items are good things—even blessings from God! But they are not as important as God. We must never let *good* things become *ultimate* things in our hearts.

190

Why Does God Command Us to Worship Him?

Isn't that vain and egotistical?

The eternal Triune God doesn't need our worship. He is complete. He lacks nothing. He is neither threatened nor diminished if humans refuse or fail to worship him.

God does command worship, however, because it is:

- Fitting
- Fulfilling

Worship of God is fitting.

As the perfect and majestic one, God deserves worship. He is worthy of all praise. Imagine how shocked you would be to watch someone spurn an exquisite gourmet feast prepared by the world's best chef, only to turn around and rave over a mediocre fast-food meal. To fail to worship the one who is worthy of infinite praise is an infinite scandal! This is why the heavens themselves shout the glory of God (Psalm 19:1). This is why God's throne is surrounded by angelic beings who forever worship him (Revelation 4:8).

God saying, "Worship me" isn't vain; it's right. It's common sense.

Worship of God is fulfilling.

The other reason God commands us to worship him is for our benefit. When we praise God we find satisfaction and joy. C. S. Lewis talked about this—how expressing our awe or wonder or appreciation to God "completes the enjoyment." Imagine not being able to cheer your favorite team after a last-second victory, or not being allowed to express affection to your beloved. Our delight and joy would be diminished.

2. In what ways is this idea that everyone worships someone or something a new concept to you?

_____

_____

_____

_____

_____

A Disciple Worships God and God Alone

3. Look at these two verses, one from the Old Testament and one from the New:

   ▶ "Bring all who claim me as their God, for I have made them for my glory. It was I who created them.'" (Isaiah 43:7, NLT)

   ▶ "For in him all things were created." (Colossians 1:16)

   According to these passages, why did God create us?

   _____

   _____

   _____

   _____

4. What does it mean to live for the glory of God?

   _____

   _____

   _____

   _____

What Psalms Teaches Us About Worship

"For me, the key to worship is simply quiet, undistracted time with my eyes closed. By setting aside a certain time of my day for God—and God alone—I am indicating in the best way I know that he is important to me. I will sit and love him whether I feel his presence or not. Of course, the Bible assures me he is with me, always, whether I sense his presence or not."
—43-year-old woman

The Old Testament Book of Psalms was the "hymn book" for the Jewish people, including Jesus. These 150 prayer-songs are beloved because they speak to every situation and emotion of life. They show that God is worthy of our worship—our attention, allegiance, affection, and adoration—no matter what we're facing.

When you read the psalms you'll notice they include loud, expressive worship and quiet introspective meditation. Whether songs of protest or praise, an individual reeling in terror or a nation rejoicing in triumph, in the psalms we see God's people:

▷ Bowing down before God (Psalm 95:6)

▷ Seeking his face (Psalm 105:3–4)

▷ Waiting for the Lord (Psalm 33:20–21)

▷ Dwelling in his house (Psalm 27:4)

▷ Lifting hands (Psalm 134:2)

▷ Shouting to him (Psalm 47:1)

▷ Singing to him (Psalm 104:33)

In short, the psalms show us that worship is not simply attending a "worship service" at some kind of "worship facility" and singing "worship songs." Worship isn't an event so much as it's a mindset, a posture of life. It's choosing to make God central. It's cultivating the moment-by-moment practice of looking to God and saying from the heart, "I want to live for your glory!"

▷ In wondrous moments it's exclaiming, "Wow! You are amazing!"

▷ In tough situations it's crying out, "I need you!"

▷ In good times it's saying, "Thank you!"

▷ In faith-testing circumstances it's whispering, "Okay (gulp!) I am trusting you."

Okay, now comes the fun part.

How Do We Engage in this Practice of Worship?

In the same way we have different personalities and relational styles, different strengths and interests, so we have different ways of worshiping or connecting with God.

In his book, *Sacred Pathways*, author Gary Thomas shows how, for some two thousand years, Christians have expressed their enjoyment and worship of God through a variety of "pathways."

Though there are surely others, he cites nine primary ways people draw near to God and express their love and devotion to him:

> "A friend of mine who was in medical school took me into the 'cadaver room' where she and other first year students learned about human anatomy by exploring bodies that had been donated to science. When she opened a 'body bag' to reveal a dissected human form, I almost dropped to my knees. I was struck, not by nausea but by awe. The complexity and intricacy of our bodies—we really are, as the Bible says, 'fearfully and wonderfully made.' In that moment, I worshiped, maybe more than I ever have in a church."—30-year-old man

▷ *Naturalists* are those who feel inspired to love God when they are out-of-doors, in natural settings.

▶ *Sensates* worship with their senses. They appreciate beautiful worship services that involve their sight (art), smell (incense), and ears (music).

▶ *Ascetics* prefer to worship in quiet solitude and simplicity.

▶ *Activists* adore God through confronting evil and battling injustice in the world.

▶ *Caregivers* worship by loving others and meeting their needs.

▶ *Traditionalists* draw closer to God and worship him through rituals, liturgy, symbols, and unchanging structures.

▶ *Enthusiasts* worship through expressive celebration.

▶ *Contemplatives* love God through peaceful adoration.

▶ *Intellectuals* praise God by studying with their minds.

5. What would you say is your primary "pathway" of worship?

_____

_____

_____

6. What would be the value of sometimes participating in worship pathways that are not your first preference?

_____

_____

_____

_____

7. What worship advice would you give a person who says, "I don't sense God. In fact, I doubt his presence in my life right now"?

_____

_____

_____

_____

Outside-the-Box Worship

Anything is worship when it is done with an eye on God and with gratitude to God.

Try these different ways of worship:

- ▶ Take a walk or hike and soak up God's creation.

- ▶ Sit and gawk at a sunset.

- ▶ Sing. Being off-key or pitchy is irrelevant, which is why Psalm 95 tells us, "Make a joyful noise!" (Psalm 95:1, ESV) and not "Perform a beautiful song."

- ▶ Climb a tree.

- ▶ Write a blogpost that would make God smile.

- ▶ Marvel at the complexity of science or the precision of an algebraic formula.

- ▶ Study a leaf, a flower, a caterpillar, a rock.

- ▶ Laughing with your toddler as he or she splashes in a puddle.

- ▶ Lie in a meadow on a cloudless night and watch shooting stars.

- ▶ Make or create something: a short story, a poem, a drawing, a painting, a sculpture, a video, a great meal, a woodworking project, an article of clothing, etc.

8. What are some other new and different ways you can think of to turn your heart to God and show your love and gratitude for him?

_____

_____

_____

_____

9. How do you feel God's Spirit prompting you to alter your worship views or practices as a result of this study?

_____

_____

_____

_____

Take-Home Reflections

Quick Reminders About Worship

Thoughts or Feelings	Way You Can React
When feeling blah or sad	Don't pretend to be upbeat when you're not. Worship isn't a pep rally. It's being your authentic self in the presence of God. As the psalms show us, sometimes that means crying out in despair (not laughing, smiling, and jumping around).
When wondering if you're doing it "right"	First, there's no single "right" way to worship. Second, God is gracious and knows your heart. When you make a genuine effort to worship God you are worshipping God. Desiring to love God is loving God.
When you can't sense God's presence	Pray something like this: "God, you promise in your Word that you are always with me. That doesn't feel true right now, but I choose to trust what you say, rather than what I sense. Thank you for being right here."
When you feel dry or stuck	It's okay to have bad days: Don't be hard on yourself. Every worshiper experiences this. People go up and down depending on the amount of sleep or good food or how healthy they are or how much stress they are under.
When you don't feel like singing—maybe due to being tone deaf or having hearing problems or over-sensitive ears	Focus on the lyrics, or be encouraged in your heart by watching others love God through song.

Life Application

An important part of discipleship is learning how to apply God's truths to your life. Below are just a few ways you can start thinking about what you've learned and apply it to your daily life.

1. Memorize our memory verse, 1 Corinthians 10:31.

   "So whether you eat or drink or whatever you do, do it all for the glory of God."

2. Ponder the chart "Worship Myths and Truths" on the next page.

3. Wrestle with one or two of these questions:

   ▶ In what new way could you worship God this week?

▶ Repetition can get stale, so how can you mix up your worship time?

　✦ A different Bible verse?

　✦ Reading a book about God?

　✦ Singing?

　✦ Focusing in on one attribute of God?

▶ What three things am I grateful for today?

▶ Where are you most dependent on God?

▶ Describe a time you felt God's power or closeness.

▶ Finish this sentence: I find myself worshipping and praising God when . . .

Worship Myths and Truths

Worship Myth	Worship Truth
Worship is a gathering at a certain time and in a certain place.	Worship is an all-day, every-day mindset. It's bowing down to God and his purpose for our lives.
That we "go" to worship.	We "live" worship, and bring it with us—or not.
Worship is a handful of "spiritual" activities such as singing, praying, taking communion, hearing sermons, etc.	All of life—even secular activities—can be worship, if we do them for the glory of God. For example, enjoying the beautiful world God created by taking a hike.
Worship is about externals such as music, song choices, body posture, how good the band or worship leader is, how expressive the congregation is, etc.	Worship is about the heart. It is setting aside quiet time alone and saying, "God, I love you. God, I trust you. God, I praise you."
God-honoring worship means having or coming away with a certain feeling.	God-honoring worship is approaching God by faith, and "in spirit and in truth" (John 4:24) whether having any sensations or not.
I am the judge of whether a time of worship was worthwhile.	I am to participate in worship—and leave judgments about its quality to God. Attempting to worship God IS to worship God. God accepts our attempts, no matter how feeble.
One kind of worship is better than others.	An infinite God can be worshiped in a variety of ways (privately, publicly; individually, corporately; silently, loudly; etc.)—whatever works for your personality and situation. No one way of worshiping is better than any other.

Topic 22: Solitude & Silence

Learning to Quiet Your Soul

"This is what the Sovereign LORD,
the Holy One of Israel, says:
'In repentance and rest is your salvation,
in quietness and trust is your strength.'"

—Isaiah 30:15

Two things are true:

▶ We are the most *connected* generation ever.

▶ Ours is the *loudest* culture in human history.

Think about it . . . we have smart phones that can do about everything but serve us

a cappuccino! With wireless technology, we can stream music and movies (and pretty much anything else) from the Internet—twenty-four hours a day, seven days a week—from just about anywhere on the planet. Would you like to sit in a bustling coffee shop and listen to your favorite band while you FaceTime with a friend on the opposite coast, text back and forth with your mom, *and* keep an eye on your Twitter feed? No problem.

But at what cost? What's all this doing to our souls? Are we addicted to noise? And is our constant connection to culture hurting our connection with God?

Here's a third true thing: As we follow Jesus to know him and his teachings and as we grow to become more like him in character, we must also do the things Jesus did. We must engage in holy habits, or spiritual disciplines. These are integral to God's mission of transformation—our own lives and the lives of others. Two of these holy habits are *solitude* and *silence*.

Bible Study

What the Bible Tells Us About Solitude

For Jesus, time in solitude was a top priority. Consider these passages, one from each of the four gospels:

▶ "After he had dismissed them, he went up on a mountainside by himself to pray. Later that night, he was there alone" (Matthew 14:23).

▶ "Very early in the morning, while it was still dark, Jesus got up, left the house and went off to a solitary place, where he prayed" (Mark 1:35).

▶ "Once when Jesus was praying in private and his disciples were with him, he asked them, 'Who do the crowds say I am?'" (Luke 9:18).

▶ "Jesus, knowing that they intended to come and make him king by force, withdrew again to a mountain by himself" (John 6:15).

"We are so afraid of silence that we chase ourselves from one event to the next in order not to have to spend a moment alone with ourselves, in order not to have to look at ourselves in the mirror."
—Dietrich Bonhoeffer

1. What conclusions do you draw from those verses?

_____

_____

_____

_____

_____

Solitude is a retreat—whether brief or long—from people and the distractions of modern life. It's the deliberate choice to withdraw from social interaction and daily "to do" lists so that you can enter an environment in which you can focus your undivided attention on the Father in heaven. When the Bible emphasizes solitude, it doesn't just mean "being alone." It means "being alone *with God*." This is important for at least three reasons:

Solitude Is Preparatory

Time alone with God can strengthen us for upcoming ministry or life challenges. Jesus spent almost six weeks alone in the wilderness before commencing his public ministry (Matthew 4:2).

Simple Ways to Find Solitude

Whether you need a few minutes of time alone with God or a more extended period, here are some tips:

- Set your alarm to go off thirty minutes before the others in your household wake up.

- Stay awake for thirty minutes after everyone else has gone to bed.

- If it's safe to do so, take a walk around your neighborhood after dark.

- Find a nearby park and "claim" an unused park bench.

- Utilize the guest room.

- At work, take advantage of an empty conference room during lunch.

- Park your car by a nearby lake.

- Find a study carrel in the library.

- Go sit in your deer stand, duck blind, or fishing camp.

- Borrow a friend's house who is on vacation.

- Go in your bedroom and lock the door.

- Sit and soak in the bathtub.

- Sit on the back porch in a rocking chair.

- Slip into a church or chapel during the week.

It's because of Jesus' example that many believers get up a few minutes early each day and have a devotional time, quiet time, or appointment with God. They see this as an important spiritual exercise—an opportunity to get their bearings, remember what's true, and reconnect with the lover of their souls before launching out into a crowded and loud world.

Discussion Questions

▶ What are your own devotional life habits? Do you have any?

▶ Have you ever experimented with extended times of silence or even a silent retreat? What was that like?

Solitude Is Revealing

When we are socially engaged, mixing and mingling with people, or handling all of the tasks at work or home, it's easy to become obsessed with what others think. Our minds fill with questions:

▶ *How am I coming across?*

▶ *Do they notice me?*

▶ *Do they like me?*

▶ *Do they consider me charming? Funny? Intelligent? Competent?*

▶ *Am I doing everything on my to-do list?*

▶ *Does God see me as a failure?*

Surrounded by people and jockeying for attention and acclaim, our motives and mission can morph. Instead of being our authentic selves, we become image-conscious. We are "on." We play to the crowd. We wear masks.

In solitude all that is stripped away. There's no one around to impress, no one around to fear. It's just us and the one who knows us through and through, the one who loves us fully and completely.

Solitude clarifies exactly what we've been looking to for our identities. Like Jesus in the wilderness, solitude forces us to deal with the temptation to find significance in

unhealthy ways. But in addition, it helps us see that God loves us unconditionally. No matter how we've failed, he loves us and is on our side, helping us to stand up again and keep going.

Discussion Questions

▶ Is the thought of solitude *exciting* to you, *excruciating*, or something in between? Why?

▶ In recent years, researchers and writers have shed light on different personality types—For example, being an introvert versus being an extrovert. Which are you? Could that be one clue as to why you either enjoy or hate solitude?

Solitude Is Restorative

> "Here then I am, far from the busy ways of men. I sit down alone; only God is here."—John Wesley

When we're tired or confused, when we have forgotten who and whose we really are, solitude can help us regain our bearings. By withdrawing, we can tune out all the other voices and hear the one voice that matters most.

In 1 Kings 19:1–4, 9–13 (NLT) we read a great example of the restorative power of solitude in the life of the prophet Elijah. After a stressful time of ministry in which he had faced down hundreds of false prophets, these events happened:

> When [King] Ahab got home, he told Jezebel [his wife, the queen] everything Elijah had done, including the way he

had killed all the prophets of Baal. So Jezebel sent this message to Elijah: "May the gods strike me and even kill me if by this time tomorrow I have not killed you just as you killed them."

Elijah was afraid and fled for his life. He went to Beersheba, a town in Judah, and he left his servant there. Then he went on alone into the wilderness, traveling all day. He sat down under a solitary broom tree and prayed that he might die.

But the Lord said to him, "What are you doing here, Elijah?"

Elijah replied, "I have zealously served the Lord God Almighty. But the people of Israel have broken their covenant with you, torn down your altars, and killed every one of your prophets. I am the only one left, and now they are trying to kill me, too."

"Go out and stand before me on the mountain," the Lord told him. And as Elijah stood there, the Lord passed by, and a mighty windstorm hit the mountain. It was such a terrible blast that the rocks were torn loose, but the Lord was not in the wind. After the wind there was an earthquake, but the Lord was not in the earthquake. And after the earthquake there was a fire, but the Lord was not in the fire. And after the fire there was the sound of a gentle whisper. When Elijah heard it, he wrapped his face in his cloak and went out and stood at the entrance of the cave.

And a voice said, "What are you doing here, Elijah?"

Discussion Questions

▶ The sound Elijah heard in verse 12, "a gentle whisper," is also translated as "a low whisper" (ESV), and "a gentle blowing" (NASB). What exactly do you think he heard in this solitary place?

▶ When you've spent time alone in the presence of God, how have you sensed him speaking to you?

▶ If you've never sensed God speaking to you what are other ways God gets your attention in "a gentle whisper"?

What the Bible Tells Us About Silence

Silence is the absence of noise and commotion. To "practice the discipline of silence" is to consciously withdraw from the ruckus of television, music, conversation, podcasts, social media, minor "emergencies" at work or home, etc. The discipline of silence is making the deliberate choice to enter into the quiet. Once there, instead of filling time and space with words, we listen attentively. We do so because as Solomon wisely noted, there is a "time to be quiet and a time to speak" (Ecclesiastes 3:7, NLT).

2. Consider these passages from the psalms and the prophets that emphasize the important role being quiet plays in the spiritual life.

▶ "Be still, and know that I am God. I will be exalted among the nations, I will be exalted in the earth!" (Psalm 46:10, ESV)

▶ "But I have calmed and quieted myself, I am like a weaned child with its mother; like a weaned child I am content." (Psalm 131:2)

▶ "But the LORD is in his holy temple; let all the earth keep silence before him." (Habakkuk 2:20, ESV)

▶ "The LORD is good to those whose hope is in him, to the one who seeks him; it is good to wait quietly for the salvation of the LORD. It is good for a man to bear the yoke while he is young. Let him sit alone in silence, for the LORD has laid it on him. Let him bury his face in the dust—there may yet be hope" (Lamentations 3:25–29).

Take five minutes to sit quietly with these verses. Slowly, carefully, simply read them several times. Let God's Word wash over you. Listen attentively. When you are done, journal some thoughts on a separate piece of paper.

Discussion Questions

▶ How can noise, talking, and busyness actually be addictive?

▶ How can you stop instinctively turning on the television when you walk in the house, or turning on your radio when you get in your car?

▶ How difficult would it be for you to go a half-day without speaking, or without immersing yourself in music and noise?

▶ Do you think there might be occasions when it's appropriate to withdraw even from written words? Can a person?

▶ What does sitting in silence make you feel? Can you name it?

3. Multiple times in the gospels, Jesus uttered the odd catchphrase "Whoever has ears, let them hear" (Matthew 11:15). What do you think he meant? Why is listening such a big deal in spirituality?

_____

_____

_____

_____

_____

_____

Cultivating the Habits of Solitude and Silence

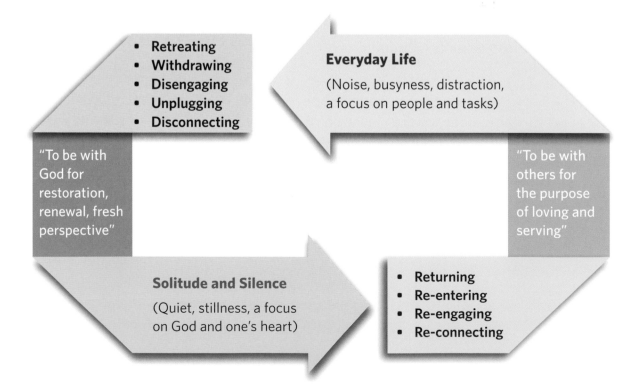

Take-Home Reflections

Here are some simple, everyday ways to build the rhythm of healthy disengagement and reengagement into our lives:

▶ Instead of staying glued to your smart phone all day, every day, put it away for short periods of time. See if you can go an hour without it, then try to go two, and then three.

▶ Set aside your "to do" list. Don't judge your worth to God on the basis of how much you accomplish.

▶ Turn off your electronics. Protect your time with God from others' demands.

▶ Resist the urge to immediately turn on the radio when you get in your car. Instead, use drive time to quietly meditate on a Bible verse.

▶ Sharpen your listening skills. Ask someone you're close to questions and really focus on their responses.

▶ Spend an evening with no television, YouTube, Netflix, etc.

▶ Set your alarm clock fifteen minutes earlier. Use that time to quietly read and contemplate Scripture.

▶ Find a solitary place and pray as the young prophet Samuel did, "Speak, LORD, for your servant is listening" (1 Samuel 3:9).

▶ Practice slipping away and being alone. If thirty minutes makes you uncomfortable, start with ten.

▶ Especially if you live in the city, devote a Saturday morning or Sunday afternoon to walking in the woods or countryside, or sitting in a quiet park.

▶ Take a break from podcasts and online sermons. Instead, sit quietly with your Bible letting God's Word and Spirit speak to your soul.

▶ Declare a 24-hour electronics fast—no gadgets, gizmos, Internet, or cable.

Carve out time with God, simply sitting together quietly and enjoying each other's presence. No words are necessary.

Life Application

An important part of discipleship is learning how to apply God's truths to your life. Below are just a few ways you can start thinking about what you've learned and apply it to your daily life.

1. Memorize this topic's verse, Isaiah 30:15.

2. Read *The Practice of the Presence of God* by Brother Lawrence. This quick read tells of a seventeenth-century French monk's attempt to maintain a quiet awareness of God at all times.

3. Set aside fifteen minutes away from distractions. Pick a Bible verse about trust (Prov. 3:5-6), hope (Psalm 31:24), or resting in God (Psalm 62:5-6). Read it slowly to yourself, thinking about each phrase. Whenever other thoughts crowd in, repeat the verse in your mind.

204

Topic 23: Bible Reading & Study

Being Rooted in God's Truth

"Your word is a lamp for my feet,
a light on my path."

—Psalm 119:105

What can be said about the Bible that hasn't already been said? Its detractors call it names we can't repeat. Its fans call it everything from "the owner's manual for life," to "letters from home," to "the story of God."

Meanwhile, God's Word touts itself as an indispensable, life-saving, life-changing, life-enhancing revelation from God (2 Timothy 3:16–17; 2 Peter 1:20–21). To help us grasp all that, it likens itself to:

- *bread* (John 6:51)—necessary for life

- *gold* and *silver* (Psalm 12:6; 19:10)—making us spiritually wealthy beyond our wildest dreams

- a *fire* (Jeremiah 20:9; Luke 24:32)—uncontainable, able to consume what is dead

- a *hammer* (Jeremiah 23:29)—able to penetrate through hard heads and shatter hard hearts

- *honey* (Psalm 19:10)—delighting to our senses

- a *lamp* (Psalm 119:105)—lighting our way in a world that has been darkened by sin and evil

- *meat* (Hebrews 5:12–14)—able to sustain and nourish mature believers with profound truth

- *milk* (1 Peter 2:2)—full of simple truths to help "baby believers" grow

- a *mirror* (James 1:23–25)—able to show us what we truly look like inside and out

- *seed* (Matthew 13:18–23)—able to grow and bear fruit when it takes root in our lives

- a *sword* (Ephesians 6:17; Hebrews 4:12)—our best weapon in fighting spiritual battles

- *water* (Ephesians 5:25–27)—able to wash us and make us pure

As the diagram on the next page shows, we are to let God's Word take root in our lives, and then let it bear fruit.

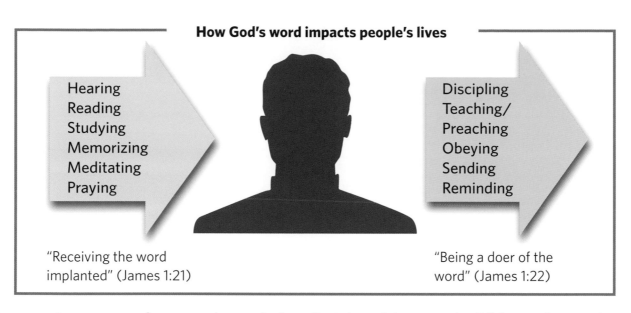

How God's word impacts people's lives

Hearing
Reading
Studying
Memorizing
Meditating
Praying

"Receiving the word implanted" (James 1:21)

Discipling
Teaching/
Preaching
Obeying
Sending
Reminding

"Being a doer of the word" (James 1:22)

Here, we just want to focus on the truth that disciples of Jesus make Bible reading and study a regular practice. They want to hear God speak. They want to know his heart and do his will. A disciple is a student and practitioner of God's Word.

Bible Study

Reading the Bible

Reading is one of the fundamental ways we process information and acquire knowledge. Consider the Bible passages in the table that starts below. They emphasize the importance of reading God's Word.

Example	Scripture
God's command to Israel's future kings, that they must be immersed in divine truth.	"He must always keep that copy with him and read it daily as long as he lives. That way he will learn to fear the Lord his God by obeying all the terms of these instructions and decrees." (Deuteronomy 17:19, NLT)
Ezra the priest's plan for helping his countrymen grow in their faith after the exile.	"They remained standing in place for three hours while the Book of the Law of the Lord their God was read aloud to them. Then for three more hours they confessed their sins and worshiped the Lord their God." (Nehemiah 9:3, NLT)
The Apostle Paul's command to Timothy, a young pastor and Paul's protégé.	"Until I come, give attention to the public reading of Scripture, to exhortation and teaching." (1 Timothy 4:13, NASB)

1. What stands out to you from these examples?

_____

_____

2. What are your own habits of Bible reading?

_____

_____

_____

3. If you are not a regular Bible reader, why? What holds you back?

_____

_____

_____

Seven Ways to Read God's Word

▶ **Prayerfully** Before you begin, ask God to speak. Ask him for "ears to hear."

▶ **Expectantly** Believe that God wants to speak to you, even more than you want to hear from him. Then be alert for his voice.

▶ **Devotionally** See your Bible reading as a personal time *with* God rather than an assignment in trying to learn new information *about* God.

> "Read it through; pray it in; live it out; pass it on."—George Gritter

▶ **Slowly** Don't be in a rush. It's not a race. You don't get a prize for finishing your reading quickly. Linger. Savor the words. Re-read them.

▶ **Comprehensively** You wouldn't buy a best-selling novel (or a work of non-fiction), let it fall open to page 134, and start reading there. Or only read the final four chapters. Why do we do that with the Bible? Resist the urge to read randomly. Read through a book at a time. (You might consider starting with the Gospels: Matthew, Mark, Luke, and John.) Don't ignore big sections of Scripture. Consider reading the entire Bible cover to cover. That's the best way to get the truest sense of who God is, and what his story is about.

▶ **Regularly** Exercising once every three weeks is better than nothing. But such a sporadic training regimen isn't likely to get you in great physical condition. In the same way, occasional Bible reading isn't the optimal way to cultivate your relationship with God or prepare for helping others know God.

▶ **Obediently** Always read with a mindset of "I will do whatever God commands."

Studying the Bible

Bible study is the practice of a disciple of Jesus in which we try to deepen our understanding of God's Word so that we can more closely align our lives to what God has revealed and commanded.

4. What intimidates you most about studying the Bible?

_____

_____

_____

Bible study is engaging one's mind, heart, and will in order to understand and apply God's Word to everyday life.

There are all kinds of ways to approach Bible study. One of the simplest, clearest, and easiest methods is the three-step method that includes

Step #1: **Observing God's Word**

Step #2: **Interpreting God's Word**

Step #3: **Applying God's Word**

Below is a chart that shows the differences between these three phases of Bible study.

Observation	Interpretation	Application
"Open my eyes that I may see wonderful things from your law." (Psalm 119:18)	"Make me understand the way of your precepts, and I will meditate on your wondrous works." (Psalm 119:27, ESV)	"I will hurry, without delay, to obey your commands." (Psalm 119:60, NLT)
Asking: What does it say?	Asking: What does it mean?	Asking: What do I need to do?
Probing	Pondering	Practicing
Exploring	Explaining	Exercising
Discovering	Digesting	Doing
Seeing	Understanding	Obeying

Sample Bible Study

Let's look at those components in more detail, by actually doing a simple Bible study of Mark 8:22–26 together. Here's the passage:

They came to Bethsaida, and some people brought a blind man and begged Jesus to touch him. He took the blind man by the hand and led him outside the village. When he had spit on the man's eyes and put his hands on him, Jesus asked, "Do you see anything?"

He looked up and said, "I see people; they look like trees walking around."

Once more Jesus put his hands on the man's eyes. Then his eyes were opened, his sight was restored, and he saw everything clearly. Jesus sent him home, saying, "Don't even go into the village."

Step #1: Observing God's Word

▶ **Pray** Ask the Spirit of God to be your teacher and to guide you into truth. Ask God for "eyes to see."

▶ **Read** Don't skim the passage the way you'd click and scroll through the Internet looking for something to catch your eye. Study the scene like a detective. What do you see? Noticing details requires conscious effort. Read the passage a second and third time. Don't read things "into" the text, but do try to draw out every relevant detail "from" the text.

▶ **Question** Dedicated Bible students bombard the text with questions. Study the chart below to discover some examples of questions you are encouraged to ask as you read the Scriptures.

▶ **Write** Record all your observations. Don't lose those "Aha!" insights by trusting them solely to your memory. Jot them down.

WHO?	Who is mentioned or involved here?
	Who seems to be the primary character?
WHAT?	What is going on or what is being said?
	What is the context for these events?
	What happened just before this?
	What is the sequence of events?
	What words (verbs, adjectives, prepositions, etc.) did the Spirit-guided author choose?
	What descriptive details do I see?
	What is the mood and setting?

WHEN?	When is this action taking place?
	When one character says or does _____, then . . .
WHERE?	Where are these events happening?
WHY?	Does the author explain why these events are unfolding?
	Does the author offer a motive for a character's words or actions?
HOW?	How do the characters respond?
	How does the scene conclude?

5. Take a few minutes to observe Mark 8:22–26. Jot down some of your observations:

_____

_____

_____

   a. Why is it important to first objectively gather data before you do anything else?

_____

_____

_____

   b. How solid will our interpretations of a passage be if we don't first carefully observe the passage? Why?

_____

_____

_____

Step #2: **Interpreting God's Word**

Once you've done the hard work of gathering facts—objectively asking what does it say and/or what do I see?—it's time to begin asking what does all this mean?

6. Suppose a friend studying Mark 8:22–26 with you said the following were things that were meaningful in the passage:

   ▶ Apart from the intercession and intervention of others, sick people will never experience Jesus' healing touch (v. 22).

- ▶ People aren't healed until they first agree to take Jesus' hand and follow him (v. 23).

- ▶ Spitting on people with disabilities helps them find healing (v. 24).

- ▶ When it comes to healing broken people, Jesus works in unique and unexpected ways (vss. 23–25).

- ▶ Divine healing is not always instantaneous (vss. 24–25).

- ▶ When Jesus takes us out of a bad situation and changes us, he does not want us going back into that same situation (vss. 23, 26).

Do you agree with any or all of those interpretations? Why or why not?

Knowing the Author's Intent

Imagine a terminally ill billionaire has drawn up her last will and testament.

After her funeral, when the will is read by a probate court, what's the goal? Is it to discover and do what she actually intended, or is it to have family factions interpret her words in five very different ways and bicker over the matter for the next twenty years?

Obviously the goal of a good attorney and a non-biased judge is to disregard what all the readers of the will want it to mean, and, instead, to discern and carry out the intent of the author of the will.

And so it is with interpreting God's Words. His intent must be our goal.

_____

_____

_____

Scholars call the science of interpretation *hermeneutics*. As with all disciplines, there are agreed-upon principles and rules to follow. Disregarding these practices can lead to unbiblical ideas and the formation of pseudo-Christian cults. Finding out how various Bible scholars who've studied the language and culture of the Bible interpret a text is valuable.

In interpreting a passage, we are asking what does God intend to communicate here? We are not asking "What do I *feel* this passage means to me?"

Avoiding Wrong Bible Interpretations

Leave our presuppositions behind.

We must beware of trying to force a passage to fit with our preexisting beliefs or experiences. Disciples should always base their beliefs on what the Bible says rather than interpreting the Bible in accordance with their beliefs.

Resist getting overly creative.

It's tempting to look for some mysterious, hidden, symbolic meaning that no one has ever seen before. It's also dangerous.

Take into account historical, cultural, grammatical, and literary realities.

Though it's one timeless story, God's Word is comprised of a variety of kinds of literature. Plus it was compiled over 2,000 years in various Near Eastern and Mid-Eastern cultural settings by some forty different human authors writing in three languages—Hebrew, Aramaic, and Greek. If we insist on reading it through twenty-first century western eyes, we will misunderstand its meaning. This requires that you . . .

Ask and answer a LOT of questions!	For example: ▸ What kind of literature is this? Poetry? History? Prophecy? Wisdom? Epistolary? ▸ Is this passage narrative (a story) or didactic (instruction)? ▸ Is this text descriptive (simply telling about things that happened in a unique setting) or prescriptive (showing what should happen in all places at all times)?
Use the whole of Scripture to help interpret the parts of Scripture.	If other passages do not corroborate your interpretation of a text, you may be on dangerous ground. We should always use clear passages to help us grasp the meanings of unclear ones. Regarding the Mark 8 passage, since there are no other healings recorded in the gospels which show Jesus laying his hands on a person a second time, we are probably wise not to read too much into this unique event. In fact, that may be a valid interpretation: Jesus deals with each person uniquely.
Consider the context of a statement or passage.	For example, to understand Jesus' command to the healed man "Don't go into the village," we need to look at comparable passages in Mark's gospel (1:44; 5:19, 43; see also Matthew 8:4 and 16:20).
Consult trustworthy commentaries on Scripture.	Seeing how Bible scholars interpret a text is a valuable help in understanding God's Word. So make use of Bible commentaries and study Bibles with notes from scholars.

7. Based on these rules of interpreting Scripture, what do you think of the "friend's" interpretations of Mark 8: 22–26 above?

_____

_____

_____

a. What would you suggest as the meaning/interpretation of the story in Mark 8:22–26?

_____

_____

_____

Step #3: Applying God's Word

Applying the Bible is the final, crucial step of Bible study. This is where we put God's truth into practice. We live it out. We seek to be doers of the Word (James 1:22). Though a single verse or passage never has multiple interpretations (meanings), it can and does have a myriad of different possible applications.

For example, a men's group studying Ephesians 5:25 and the command to "love your wives, just as Christ loved the church" all agreed that the timeless *principle* there is that husbands are called to love their wives unconditionally and sacrificially. But their individual *applications* of that principle will look very different. For example,

> ▶ Bob has decided to back out of his fishing trip, and stay home to do three "honey do" projects that his wife Elizabeth has been begging him to do for months.

> ▶ Stephen feels nudged to apologize to his wife Ellen for being a slob and for not helping around the house. He wants to give her a weekend at a nice hotel.

How to Find Good Applications

After you have carefully observed a Bible passage and prayerfully determined what truth God meant to convey through it, you need to state that truth in the form of a broad "now" principle (like the guys did above). This serves as a kind of "bridge" between interpretation and application.

For example, in the case of our passage, Mark 8:22–26:

> ▶ **Observation** When some people brought a blind man to Jesus and requested he touch and heal the man, Jesus did so, in two phases.

> ▶ **Interpretation** Jesus demonstrated unique compassion and power to those who needed his touch.

8. What broad timeless principle do you see in this passage?

_____

_____

a. Finally, what **application(s)** do you get from the story of Jesus healing the blind man?

_____

_____

_____

Take-Home Reflections

The growing, fruitful disciple of Jesus makes it a practice to read and study God's Word. He or she has the attitude expressed by John Wesley:

> "I want to know one thing—the way to heaven; how to land safe on that happy shore. God Himself has condescended to teach the way: For this very end he came from heaven. He hath written it down in a book. O give me that book! At any price, give me the book of God! I have it: Here is knowledge enough for me. Let me be a man of one book."

D. L. Moody on Why and How to Study the Bible

▶ "Someone has said that there are four things necessary in studying the Bible: Admit, submit, commit and transmit."

▶ "What we need as Christians is to be able to feed ourselves. How many there are who sit helpless and listless, with open mouths, hungry for spiritual things, and the minister has to try to feed them, while the Bible is a feast prepared, into which they never venture."

▶ "Depend upon it, my friends, if you get tired of the Word of God, and it becomes wearisome to you, you are out of communion with Him."

▶ "The more you love the Scriptures, the firmer will be your faith. There is little backsliding when people love the Scriptures."

Classic Bible Study Application Questions:

- Is there an overt command here to obey?
- Is there a promise to claim?
- Is there a new truth about God in which I can trust?
- Is there a sin to avoid?
- Is there a behavior to renounce?
- Is there an attitude to embrace?
- Is there an example to follow?
- Is there a prayer to express?

▶ "Bear in mind there is no situation in life for which you cannot find some word of consolation in Scripture."

▶ "The best law for Bible study is the law of perseverance."

▶ "So few grow, because so few study."

▶ "When I pray, I talk to God, but when I read the Bible, God is talking to me; and it is really more important that God should speak to me than that I should speak to Him. I believe we should know better how to pray if we knew our Bibles better. What is an army good for if they don't know how to use their weapons?"

▶ "I thank God there is a height in [the Bible] I do not know anything about, a depth I have never been able to fathom, and it makes the Book all the more fascinating."

Life Application

An important part of discipleship is learning how to apply God's truths to your life. Below are just a few ways you can start thinking about what you've learned and apply it to your daily life.

1. Memorize our memory verse, Psalm 119:105.

   "Your word is a lamp for my feet, a light on my path."

2. Review "D. L. Moody on Why and How to Study the Bible" on the previous page. Which of the individual points represent something you already do? Which represent something you would like to do? Determine which of the "want to" points you will immediately incorporate into your Bible study practices.

3. Read the following article about "Scripture Memory."

Scripture Memory

A lot of people (especially people who are upwards of 30 years old) are inclined to think *I can't memorize a bunch of Bible verses!*

Not true! Think of all the information, all the facts you've already got stored in your mind—computer passwords, pin numbers, funny lines from movies, phone numbers, important dates (like your anniversary—right, guys?), addresses, etc. And that doesn't include all the song lyrics you know by heart.

The truth is we *can* memorize Scripture. The only question is *will* we?

Why does Scripture memory matter?

Internalizing God's truth is life-changing! It:

▶ Gives us victory over sin. Psalm 119:11 says that when we hide God's Word in our hearts, it is a great defense against temptation. Jesus proved this in his own wilderness struggle against the devil (Matthew 4:1–11).

▶ Radically affects our lives by helping renew our minds (Romans 12:1)

▶ Helps us overcome worry; God promises to flood our lives with peace when our minds are fixed on him and his Word (Isaiah 26:3; Philippians 4:6–8).

▶ Gives us confidence when we share our faith (1 Peter 3:15). No longer will we feel tongue-tied or wonder what to say in a conversation about spiritual matters.

When is the best time to memorize?

Most people find the best times are probably just before going to bed, or when you first wake up in the morning. But it may be that your mind is sharpest at 2:15 in the afternoon, or around lunchtime. The point is, there is no "right" time. Just do it whenever you can really focus and concentrate. NOTE: Some people like to memorize while running or walking (*Warning! You can twist an ankle doing it this* way!)

How much Scripture should I memorize?

Don't get too ambitious and try to memorize all four gospels the first week (at least not in Greek). Shoot for one or two verses per week, and keep reviewing them until you really have them down.

What is the "trick"?

Now we get down to the nitty-gritty. Here are some tips for getting God's Word into your mind and heart:

▶ Pick out the verse you intend to memorize.

▶ Read the chapter that contains the verse so that you understand the context—what's going on in the background.

▶ Include the reference (example, Psalm 119:105) as part of the verse. Say this *before* reading the verse and again *after* you've finished. This is important because it helps you remember exactly where the verse is located. Then you won't get in situations where you end up saying, "Well, I don't remember where that verse is, but I know it's in the Bible *somewhere.*"

▶ Read the verse several times out loud. This gives you the flow of the verse.

▶ Break the verse into chunks, memorizing phrase by phrase. Say the reference by itself. Then the reference and the first "chunk." Then the reference, the first, and the second part of the verse. And so forth, until you've said the reference, the whole verse, and the reference again.

▶ Carefully write the verse on an index card, note pad, or in your mobile phone, thinking about it as you go. This helps cement it in your mind. For visual learners, writing the verse works better than merely saying it over and over. Once you've written the verse down, take it with you everywhere you go and . . .

▶ Review your pants off! (Not *literally*, of course, but several times each day during the next two or three days).

That's all there is to it. Isn't that simple?

A final reminder

God will help you as you memorize. He wants his Word to take root and bear fruit in your life even more than you do. (See Deuteronomy 6:6 and Colossians 3:16.)

You can count on his help!

216

Topic 24: Prayer

Communing with God

"Pray in the Spirit on all occasions with all kinds of prayers and requests. With this in mind, be alert and always keep on praying for all the saints."

—Ephesians 6:18

What if you had a friendship with someone you could call any time, night or day? A friend who met with you regularly and allowed you to talk non-stop for ten, twenty, thirty minutes—or more—and never asked you to stop? Or maybe you just send out a quick call or text now and then, and no matter what, that friend was always there to answer. Suppose as well that this friend reached out to you to give you guidance, support, love, and encouragement—even when you didn't call and ask for it first.

You would feel deeply loved by that friend, right? Happily, that's a description of how any of Christ's followers can approach God.

In this lesson, we're going to see that disciples of Jesus imitate Jesus in the way he prayed.

"Pray until you can pray; pray to be helped to pray and do not give up praying because you cannot pray. For . . . when you think you cannot pray that is when you are praying."
—Charles Spurgeon

Bible Study

What Is Prayer?

In its purest essence, prayer is simply communing with the One (see Exodus 33:11) who is nearer to us than we realize (Acts 17:28). Biblical prayer can be silence or it can be an ongoing dialogue with God (1 Thessalonians 5:17). It's less a way to get stuff, and more a way to draw close to the Father in heaven.

1. How have you experienced praying to God?

_____

_____

_____

_____

Why do we pray?

Prayer is a mystery. God is *all-knowing*. We can't tell him things he doesn't already know. And he is *sovereign*—working and weaving everything everywhere together to accomplish his perfect eternal purposes. These truths make us ask: Why do I even need to pray?

And yet, for reasons we can't fully understand, *God commands us to pray*: "Devote yourselves to prayer, being watchful and thankful" (Colossians 4:2). Furthermore, God tells us that *our prayers are eternally significant*: "Confess your sins to each other and pray for each other so that you may be healed. The earnest prayer of a righteous person has great power and produces wonderful results" (James 5:16, NLT).

2. What results have you seen from praying?

_____

_____

_____

The following list surely isn't exhaustive. But here are a few reasons prayer is so essential to followers of Jesus.

Prayer is how we approach God.

"Draw near to God and He will draw near to you" (James 4:8, NASB). Never forget that God longs for a relationship with us. Proverbs 15:8 tells us, "The LORD . . . delights in the prayers of the upright" (NLT). Even if we don't know what to say, God's Spirit prays for us (Romans 8:26). When we approach God with respect, we need not worry about praying wrong.

Prayer aligns us with God's purposes for our lives.

If we are wise, we recognize that God, being good and loving, desires our best. Consequently, a big part of prayer is learning to relinquish our desires and say "your will be done" (Matthew 6:10). As C. S. Lewis said, "If God had granted all the silly prayers I've made in my life, where would I be now?"[1] In another place Lewis said, "Prayer doesn't change God, it changes me."

Prayer is an expression of faith.

"Without faith it is impossible to please God, because anyone who comes to him must believe that he exists and that he rewards those who earnestly seek him" (Hebrews 11:6). Behind all true prayer is a belief that there is one who is there, one who hears; in all true prayer is an admission of "you are the One I need; you are the One who can help; you are the One I trust."

Prayer gives peace.

"Do not be anxious about anything, but in everything by prayer and supplication with thanksgiving let your requests be made known to God. And the peace of God, which surpasses all understanding, will guard your hearts and your minds in Christ Jesus" (Philippians 4:6–7, ESV).

Prayer is powerful.

Though we don't understand exactly how prayer works—only that it isn't a magic formula or guarantee—there are plenty of examples in Scripture and in more recent history of *prayer making a difference*. For instance, when Hezekiah was dying, he prayed and wept. God heard and told the prophet Isaiah: "Go and tell Hezekiah, 'This is what the LORD, the God of your father David, says: I have heard your prayer and seen your tears; I will add fifteen years to your life'" (Isaiah 38:5).

Prayer changes things—at the very least it changes us.

"In the name of Jesus, amen"

Praying "in the name of Jesus" means more than mindlessly tacking that phrase on to the ends of our prayers. Biblically, a name represents all that a person is and stands for. Doing anything in a person's name means to do that thing as if he or she were doing it. To pray in Jesus' name means praying the kind of prayers Jesus would pray. An "in the name of Christ" prayer should reflect who Jesus is—his person and works.

---

1 C. S. Lewis, *Letters to Malcolm: Chiefly on Prayer* (Fort Washington, PA: Harvest Books, 1973): 28

3. What specific factors motivate you to pray?

_____

_____

_____

As with any close relationship, prayer needs to be more than, "Can you give me this? And that? And that?" A running conversation with the Almighty should include the same kinds of exchanges found in any intimate relationship:

▶ Expressions of appreciation and admiration

▶ Careful listening

▶ Revealed hopes and dreams

▶ Admissions of disappointment, frustration, and struggle.

Prayer is an ongoing, back-and-forth conversation that leads to intimacy with God.

How Should We Pray?

Take a few moments to carefully and thoughtfully read these verses that tell us *how* to pray:

In faith	"I tell you, you can pray for anything, and if you believe that you've received it, it will be yours" (Mark 11:24, NLT).
In the name of Jesus	"I will do whatever you ask in my name, so that the Father may be glorified in the Son" (John 14:13).
According to God's will	"This is the confidence we have in approaching God: that if we ask anything according to his will, he hears us. And if we know that he hears us—whatever we ask—we know that we have what we asked of him" (1 John 5:14–15).
Unceasingly	"Pray continually" (1 Thessalonians 5:17).
Confidently	"Therefore let us draw near with confidence to the throne of grace, so that we may receive mercy and find grace to help in time of need" (Hebrews 4:16, NASB).
Stubbornly	"Then Jesus told his disciples a parable to show them that they should always pray and not give up" (Luke 18:1).
With the help of the Spirit	"In the same way, the Spirit helps us in our weakness. We do not know what we ought to pray for, but the Spirit himself intercedes for us through wordless groans" (Romans 8:26).

Stop and think about this last point for a moment. The Spirit helps us to pray. This is a huge comfort. When we're clueless, he knows. When we can't, he can!

220

4. Based on these verses and truths, how would you evaluate your prayer life of late?

_____

_____

_____

5. The Bible gives some explicit warnings about how *not* to pray. What actions or attitudes cited in the following verses are clear hindrances to God-honoring prayer? Write your answer on the blank spaces in the chart.

Passage	What's the snare to God-pleasing prayer?
Luke 8:9-14	
Psalm 66:18-20	
James 4:2-3; 1 Peter 3:7	
Matthew 6:5-8	
James 1:5-7	
Isaiah 29:13	

Are there "rules" regarding the details of praying?

The short answer is no. In Scripture we see:

Prayers from all kinds of people:

▶ Children (1 Samuel 3:10)

▶ Elderly widows (Luke 2:36–38)

▶ Kings (Psalm 139)

▶ Frightened people (Jonah 1:14)

▶ Military leaders (Joshua 7:6–9)

▶ Broken adults (Judges 16:28)

People praying:

▶ Alone (Matthew 14:23)

▶ In groups (Acts 1:14)

People crying out to God:

▶ In bed (Psalm 63:6)

▶ On the beach (Acts 21:5)

▶ On mountainsides (Luke 6:12)

▶ Outdoors (Genesis 24:11–12)

▶ At the temple (Luke 18:10)

Time people prayed:

▶ Fixed-hour prayers (Psalm 55:17)

▶ Midnight prayers (Acts 16:25)

▶ Morning prayers (Psalm 5:3)

People praying while:

▶ Sitting (2 Samuel 7:18)

▶ Standing (Mark 11:25)

▶ Kneeling (Acts 9:40)

▶ Lifting hands toward heaven (1 Kings 8:22)

The Prayer Life of Jesus

- He prayed in the early morning (Mark 1:35).
- He prayed in the evening (Mark 6:46–47).
- He spent whole nights praying (Luke 6:12).
- He prayed in lonely places (Luke 5:16).
- He agonized in prayer (Luke 22:39–46).
- He died praying (Luke 23:46).
- He praised the Father in his prayers (Matthew 11:25).
- He thanked the Father in prayer (John 11:41).
- He prayed for the will of the Father (Matthew 26:39).
- He prayed for his followers (John 17:9).
- He prayed forgiveness for his enemies (Luke 23:34).
- He prayed for children (Matthew 19:13–15).
- He prayed for himself (John 17:1).

Believers praying:

▶ Silently (1 Samuel 1:13)

▶ In a loud voice (Ezra 3:11–13)

▶ With joy (Philippians 1:4)

Jesus prayed:

▶ Through tears (Hebrews 5:7)

▶ While looking up (John 11:41)

▶ With his face to the ground (Matthew 26:39)

Basically, there are no hard and fast rules to follow. What matters is engaging God. Giving him your attention. Talking to and communing with him—everywhere and all the time.

6. How do you like to pray—when, where, body posture, etc.?

_____

_____

_____

What should we pray about?

Jesus gave his followers some guidelines for prayer in Matthew 6:9–13—not a mantra to memorize and repeat mindlessly, but a short outline for conversing with God. Look at the parts of the so-called "Lord's Prayer:"

> "Some people think God does not like to be troubled with our constant coming and asking. The way to trouble God is not to come at all."—D. L. Moody

Statement or Request	Focus	Explanation
"Our Father in heaven . . .	God's nature	Our prayers are directed to a loving father who wants the best for his children and whose heart we can trust.
hallowed be your name . . .	God's glory	Our prayer should always focus on bringing honor and praise to God.
your kingdom come . . .	God's kingdom	Our prayers ought to seek the righteous rule of God in every part of life.
your will be done, on earth as it is in heaven . . .	God's will	Our prayers must always submit to the higher plan and wiser purposes of God.
Give us today our daily bread . . .	God's provision	Our prayers need to be humble and dependent, looking to God to meet our needs.
And forgive us our debts, as we also have forgiven our debtors . . .	God's mercy	Our prayers acknowledge our constant need to receive and dispense grace.
And lead us not into temptation, but deliver us from the evil one."	God's protection	Our prayers recognize the sobering reality of evil.

7. How could you apply Jesus' "Lord's Prayer" outline to your own life today?

_____

_____

_____

Take-Home Reflections

It's easy to get so preoccupied with "answers" to prayer, we forget that the goal is communing with God. Inherent in all prayer is an acknowledgement of God. Permeating all prayer should be an enjoyment of God. Prayer is trusting that God knows what is best for us, even if we can't see it.

Prayer is lingering in the divine presence. It can be wordless. The point is to pay attention to God. Draw near. When you get right down to it, he is our hearts' truest, deepest desire, not some lesser blessing he can provide.

Go ahead and offer up prayers for needs and "stuff." But remember: even if God's response is "Wait" or "Not yet" or even "No," the biggest blessing is that you are getting to spend time with your Creator!

> "In prayer it is better to have a heart without words than words without a heart."—John Bunyan

Think of it as a gift when God answers in a way you don't expect or even desire. It means you get to respond to God's response. If his answer is "no," you can, by faith, thank God for wisely and lovingly protecting you from something hurtful or detrimental that you can't see. If the outcome is still pending, you can bring the subject up again at a later date (Luke 18:1–8). If God gives you what you seek, you get to come back and express thanksgiving and gratitude.

The lesson in all this? God offers you marvelous gifts through prayer. But don't settle for mere gifts when the Giver also offers you himself. Focus on the Giver, not the gift.

Life Application

An important part of discipleship is learning how to apply God's truths to your life. Below are just a few ways you can start thinking about what you've learned and apply it to your daily life.

1. Memorize our memory verse, Ephesians 6:18.

   "Pray in the Spirit on all occasions with all kinds of prayers and requests. With this in mind, be alert and always keep on praying for all the saints."

2. Read Paul's prayers in Ephesians 1:15–23 and 3:14–21.

3. Ask your group, spouse, or a friend to work through the exercise on the following page with you.

> "The main lesson about prayer is this: Do it! Do it! Do it! You want to be taught to pray? My answer is: pray."—John Laidlaw

Pray Honestly and Boldly

One great thing about group prayer times is that they give us an opportunity to pray specifically and boldly about the real issues going on here and now, in our own lives. Use the sample prayer requests below to spark or broaden your thinking, and to help *focus* your own prayer requests.

Sample Prayer Requests

▶ I need more joy in my life. Would you pray that I could recapture a sense of spiritual awe and delight?

▶ My spiritual life is kind of blah. Please pray that I'll recapture my desire to live for God.

▶ I have a family member or friend who needs Christ. Pray that God will use me to reach him/her. Pray that I'll be sensitive and available.

▶ I'm realizing there are certain areas of my life that I need to surrender (or re-surrender) to God. I'm struggling! Please pray that I'll take this step.

▶ There's an unresolved conflict that is affecting one of my primary relationships. Pray that I'll do right—do everything within my power this week to begin to address it and fix it.

▶ I'm facing a big, life-decision. I sure could use wisdom.

▶ Lately, I haven't been taking care of my heart or making my relationship with Christ my top priority (Proverbs 4:23). Pray that I'll exercise the discipline to live more like Mary and less like Martha (Luke 10:38-42).

▶ I keep tripping over the same temptation(s). Pray that I will lean on God's strength this week to say "NO!"

▶ I need more boldness in my faith.

▶ I'm discouraged about _____. Pray that I will bounce back.

▶ I feel like I'm under attack. Pray that I'll be alert and wise.

▶ Pray that I have courage to invite _____ to church or my small group.

▶ I don't feel right now like I know God very well. Pray that he'll reveal himself to me and that I'll have eyes of faith to see and ears to hear what he's saying to me.

▶ Our/my finances are not in the greatest shape. Pray that God would show what needs to be done.

▶ I feel far away from God. Pray that I'll make my way back.

▷ Pray that I'll have the courage to look hard at my life and to identify wrong attitudes or actions. And that with God's help, I'll begin to make changes.

▷ My life feels chaotic and out-of-control. Would you pray that I'd find a healthier balance?

▷ Pray that I'd be the kind of spouse I need to be (loving, selfless, thoughtful, kind, etc.).

▷ Pray for me this week as a parent. I need strength/patience/gentleness/ wisdom, etc.

▷ I'm anxious about _____. Pray that I'll experience God's perfect peace this week.

▷ I have an important relationship that needs some work. Pray that I will have supernatural wisdom to know what to do, the courage to do right, and that my actions will be rooted in love.

▷ I need to confront someone in love. Pray that I'll know what to say and how to say it.

▷ I feel guilty about _____. Pray that I can get to the bottom of this and resolve it.

▷ My faith is really weak and shaky. Pray that I'll keep clinging to God.

▷ I'm angry about _____. Pray that I'll process and deal with these things in a God-honoring way.

▷ I'm realizing I've buried some old hurts and wounds and it's affecting my life and relationships. Would you pray that I can deal healthily with these things and move forward?

▷ I need to ask forgiveness from someone I've wronged. Pray for the grace and courage to do this ASAP.

▷ I'm going through some trials just now—pray that I'll respond in a mature way— that I'll *grow* and not *grumble*.

▷ I pray you would heal _____. Give me the strength to help this person. If it is not your will to heal now, please give us all comfort, courage, and peace as we walk through this tough time.

If you don't know what kinds of things to pray for, let this spark your thinking. If you're reluctant to open up, take a risk. Alfred Lord Tennyson said it best: "More things are wrought by prayer than this world dreams of."

Topic 25: Discerning God's Will

Figuring Out What God Wants You to Do

"Do not conform to the pattern of this world,
but be transformed by the renewing of
your mind. Then you will be able to test
and approve what God's will is—
his good, pleasing and perfect will."

—Romans 12:2

Read the hypothetical situations described below. Try to identify what these three very different situations have in common.

▶ A new bestselling book by a well-known celebrity is creating a firestorm of controversy. Titled *Chruddism* it offers a new kind of spirituality that blends the teachings of Christ with the tenets of Buddhism. Several of your Christian friends have read it, and say they loved it—that it opened up their eyes to some truths they'd never thought of before. What is your response?

▶ A bright high-school senior with test scores through the stratosphere has been offered full scholarships to three very different but equally prestigious colleges. There's much to commend each one. She likes them all, and is freaking out about which one is the best decision. What is your advice?

▶ You've been asked to help out with the shut-in ministry at your church. There is a huge need there, and you worked with senior citizens when you were in college. Part of you feels like this would be a good thing; another part of you just feels tired and frazzled. Your thoughts vacillate wildly between *I probably should do this* and *I already feel pulled in ten directions.* In the end, what is your response?

Did you figure out the common thread through all these examples? In each of the situations above, what's needed is *discernment*.

1. Name a situation in your life that causes you to struggle with what's right and true, or what may be the best course of action.

_____

_____

What Is Discernment?

Biblically speaking, discernment is the ability God's Spirit gives us to distinguish and decide between that which is true, wise, and good and that which is false, foolish, and evil.

God wants *all* of his children to have and exercise this ability. Consider these passages from the apostle Paul, written to the ancient Christians in Colossae and Philippi:

▶ "So, from the day we heard, we have not ceased to pray for you, asking that you may be filled with the knowledge of his will in all spiritual wisdom and understanding" (Colossians 1:9, ESV).

▶ "This is my prayer: that your love may abound more and more in knowledge and depth of insight, so that you may be able to discern what is best and may be pure and blameless for the day of Christ" (Philippians 1:9–10).

Bible Study

2. What does Paul request for Christians here? What ability does he want them to develop?

_____

_____

In 1 Corinthians 12, the apostle Paul discusses spiritual gifts—special God-given abilities for building up the body of Christ. Here we discover some Christians are given a special ability to discern between right and wrong, spiritual truth and spiritual error. It's like the Holy Spirit functions in their life like a built-in "bad theology detector."

"He gives one person the power to perform miracles, and another the ability to prophesy. He gives someone else the ability to discern whether a message is from the Spirit of God or from another spirit. Still another person is given the ability to speak in unknown languages, while another is given the ability to interpret what is being said." (1 Corinthians 12:10, NLT)

3. Do you know any Christians with this extra-special ability to correctly analyze situations and messages and say, "That's a bad idea" or "That works well with biblical teachings"? Give an example or two.

_____

_____

_____

What Is True, Wise, and Good

Here are four truths about figuring out what is true, wise, and good:

Truth #1: God's will is discernible.

Some believers act like God's will is accessible only to a few eccentric spiritual geniuses who have figured out how to "hack into the Almighty's heavenly database."

Not true. God is not trying to turn our lives into a frustrating search. We can discern his purposes for us. He *wants* us to know his will—so that we can do it!

4. Look at what our memory verse for this lesson tells us: "Do not conform to the pattern of this world, but be transformed by the renewing of your mind. Then you will be able to test and approve what God's will is—his good, pleasing and perfect will" (Romans 12:2).

   How would you explain this verse to a child?

Dangerous Assumptions About the Will of God

- He probably wants to send me to someplace miserable.

- I'll have to marry a boring, mean, or unattractive person. Or I'll never get married!

- He'll have me do something dreadful—something that I hate.

- His plans for my life won't be nearly as exciting as *my* plans for my life.

- I'll probably end up poor.

- Obeying God will take all the fun out of life.

- He'll make me suffer.

- His will likely involves a frustrating existence in a foreign country.

_____

_____

_____

Clearly God desires for us to know his will today. He may not reveal his will for tomorrow, next month, or next year. But he gives us what we need to know now. We see this in the prayer of the Spirit-led psalmist: "Teach me to do Your will, for You are my God; let Your good Spirit lead me on level ground" (Psalm 143:10, NASB).

Truth #2: God's will is good.

Now we get to the heart of the issue. So many times Christians cringe at the phrase "the will of God," because they equate that with hard or bad things (see "Dangerous Assumptions About the Will of God"). We assume that if we seek hard after God's will, we just might find it, and that will involve all sorts of unpleasantness!

5. Consider the following passages:

▶ "For the LORD God is a sun and shield; the LORD bestows favor and honor; no good thing does he withhold from those whose walk is blameless" (Psalm 84:11).

▶ "Give thanks to the LORD, for he is good; his love endures forever" (Psalm 107:1).

▶ "'For I know the plans I have for you,' says the LORD. 'They are plans for good and not for disaster, to give you a future and a hope'" (Jeremiah 29:11, NLT).

▶ "He who did not spare his own Son, but gave him up for us all—how will he not also, along with him, graciously give us all things?" (Romans 8:32).

What conclusions might we draw from these passages about the will of God?

_____

_____

_____

_____

Someone has observed, if we really believed our heavenly Father's character is 100-percent good, every hour of every day, we'd trust his will, no matter what. And if we trusted his heart, we would *do* his will eagerly, as Jesus did (Matthew 26:42).

Here's what we have to believe: In following the way of Christ wholeheartedly, we find a life that simultaneously honors God, blesses others, and brings happiness to our own soul. Outside of embracing and doing the will of a good God, we will never find all of that.

6. Why is it a struggle for people to believe in God's love and care for us?

_____

_____

_____

_____

Truth #3: **Discerning God's will requires God's resources.**

These resources include God's Word, God's Spirit, as well as other resources.

God's Word

God doesn't give his children a detailed blueprint for life. Nobody gets a comprehensive itinerary for the next twenty, forty, or sixty years. Instead God gave us his Word.

What exactly is the Bible? Maybe we should start with what the Bible is not. It's not a day-planner. It's not going to give you explicit instructions for every situation of life—like whether you should wear your red shirt or your green one!

Rather, the Bible is the wild-but-true story of God. It's like a photograph album or scrapbook of sorts. It gives us glimpses and remembrances of what God is like and how he's acted in history. It's also a love letter full of divine promises. And further, it's a show-and-tell of the best and worst ways to live.

7. What would happen to our relationship with God if instead of the Bible, God gave each of his children a personalized app that dinged and buzzed moment-by-moment to tell us exactly what to think, do, and say in every situation?

A Couple of Discernment Reminders:

- When you embark on a new path that you really sense is God's will and some people push back, be firm but gracious. Say something like: "I may not be hearing perfectly from God, but I am going this direction because at this moment, this is what I genuinely believe God is leading me to do."[1]

- Sometimes God leads us down paths that are hard or seem like big mistakes. We can't measure the will of God by how things look in the moment. If you're in that spot, follow the next thing God reveals. If you keep trusting and walking, by the end of your life (or at least in the life to come), you will be able to see how God used even those painful periods for his glory, and yours and others' good.

---

1 If ten of your wisest, most trusted friends are discouraging your chosen course of action, that's a different story!

_____

_____

_____

_____

8. It has been said, "About ninety percent of God's will for our lives is already spelled out in his Word. The other ten percent is just details." Based on what you know of God's Word, what are some things that you know for sure are the will of God for your life today?

_____

_____

_____

_____

_____

God's Spirit

9. Read these words of Jesus:

   "When he, the Spirit of truth, comes, he will guide you into all the truth. He will not speak on his own; he will speak only what he hears, and he will tell you what is yet to come." (John 16:13)

   What is the role of the Holy Spirit in helping us discern God's truth and/or God's will?

   _____

   _____

   _____

   _____

10. In John 16, Jesus talks about "the Spirit of Truth." In John 17, Jesus says, "Your Word is truth" (v. 17). Do you think there could ever be a time when God's Spirit and God's Word would lead us in two different ways?

   _____

   _____

   _____

   _____

We want to be able to see our whole future in front of us. We'd prefer a detailed itinerary for life. Instead, God gives us a flashlight and a reliable guide. The flashlight is his Word (see Psalm 119:105), and the guide is his Spirit. That's because he wants us to "live by faith, not by sight" (2 Corinthians 5:7). We need to make our decision on what is revealed to us today. God may take us another direction tomorrow, but that's okay. Remember: God is not trying to hide his will. He wants you to know his will for you today more than you seek to know it.

Other Resources for Discerning the Will of God

Tool	Definition	Danger
Godly counsel "Plans fail for lack of counsel, but with many advisers they succeed" (Proverbs 15:22).	Seeking input and advice from spiritually wise friends and experienced mentors	▸ People are fallible and sometimes suggest wrong or unwise actions. ▸ We tend to gravitate toward those who will tell us what we want to hear
Sovereign circumstances "We may throw the dice, but the Lord determines how they fall" (Proverbs 16:33, NLT; see also Romans 8:28 and Ecclesiastes 7:13–14).	Observing life events and prayerfully considering how God might be leading you through his providential acts	▸ Obstacles don't always mean "stop." ▸ Open doors don't always mean "go."
Holy contentment "Let the peace that comes from Christ rule in your hearts" (Colossians 3:15, NLT).	Paying close attention to your heart and to the course of action that brings an undeniable sense of "peace" and/or rightness	▸ Sometimes God's will is scary and not peaceful—consider Jesus wrestling with God's will and sweating blood in Gethsemane (Luke 22:44).
Divine compulsions "Now, compelled by the Spirit, I am going to Jerusalem, not knowing what will happen to me there" (Acts 20:22; see also Romans 8:14).	Noticing inner promptings, checks on your spirit, impressions, or "nudges" by the Holy Spirit to do (or not do) a certain thing	▸ Not every internal urge is from God. ▸ Any whim or notion needs to be prayerfully and carefully analyzed in light of God's Word—that's part of discernment!
Common sense "Good sense is a fountain of life to him who has it, but the instruction of fools is folly" (Proverbs 16:22, ESV).	Taking into account reason, facts, and logic. For example, realizing as a 6-foot 6-inch, 250-pound guy, you probably weren't meant for a career as a jockey	▸ God's ways are higher than ours. ▸ Sometimes God's might seem crazy. For example, having your fiancée tell you that God made her pregnant—Matthew 1:18–19.

11. What's your experience with discerning God's will via these means?

_____

_____

_____

_____

12. How could you use these tools and resources in your current search to know God's will in a certain situation?

_____

_____

Here's a final truth about discovering the truth and/or will of God.

Truth #4: Discerning God's will requires effort on our part.

Much of God's will for your life is already quite clear.

> "Trust in the Lord with all your heart; do not depend on your own understanding. Seek his will in all you do, and he will show you which path to take" (Proverbs 3:5–6, NLT).

- ▶ You were *created* to:
  - ✦ Glorify God (Isaiah 43:7)
  - ✦ Love him with all your heart (Mark 12:28–30)

- ▶ You've been *called* to:
  - ✦ Follow Jesus and help others learn to do likewise (Matthew 28:18–20)

- ▶ You're *commanded* to:
  - ✦ Love others (John 13:34–35)
  - ✦ Serve others with all the blessings God has given you (1 Peter 4:11).

> God always speaks clearly, but we don't always hear clearly.

Those things will always be true, no matter where you go to college, whom you marry, what career you choose, or where you decide to live. In other words, most of the "what?" is clear. All that remains now is discovering the details (How? Where? When? With whom?). This involves cultivating the ability to use the resources God has given to develop the ability to hear God's voice and follow his specific leaning. What's your part in discovering those details?

Pray

"If any of you lacks wisdom, you should ask God, who gives generously to all without finding fault, and it will be given to you. But when you ask, you must believe and not doubt, because the one who doubts is like a wave of the sea, blown and tossed by the wind. That person should not expect to receive anything from the Lord" (James 1:5–7).

13. According to James, why is believing in God's generosity important for someone seeking God's direction?

_____

_____

_____

_____

_____

Recognize and Relinquish

Because of our unique personalities and life experiences, we each have tendencies, biases, predispositions, "default" ways of reacting, unconscious habits, and compulsive behaviors (sometimes bordering on addiction).

For example, maybe your natural instinct is to play the role of rescuer, and so you keep falling into bad relationships. Or maybe because of your own chaotic childhood you have a tendency to try to control everything about your own child's life. If so, it could be that some of your parenting decisions are rooted more in fear than in the will of God. Or maybe your high salary is less a blessing to you, and more a master—so that when the opportunity arises for you to pursue your dream job (at about half the income), you feel like you can't even consider it. You get antsy, even terrified at the thought of walking away from such a financial safety net. Maybe, in truth, it's money, not God, that's directing your life.

Whatever your particular struggle, it's important to recognize it. Only by first identifying the deep issues of your heart, can you consciously relinquish those things and trust God. Some struggles are long-term, or as C. S. Lewis calls them, "afflictions." In those instances, recognizing and relinquishing is a continual process.

14. What is one tendency or natural instinct you have that probably fights against your ability to discern the will of God in your life?

_____

_____

_____

_____

Take-Home Reflections

Take Action

Someone has wisely noted that it's impossible to steer a parked car. Get moving on the clear things. Stop waiting for a detailed twenty-year plan (that's never going to drop from heaven). Instead, trust God and take a step of faith. Then another and another. All along the way, ask the Lord to guide you and re-route you if you get off course. Don't get fixated on the destination you imagine, or you will end up feeling hurt and betrayed by God.

Sometimes God leads us down paths that don't appear to turn out well. That's okay.

Just follow the next thing God reveals. By the end of your life, you will see how the painful things in life are also used by God.

Unlike the original followers of Christ, we do not have Jesus physically with us. We don't have the privilege of watching and listening to him talk in person. We live in a loud, noisy world that offers us a million options.

And so we need discernment. We need to cultivate the ability to open the Word of the Lord and be sensitive to the Spirit of the Lord. That's how we know what's true, and what we need to do.

Life Application

An important part of discipleship is learning how to apply God's truths to your life. Below are just a few ways you can start thinking about what you've learned and apply it to your daily life.

1. Memorize our verse, Romans 12:2:

2. Review the table on the next page, "When God's Will Isn't Black and White."

3. Wrestle with one or two of these questions:

   ▶ Why is it often so hard to know what is the best course of action?

   ▶ What do you think of the statement that if we are not already doing the things God has clearly shown us to do, why would he reveal any more of his will for our lives?

   ▶ How can other spiritual practices like solitude and silence (Topic 22) or fasting (Topic 26) be helpful in hearing God and finding guidance for life?

   ▶ How do you handle conflicting feelings and competing impulses?

   ▶ What big, confusing decisions are you facing now?

   ▶ If you are at a crossroads, answer these questions: What gives you a deep sense of joy, significance, and satisfaction? What habits and activities do you walk away from saying, "I sense God's pleasure every time I do that"?

   ▶ Do you think you have the spiritual gift of discernment?

If you love God, you'll stop in the right place even if you make mistakes along the way.

When God's Will Isn't Black and White

The Bible gives explicit instruction regarding lots of things. What about when we're facing a choice the Scriptures don't specifically address? Consider these ten principles in trying to discern what to do.

Ask Yourself	Scripture	Principle
Will this bring glory to God?	1 Corinthians 10:31	I am to live my life in such a way that God always gets the glory he deserves.
Am I trusting God, relying on my own wisdom, or trying to please someone else?	Proverbs 3:5–6, NLT; cf. 2 Corinthians 5:9–10	Biblical faith resists both the temptation to be a "men-pleaser" and the urge to rely on worldly wisdom.
Is this a case of "If it seems too good to be true, it probably is"?	Proverbs 14:12	We live in a confusing world influenced by a destructive deceiver whose goal is to ruin our lives. We should be careful and prayerful!
Could my faith be damaged or my character corrupted by this choice?	1 Corinthians 15:33	I will be influenced by environments I choose and the company I keep.
How does this square with my calling to pursue holiness?	1 Peter 1:14–15	As disciples, we are called to be different (in attitudes and actions) from those around us.
Would this decision harm Christ's reputation or my own as his disciple?	Ephesians 5:3	We must be above reproach in all we do.
Could this be the first step on the path to spiritual or moral danger?	Proverbs 4:14–15	We must be alert, recognizing the weakness of our flesh and the power of sinful desires.
Would this action send the wrong signal to a "weaker" believer who might copy my behavior and violate his or her conscience?	1 Corinthians 8:9	The law of love requires that I sometimes voluntarily (and selflessly) limit my freedom for the sake of others.
Even if this isn't "sinful," is it "wise"?	1 Corinthians 10:23	Some things are "okay," others are "good," and still others are "best." Disciples are called to pursue the best!
Do older and wiser believers agree with my chosen course of action?	Proverbs 12:17	It is foolish (and prideful) not to seek out and heed the wise counsel of godly men and women we respect when facing a tough decision.

Topic 26: Fasting

Cultivating an Appetite for the Things of God

"'Even now,' declares the LORD, 'return to me with all your heart, with fasting and weeping and mourning.'"

—Joel 2:12

Maybe you've heard spiritually minded people speak about *fasting*. Or perhaps you've got friends who have given up certain foods or habits for Lent. What's all that about? And more importantly, why is fasting such an important practice for the disciples of Jesus?

In this lesson, we want to examine this obscure, often misunderstood practice.

▶ What is it?

▶ Why is it important?

▶ How do we practice it?

When you hear the word "fasting," what thoughts and images come to mind?

_____

_____

_____

What is fasting?

The Old Testament Hebrew verb "to fast" is *tsoom*. It means, as we might expect, to abstain from food. The comparable New Testament Greek word is *nēsteuō*. This word has the added nuance of meaning "to be empty."

Biblical fasting, then, as defined by most people, is choosing to go without food—and sometimes drink—for a specified length of time. There are other types of fasts, but we'll start with food.

238

Bible Study

1. What's the longest time you ever went without eating? What were the reasons?

_____

_____

_____

Why Is Fasting Important?

The Bible seems to set forth at least four purposes for fasting.

Purpose #1: **To show sorrow for sin, whether personal or national.**

In the table below, read the verses in the right column, and in the left, write down who it is that is fasting to show sorrow for sin. Identify whether this is an example of personal or national sorrow.

Who is expressing sorrow?	Scripture
	"When they had assembled at Mizpah, they drew water and poured it out before the Lord. On that day they fasted and there they confessed, 'We have sinned against the Lord'" (1 Samuel 7:6).
	"So I turned to the Lord God and pleaded with him in prayer and petition, in fasting, and in sackcloth and ashes. I prayed to the Lord my God and confessed: 'Lord, the great and awesome God, who keeps his covenant of love with those who love him and keep his commandments, we have sinned and done wrong. We have been wicked and have rebelled; we have turned away from your commands and laws'" (Daniel 9:3-5).
	"Then Ezra withdrew from before the house of God and went to the chamber of Jehohanan the son of Eliashib, where he spent the night, neither eating bread nor drinking water, for he was mourning over the faithlessness of the exiles" (Ezra 10:6, ESV).
	"They said to me, 'Those who survived the exile and are back in the province are in great trouble and disgrace. The wall of Jerusalem is broken down, and its gates have been burned with fire.' When I heard these things, I sat down and wept. For some days I mourned and fasted and prayed before the God of heaven" (Nehemiah 1:3-4).

2. Why not just pray about sin? Why the added step of denying oneself food?

_____

_____

_____

_____

Purpose #2: **To attempt to hear from God and/or to seek his intervention.**

Fasting can help us focus on seeking God and listening to hear his voice.

Circumstance	Scripture
When Esther was going to ask the Persian king to spare her fellow Jews.	"Go, gather all the Jews to be found in Susa, and hold a fast on my behalf, and do not eat or drink for three days, night or day. I and my young women will also fast as you do. Then I will go to the king, though it is against the law, and if I perish, I perish" (Esther 4:16, ESV).
Before the Jewish exiles began the trip back to their homeland.	"And there by the Ahava Canal, I gave orders for all of us to fast and humble ourselves before our God. We prayed that he would give us a safe journey and protect us, our children, and our goods as we traveled. For I was ashamed to ask the king for soldiers and horsemen to accompany us and protect us from enemies along the way. After all, we had told the king, 'Our God's hand of protection is on all who worship him, but his fierce anger rages against those who abandon him.' So we fasted and earnestly prayed that our God would take care of us, and he heard our prayer" (Ezra 8:21–23, NLT).

3. Imagine you had a friend who said, "Fasting seems like you're just trying to manipulate God—_Look at how serious I am—I'm not even eating! Now, God, you have to give me what I'm asking for!_" How would you respond to this friend?

_____

_____

_____

_____

Purpose #3: To seek discernment for a looming decision or guidance for next steps.

Circumstance	Scripture
Paul, immediately after his conversion.	"He remained there blind for three days and did not eat or drink" (Acts 9:9, NLT).
The church, before sending out missionaries.	"Now in the church at Antioch there were prophets and teachers: Barnabas, Simeon called Niger, Lucius of Cyrene, Manaen (who had been brought up with Herod the tetrarch) and Saul. While they were worshiping the Lord and fasting, the Holy Spirit said, 'Set apart for me Barnabas and Saul for the work to which I have called them.' So after they had fasted and prayed, they placed their hands on them and sent them off" (Acts 13:1–3).
Paul and his cohorts, before appointing and commissioning church leaders.	"They preached the gospel in that city and won a large number of disciples. Then they returned to Lystra, Iconium and Antioch, strengthening the disciples and encouraging them to remain true to the faith. 'We must go through many hardships to enter the kingdom of God,' they said. Paul and Barnabas appointed elders for them in each church and, with prayer and fasting, committed them to the Lord, in whom they had put their trust" (Acts 14:21–23).

4. How and why might fasting help you have clarity when you face big decisions?

_____

_____

_____

_____

Purpose #4: To practice self-control.

"For this very reason, make every effort to add to your faith goodness; and to goodness, knowledge; and to knowledge, self-control; and to self-control, perseverance; and to perseverance, godliness; and to godliness, mutual affection; and to mutual affection, love. For if you possess these qualities in increasing measure, they will keep you from being ineffective and unproductive in your knowledge of our Lord Jesus Christ" (2 Peter 1:5–8).

> "Fasting is abstaining from anything that hinders prayer."
> —Andrew Bonar

Remember the idea that the Greek word for fasting, *nēsteuō*, also means "to be empty"? This is why fasting is important to disciples of Jesus. Sometimes we "fill up" on the wrong things. We become so satiated with earthly things, we don't have appetite or room for the things of God.

> "Prayer is reaching out after the unseen; fasting is letting go of all that is seen and temporal. Fasting helps express, deepen, confirm the resolution that we are ready to sacrifice anything, even ourselves to attain what we seek for the kingdom of God."
> —Andrew Murray

When we choose to do without something to which we've grown accustomed, and perhaps even attached, we feel empty and needy. *And that's a good thing, not a bad thing!* The goal with fasting is to take our emptiness and our restless powerful longings to Jesus, who alone can satisfy. The point is to deprive ourselves, to exercise self-control over any and all powerful appetites so that we can focus more fully on God and cultivate our love for and trust in him.

What is something that would be hard for you to give up—even temporarily?

How Does Fasting "Work"?

In the Old Testament, only one fast a year was commanded—the Day of Atonement (Leviticus 16:29, 31; 23:27–32). Late in Jewish history, other fasts were instituted (Esther 9:31; Zechariah 8:19). All other

NOTE
Fasting is not a statement about God's good gifts. When we choose to abstain from food or sex or technology, we are not denigrating those things. Each, when viewed and used properly, is a wonderful blessing from God. Fasting is one way to help us make sure those good things don't become paramount things. Fasting helps us redirect our desires toward the only one who can truly satisfy us.

fasting was personal and/or voluntary. Since the Jewish people saw sunset as the end of the day, they would often eat supper just before sunset, then fast until supper after sunset the following day (thus skipping a breakfast and a lunch).

In the New Testament we don't find any explicit commands to fast. We note that Jesus fasted (Matthew 4:2) and he assumed his disciples would (Matthew 6:16–18; Luke 5:33–35). From the passages already given, we know that Paul participated in the spiritual practice of fasting.

> "Fasting, if we conceive of it truly, must not be confined to the question of food and drink; fasting should really be made to include abstinence from anything which is legitimate in and of itself for the sake of some special spiritual purpose. There are many bodily functions which are right and normal and perfectly legitimate, but which for special peculiar reasons in certain circumstances should be controlled. That is fasting."
> —Martyn Lloyd-Jones

ROSE GUIDE TO DISCIPLESHIP

242

5. What would be some good reasons for you to fast in your life right now?

_____

_____

_____

_____

_____

6. What would be some wrong reasons to fast?

_____

_____

_____

_____

_____

7. What's your biggest takeaway from this lesson?

_____

_____

_____

_____

> "The purpose of fasting is to loosen to some degree the ties which bind us to the world of material things and our surroundings as a whole, in order that we may concentrate all our spiritual powers upon the unseen and eternal things."
> —O. Hallesby

© Bristol Works, Inc.   www.rose-publishing.com   May be reproduced for classroom use only, not for sale.

Take-Home Reflections

Tips and Reminders for the Spiritual Discipline of Fasting

▶ If you have a chronic medical condition or are pregnant, check with your physician first.

▶ Drink plenty of water.

▶ Start small—instead of fasting for a day, fast for one meal.

▶ Consider fasting from a particular kind of food to which you feel unhealthily attached such as desserts or caffeine.

▶ Remember that fasting from things we *want*—such as entertainment—can sometimes be harder than things we really *need*—like food.

▶ Remember fasting isn't magic, and it doesn't obligate God to give you what you seek (2 Samuel 12:16–20).

▶ Use missed meal times—prep, cooking, eating, and clean-up—as opportunities to draw near to God and pray.

▶ Don't be legalistic. If not drinking coffee gives you a splitting headache, then drink your morning java!

▶ Don't make a public declaration of your fasting (Matthew 6:16–18).

▶ Don't limit fasting to food. You may abstain from shopping, the Internet, social media, excessive exercise, going to movies, email, watching sports, even sex with your spouse for a brief time (1 Corinthians 7:5).

▶ Break your fast carefully. Don't gorge on whatever you've been fasting from.

Life Application

An important part of discipleship is learning how to apply God's truths to your life. Below are just a few ways you can start thinking about what you've learned and apply it to your daily life.

1. Memorize our memory verse, Joel 2:12.

2. Read and consider Isaiah 58:6–7.

3. Wrestle with one or two of the following:

▶ Does the thought of doing without certain things—even temporarily— make you fidgety or nervous?

▶ What things do you turn to when you begin to feel restless or empty?

▶ What "wants" in your life would you find most difficult to deny yourself?

▶ The purpose of fasting, or abstaining from a thing, is to loosen that thing's grip on your soul. Fasting is an external practice meant to restore or foster internal health. Agree or not? Why?

▶ When it comes to you personally, would fasting from food be the best way to restore or foster internal health? Or would another form of fasting be more effective? Why?

Topic 27: Giving

Understanding Generosity and Stewardship

"Remember this: Whoever sows sparingly
will also reap sparingly, and whoever sows
generously will also reap generously. Each of you
should give what you have decided in your heart
to give, not reluctantly or under compulsion, for
God loves a cheerful giver."

—2 Corinthians 9:6–7

A Parable

In 1980 two brothers received a large inheritance from their father's estate. One son took his $150,000 and went on a lavish spending spree. He bought himself a sports car, a ski boat, assorted other gadgets and toys. He took exotic trips. In eighteen short months, his money was gone.

> How we handle money speaks volumes about what and who we really believe.

The other son took his money and decided to invest it. He did some research, and then used half his windfall to buy stock in two "up-and-coming" companies. Maybe you've heard of them: a software company called Microsoft? A computer company named Apple? With the other half of his unexpected blessing he created a foundation that has built schools in India and drilled water wells in Africa.

Both brothers were given a great gift, but only one was wise. One brother, in his short-sighted selfishness, blessed a car dealer, a ski boat salesman, and some hotel owners. There's no telling how many thousands of lives the other brother is continuing to bless with his visionary generosity.

You may not know that Jesus talked more about money than He did about heaven and hell combined! Meaning, we *have* to study this subject. If we avoid it, we ignore a major discipleship issue.

Perhaps money has never been an issue for you . . . you're rolling in the dough . . . you have a big closet in your house full of cash and you're like a broken ATM when it comes to helping others.

More likely, as with most people, money is an ongoing stressor in your life. Whether it's:

- ▶ Saving, "Yeah, right!"
- ▶ Spending, "Somebody stop me!"
- ▶ Investing, "Who are you kidding?!"
- ▶ Borrowing, "I'm in debt up to my eyeballs!"
- ▶ Giving, "Sorry, there's nothing left to give!"

> "If you have something you can't give away, perhaps you don't own it. Maybe it owns you?"
> —Howard Hendricks

Just the mention of this topic leaves most people feeling uncomfortable or discouraged.

This is a lesson about money, and about cultivating the wise and joyous habit of being generous and making a difference with our finances.

Bible Study

1. Why do you think this subject of money causes such tension within people? Why such awkwardness between people?

_____

_____

_____

_____

Three Encouraging Truths About Money:

Truth #1: **God is generous with his children; he promises to provide for *all* of our needs.**

2. Look up and read these verses: Psalm 145:16; Matthew 7:11; and Philippians 4:19. What strikes you most about these statements and promises?

_____

_____

_____

246

Truth #2: **God gives generously to his people so that we can give generously to others.**

This principle goes all the way back to the calling of Abraham. God promised to bless him, and then said "and you will be a blessing" (Genesis 12:2). In other words, don't hoard—give! Be a conduit of God's blessings, not a black hole.

3. Take a moment to read 2 Corinthians 9:6–11, the passage from which we get our memory verse for this topic. What does Paul mean when he uses the agricultural imagery of "sowing and reaping?"

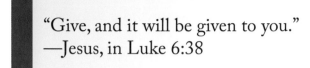

"Give, and it will be given to you."
—Jesus, in Luke 6:38

_____

_____

_____

_____

You don't have to be a farmer to realize that if you only plant a few seeds, you'll only get a small harvest. The more you put into the ground, the more you stand to receive back from the ground. This is also true in the spiritual realm. The blessings may not be financial, but there is a return.

Truth #3: **God says he blesses the generous.**

Did you happen to note all the promises of blessing in the passage you just read? God said that those who sow generously by giving generously to the work of God will:

▶ Have what they need to live (v. 8)

▶ See increasing fruit from their sacrificial contributions (vss. 8, 11)

▶ *Receive* more in order to be able to *give* more (v. 11)

A careful reading of the New Testament shows that the Lord calls his followers to selflessly and generously share with others the blessings that he has placed in their care. Disciples don't stockpile money and things—they share. They invest in eternal causes for the glory of God, for the good of others, and for their own spiritual well-being.

Let's look at an incident from Jesus' life and ministry that can help us get a grip on the subject of money—ironically, by showing us how to *loosen* our grip on it. Here's the scene:

"Jesus sat down opposite the place where the offerings were put and watched the crowd putting their money into the temple treasury. Many rich people threw in large amounts.

But a poor widow came and put in two very small copper coins, worth only a few cents.

"Calling his disciples to him, Jesus said, 'Truly I tell you, this poor widow has put more into the treasury than all the others. They all gave out of their wealth; but she, out of her poverty, put in everything—all she had to live on.'" (Mark 12:41–44)

4. What do you notice about this scene—what stands out to you?

_____

_____

_____

_____

A word of explanation: At the temple in Jerusalem, in the Court of the Women, were thirteen trumpet-shaped collection receptacles for receiving worshipers' offerings. Copper coins were the smallest Jewish coin in circulation. Two were equal to $1/64$ of what a common laborer would make in a day.

Notice the contrast that Jesus noticed:

Many Rich People	One Poor Widow
They gave large amounts.	She gave two very small copper coins.
They gave out of their surplus—literally, out of their excess, their leftovers.	She gave out of her poverty—literally, out of her need or lack. She gave everything she had, all that she had to live on.
They made contributions—granted, sizable ones.	She made a sacrifice.
Not particularly noteworthy to Jesus.	Remarkable to Jesus—"Come see this!"

Why does Jesus single out this obscure woman who gave such a paltry sum? What's his point? It's this:

Followers of Jesus honor God, bless others,
and find great reward in giving!

Cultivating a Generous Attitude

How can we cultivate this kind of attitude that leads us to give so generously? We have to do three things:

#1: Recognize that "your" stuff is really not your stuff.

Carefully read the following verses:

- ▶ "The whole earth is mine" (Exodus 19:5).

- ▶ "Everything under heaven belongs to me" (Job 41:11).

- ▶ "The earth is the LORD's, and everything in it" (Psalm 24:1).

- ▶ "'The silver is mine and the gold is mine,' declares the LORD Almighty" (Haggai 2:8).

5. If God is the true owner of *everything*, what does that mean as far as "your" paycheck, possessions, property, portfolio, etc.?

_____

_____

_____

Do you see it? The Bible teaches that "our" stuff is not really our stuff. It all belongs to God. He's the owner of it all and we are simply caretakers, managers, or stewards—trustworthy servants (1 Peter 4:10; 1 Corinthians 4:2, 6:20).

6. How does this truth—understood and embraced—change the way you look at your spending decisions?

_____

_____

_____

Since God owns it all, *every* money decision is a spiritual decision. Here's an example of how this mindset works out in a believer's life: When John Wesley, the founder of the Methodist Church, was told that his home had been destroyed by fire, he responded: "The Lord's house burned. One less responsibility for me!"

The Bible Says Money Is . . .	Our Reaction . . .
A blessing from God (Proverbs 10:22).	Be thankful!
A stewardship (Psalm 24:1; Romans 14:12).	Be responsible!
A test (Luke 12:48; 16:9-12).	Be faithful!
An indicator (Matthew 6:21).	Be aware of what you truly value.
A false hope (Proverbs 11:4; 1 Timothy 6:17).	Be wise!
A danger (Matthew 6:24; 13:22; 19:23; 1 Timothy 6:9-10).	Be wary!
A tool for honoring God and blessing others (Proverbs 3:9; Matthew 6:20).	Be generous!
A testimony (John 3:16; Ephesians 5:1).	Be sacrificial.

#2: Remember that giving is transformative.

What motivated this poor widow? She could have come up with a hundred reasons not to give. And so could we. So why did she do it? Why should we give?

7. What would you say are the best reasons to share the financial resources God has blessed you with?

_____

_____

_____

_____

Giving changes lives—including our own. Our generosity furthers the work of God. Just as importantly, practicing generosity changes us. It fosters trust that God will re-supply the money that we give away. Giving also combats our tendency to look to money for security, peace of mind, and happiness.

8. Read the following passage:

"But people who long to be rich fall into temptation and are trapped by many foolish and harmful desires that plunge them into ruin and destruction. For the love of money is the root of all kinds of evil. And some people, craving money, have wandered from the true faith and pierced themselves with many sorrows" (1 Timothy 6:9–10, NLT).

250

a. Record your thoughts on the lines below:

_____

_____

_____

_____

b. What are the spiritual benefits of giving money to the Lord?

_____

_____

_____

_____

_____

#3: Regard giving as the safest and wisest investment of all.

We look at the annual *Forbes* List of "The 500 Richest People in the World" and are tempted to think: "These guys and gals have got it made. They're set! They're secure. If only I had money like that . . . "

> Generosity has nothing to do with your income and everything to do with your character.

Here's the truth: Even though our financial lingo includes terms like *securities*, *safety net*, *guaranteed returns*, and *futures*, Jesus tells us of the tremendous fragility of worldly wealth (Matthew 6:19–24). The markets are volatile. Scammers are everywhere. To put our hope in worldly riches is not only wrong, it's foolish.

Wise Warnings About Wealth

- "Prosperity knits a man to the world. He feels that he is 'finding his place in it,' when really it is finding its place in him." —C. S. Lewis

- "Money never stays with me. It would burn me if it did. I throw it out of my hands as soon as possible, lest it should find its way into my heart."—John Wesley

- "The fellow that has no money is poor. The fellow that has nothing but money is poorer still."—Billy Sunday

- "I am obliged to tell you that God does not need anything you have. He does not need a dime of your money. It is your own spiritual welfare at stake in such matters as these. . . . You have the right to keep what you have all to yourself—but it will rust and decay, and ultimately ruin you." —A. W. Tozer

James chided the rich, "You have hoarded wealth in the last days" (James 5:3). William Barclay translated this sentence, "You have piled up wealth in a world that is coming to an end."

Isn't that tragic? It's the classic bad investment—like putting all you've got in the stock market—the day before it crashes! You amass a huge fortune, only to leave it all behind, or see it all disappear. What a waste!

Jesus made it clear it's not wrong to accumulate wealth. In fact, it's good so long as it's the right kind of wealth stored up in the right place.

> "But store up for yourselves treasures *in heaven*, where moths and vermin do not destroy, and where thieves do not break in and steal" (Matthew 6:20).

9. Someone once paraphrased Jesus' words this way: "You can't take it with you, but you *can* send it on ahead!" How do we "send our wealth on ahead to heaven"?

Where should I give? To whom should I direct my support?

- Your family (1 Timothy 5:8)
- Your local church body to support collective ministry efforts and to support those who give themselves fully to God's work—missionaries, pastors, etc. (Acts 5:1-4)
- The poor (Proverbs 19:17)
- Christian brothers and sisters who are facing hard times (Galatians 6:10)
- Neighbors who are in trouble (Luke 10:30-37)
- Organizations and groups distinct from the church that are engaged in Christian ministry and advancing the kingdom of God
- Agencies devoted to relief work, helping the suffering

_____

_____

_____

_____

There is much, much more we could say about money and giving[2]. We've only scratched the surface on what the Bible teaches. To summarize, we've said that followers of Jesus practice sacrificial giving by consistently doing three things. They:

▶ Recognize "their" stuff is not really their stuff.

▶ Remember that giving is transformative.

▶ Regard giving as the safest and wisest investment of all.

---

2   *God and Money* by John Cortines and Gregory Baumer is an excellent resource for money planning. It outlines a simple framework and seven key principles for implementing radical generosity. *God and Money* is available at www.rose-publishing.com.

Take-Home Reflections

How the Average Person Spends Money[3]

After taxes, out of every dollar spent, families and/or individuals spend

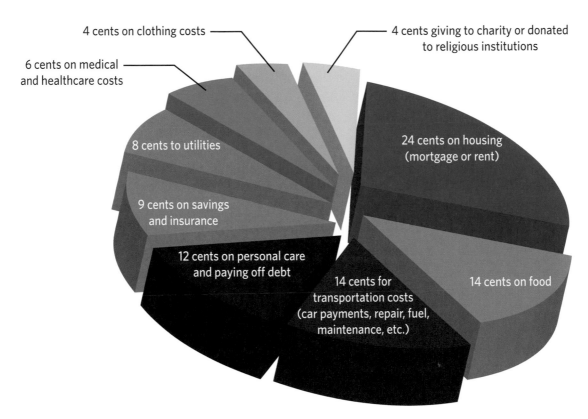

4 cents on clothing costs

4 cents giving to charity or donated to religious institutions

6 cents on medical and healthcare costs

8 cents to utilities

24 cents on housing (mortgage or rent)

9 cents on savings and insurance

12 cents on personal care and paying off debt

14 cents for transportation costs (car payments, repair, fuel, maintenance, etc.)

14 cents on food

"I do not believe one can settle how much we ought to give. I am afraid the only safe rule is to give more than we can spare. In other words, if our expenditure on comforts, luxuries, amusements, etc., is up to the standard common among those with the same income as our own, we are probably giving away too little. If our charities do not at all pinch or hamper us, I should say they are too small."—C. S. Lewis

Life Application

An important part of discipleship is learning how to apply God's truths to your life. Below are just a few ways you can start thinking about what you've learned and apply it to your daily life.

1. Memorize our verse, 2 Corinthians 9:6–7.

2. Look up the verses listed in "Ten Truths for Honoring God with Money." Prayerfully ask

---

3   U.S. Bureau of Labor Statistics, Consumer Expenditure Survey

God to show you an action step for each principle.

3. Wrestle with one or two of the following questions:

▶ What does it look like for you to "store up treasures in heaven"?

▶ God says to give to people who cannot repay us. Why do you think this is?

▶ God promises to meet our needs. Which promise speaks to you the most and why?

▶ God gives a lot of promises of reward to those who give. What is God saying to you?

▶ What are the dangers of putting our trust in money? If we trust in money rather than God, what happens?

▶ Is God inviting you to give to something? Make a list of possible people or organizations or types of organizations.

Ten Truths for Honoring God with Money

Biblical Principle	Passage	My Practical Action Step:
Determine to trust God, not money.	Revelation 3:17–21; Deuteronomy 8:18	
Am I trusting God, relying on my own wisdom, or trying to please someone else?	Proverbs 3:5–6, NLT; cf. 2 Corinthians 5:9–10	
Focus on the things that are most important.	Matthew 22:37–39; Proverbs 15:16–17	
Always remember God's enduring faithfulness.	Romans 8:32; Jeremiah 29:11	
Ask God to meet your financial needs.	Proverbs 30:8–9; Matthew 6:11	
Solicit divine wisdom in money matters.	James 1:5	
Act responsibly and with integrity in your handling of God's finances.	Romans 13:7	
Invest in eternal things.	Luke 12:33; Matthew 6:33	
Be generous and share what you have with others.	Deuteronomy 15:7; 2 Corinthians 9:6–7	
Cultivate contentment.	1 Timothy 6:7–8; Acts 20:33–35	
Praise God for his many generous blessings.	Psalm 112:1–5	

Topic 28: Service

Laying Down Your Life for Others

"Each of you should use whatever gift you have received to serve others, as faithful stewards of God's grace in its various forms."

—1 Peter 4:10

The parents at Bayside Church approached their minister and church board with a request that the church hire a new youth pastor. "We're a young church that's filled with preadolescent kids," they reasoned, "We're located just two blocks from Bayside High. We should get someone to come in and work with our teens and shepherd them through the tough teen years."

The board agreed. After much prayer and a regional search lasting several months, Bayside hired Jason, a sharp, energetic guy with teens of his own to come and serve in this capacity.

Everything was great for three months. The new youth pastor spent time asking lots of questions, meeting families, getting to know kids, becoming familiar with the community. Then he called a parents' meeting. In that meeting, he presented an ambitious plan built around youth small groups. It's a plan that calls for a *lot* of adult volunteers.

The next day several parents called the church office. "We hired this guy to minister to our teens. But now he's asking *us* to sign up to work with them!" they complained. "Doesn't he understand the job description of a minister!?"

1. What do *you* think of when you hear the word "minister"? Write down any words, phrases, images, or thoughts that come to mind:

_____

_____

_____

_____

_____

"One of the principal rules of religion is, to lose no occasion of serving God. And, since he is invisible to our eyes, we are to serve him in our neighbour; which he receives as if done to himself in person, standing visibly before us."
—John Wesley

Check out the Apostle Paul's description of how Jesus designed his church to function. (Note: It's the passage that Jason uses to guide his own ministerial philosophy):

"He gave the apostles, the prophets, the evangelists, the shepherds and teachers, to equip the saints for the work of ministry, for building up the body of Christ" (Ephesians 4:11–12, ESV).[4]

2. According to these verses, what is the role of church leaders? What is the role of "the saints"—regular church members?

_____

_____

_____

_____

_____

How about that? According to this passage, it isn't the professional clergy who are supposed to do all the hands-on working and serving and ministry. It's the saints—regular church members. The Apostle Paul describes a system in which pastors and teachers and other church leaders spend their time and efforts "equipping"—training and encouraging—the members of the congregation.

---

4   The NIV translates this last phrase "to equip his people for works of *service.*" All through the New Testament those two words—ministry and service—are used interchangeably. To minister is to serve. To serve is to minister. All of God's people are to work at serving.

3. Read the following examples of churches.

▶ a church with five very gifted and talented staff members and a congregation that mostly sat back and watched the professional clergy use their gifts

▶ a church staff of three pastors committed to helping 100 willing and available volunteers discover and develop and use their gifts to minister to others

Explain which church would have the biggest impact and why.

_____

_____

_____

_____

_____

In this lesson we will see three things about ministry or service:

▶ Disciples are *called* to serve

▶ Disciples are *gifted* to serve

▶ Disciples must be *obedient* to serve.

Bible Study

Disciples Are Called to Serve

▶ "For even the Son of Man did not come to be served, but to serve, and to give his life as a ransom for many" (Mark 10:45).

▶ "In your relationships with one another, have the same mindset as Christ Jesus: Who, being in very nature God, did not consider equality with God something to be used to his own advantage; rather, he made himself nothing by taking the very nature of a servant" (Philippians 2:5–7).

▶ "You, my brothers and sisters, were called to be free. But do not use your freedom to indulge the flesh; rather, serve one another humbly in love" (Galatians 5:13).

It's clear that Jesus came to serve. It could be argued from Mark 10:45 that his entire life was one continuous act of service. It's also clear that those who follow Jesus are expected to act like Jesus.

4. What can make it difficult to follow Jesus and serve others?

_____

_____

_____

Disciples Are Gifted to Serve

In four different places—1 Corinthians 12, Romans 12, Ephesians 4, and 1 Peter 4, the Scripture speaks of something called *spiritual gifts*. A spiritual gift is best defined as a God-given ability for service to and through the body of Christ.

> "The Great Commission is the greatest command, given by the greatest Commander, to the greatest army, for the greatest task ever. . . . Unfortunately, some have forgotten that the God who assigned us this great task also assigned us the means to fulfill the task—people, men and women whom God has equipped to fulfill that task, men and women with God-given gifts—spiritual gifts." —Larry Gilbert

God sees to it that every believer has at least one gift (1 Corinthians 12:11, 18; 1 Peter 4:10). These supernatural abilities aren't given to call attention to the individuals who have them, but to glorify God and bless others. All these divine abilities are important for the healthy functioning of the body. The Greek word for these gifts is *charisma*—a form of *charis*, the word translated "grace." God distributes these gifts, or graces, as he sees fit, and never on the basis of merit (1 Corinthians 12:4–6, 11).

Most Common Christian Understanding of the Gifts:

▶ Some believers hold firmly that these four gifts were limited to a period between Jesus' ascension and the death of the last Apostle, Jesus' beloved disciple John (about AD 90). People who hold this view are known as *cessationists*.

▶ Other Christians affirm the continuation of all of the gifts. They are *continuationists*.

▶ Many other believers fall in an in-between category, "open but cautious."

▶ Still others believe that some of the four gifts continue, while others have ceased.

Whatever view we take, we must remember that according to Paul, the spiritual gifts are meant to promote the unity of the body (1 Corinthians 12:12; Ephesians 4:12–13). In the letters of Paul, the unity of the body is necessary for the church's growth. The alternative, disunity and spiritual arrogance, tears down the church.

5. Up until now, what has been your understanding of spiritual gifts?

_____

_____

_____

_____

Disciples Are Obedient to Serve

> "Trying to do the Lord's work in your own strength is the most confusing, exhausting, and tedious of all work. But when you are filled with the Holy Spirit, then the ministry of Jesus just flows out of you." —Corrie Ten Boom

Our verse for this lesson says: "Each of you should use whatever gift you have received to serve others, as faithful stewards of God's grace in its various forms" (1 Peter 4:10).

In Bible times a steward was the most trusted servant in a household. This individual was given authority over the master's estate and possessions. Anyone in the household with needs would ask the steward, who would then dispense whatever was needed.

The "Sweet Spot" of Service

Sometimes needs arise and we have to do things we may have zero desire to do or engage in tasks for which we are not exactly gifted. But when we get to address real *needs* that we have a *passion* to solve using our unique *gifts* and abilities, that's a very special blessing.

The apostle Peter tells us that the Lord has given each disciple a spiritual gift which others need (1 Corinthians 12:7). When we use our gift(s), we, in effect, dispense God's grace to others.

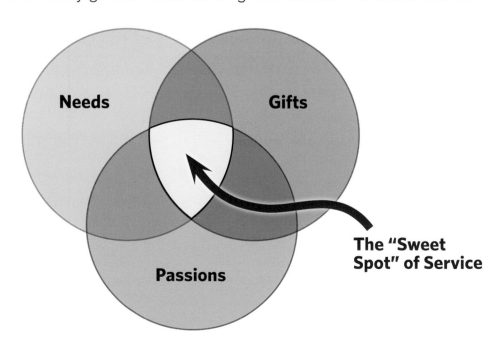

Needs

Gifts

Passions

The "Sweet Spot" of Service

Do you know what your spiritual gifts are? You can prayerfully discover your gifting in a variety of ways:

▶ *Examination* (via spiritual gift questionnaires—like the one on the following two pages)

▶ *Evaluation* (of your Christian history and experiences); *experimentation* with various new ministries

▶ *Enjoyment* (considering which acts of service have been most fulfilling to you)

▶ *Effectiveness* (considering where you have seen the most fruitfulness in ministry)

As with faith, prayer, and evangelism, it's not enough merely to study this topic. Being a follower of Jesus means rolling up your sleeves and diving in. We have to take action and get busy.

6. Now that you've studied a bit about this idea of being called and gifted to minister to others, what—specifically and practically—does service look like in your life today? What would you like it to look like in the days to come?

_____

_____

_____

_____

_____

_____

_____

_____

_____

_____

Take-Home Reflections

Good Reasons to Serve	Bad Reasons to Serve
Jesus served and we're called to be like him.	To avoid looking like a slacker
"Servant" is every disciple's new, true identity.	To alleviate guilt or pressure that others are laying on me
God has graced us with important abilities, skills, experiences, and blessings.	To show myself spiritually superior to those who don't serve
The world is a needy place. Jesus called us to serve the needy.	To put others in my debt
We are transformed as we engage in the process of serving others.	To try to win God's approval—and to avoid his displeasure for not serving
Serving is rewarding (both now and forever).	To compel others to serve me in return

Life Application

An important part of discipleship is learning how to apply God's truths to your life. Below are just a few ways you can start thinking about what you've learned and apply it to your daily life.

1. Memorize our memory verse, 1 Peter 4:10.

   "Each of you should use whatever gift you have received to serve others, as faithful stewards of God's grace in its various forms."

2. Read carefully and meditatively the story of Jesus washing his disciples' feet in John 13. On a separate sheet of paper journal any insights or "aha!" moments.

3. Complete the "Spiritual Gift Questionnaire" that follows.

Spiritual Gift Questionnaire

This questionnaire is one of many tools to help you discern where you fit in the church's many ministries. It can help you to either learn or confirm areas of affinity—areas that you naturally tend to focus on. But as with most spiritual gifts tests, it is not meant to definitively tell you what your gift is. Simply knowing your spiritual gifts is not the goal, but rather knowing how to serve God as a member of Christ's body and serve are the real goals.

> Ask God for guidance and wisdom to find your place in the church's ministry.
> Your life experience can be a good guide to find your interest and abilities.
> Be mindful of the needs of your church. Sometimes, God will call you to minister—serve—in places you might not prefer. The calling may be temporary or long term.
> Be ready, willing, and courageous. Obedience is challenging.
> Listen to the encouragement, wisdom, and guidance of other members of the body of Christ.
> Be prayerful about finding God's will for you.

For each question, choose a response between 0 and 3 as follows:

3 Consistently, almost always true   **2** Most of the time, usually true   **1** Some of the time, once in a while   **0** Not at all, never

---

1. _____ I am able to communicate effectively the message of salvation through Christ Jesus.

2. _____ I make critical decisions when necessary.

3. _____ I rejoice when meeting needs through sharing my possessions.

4. _____ I enjoy studying.

5. _____ I thrive when trusting God in difficult situations.

6. _____ I actively meet physical and practical needs.

7. _____ I can analyze events or ideas from different points of view.

8. _____ I naturally encourage others.

9. _____ I am acutely in tune with the emotions of other people.

10. _____ I am a cheerful giver.

11. _____ Yielding to God's will gives me great joy.

12. _____ It is very important for me to do things for people in need.

13. _____ I can identify those who need encouragement.

14. _____ I am sensitive to the hurts of people.

15. _____ I am sensitive to new truths and to how they apply to specific situations.

16. _____ I have experience with organizing ideas, resources, time, and people effectively.

17. _____ I am able to discern when sermons or teachings do not conform to the Scriptures.

18. _____ I can trust in God even in very difficult moments.

19. _____ I can discern where God wants a group to go and help it get there.

20. _____ I have the ability and desire to teach.

21. _____ I am sensitive to what people need.

22. _____ I have experience making effective and efficient plans for accomplishing the goals of a group.

23. _____ I can explain Scripture in simple and accessible ways.

24. _____ I spend time digging into facts.

25. _____ Sharing Christ with nonbelievers comes naturally to me.

26. _____ I can discern the motivation of persons and movements.

27. _____ I can delegate and assign meaningful work.

28. _____ I detect when people experience stress and distress.

29. _____ I desire to give generously and unpretentiously to worthwhile projects and ministries.

30. _____ I can relate God's truths to specific situations.

31. _____ I can organize facts into meaningful relationships.

32. _____ I can detect honesty (and dishonesty) when people share their religious experiences.

33. _____ I look for ways to encourage and comfort others around me.

34. _____ I am able to help people flourish in their ministries.

35. _____ I can make complex ideas and doctrines simple and accessible to others.

36. _____ I look for opportunities to establish relationships with non-believers.

Write your answer for each question, then add your answers for each gift. Pay attention to 2's or 3's. These are likely the gifts you are currently leaning toward.

Gift	Question Number	Your Answer	Total
Discernment	17		
	26		
	32		
Exhortation	8		
	13		
	33		
Evangelism	1		
	25		
	36		
Faith	5		
	11		
	18		
Giving	3		
	10		
	29		
Guidance	16		
	22		
	27		
Help/Serving	6		
	12		
	21		
Knowledge	4		
	24		
	31		
Leadership	2		
	19		
	34		
Mercy	9		
	14		
	28		
Teaching	20		
	23		
	35		
Wisdom	7		
	15		
	30		

Topic 29: Evangelism

Sharing the Message of Your New Life in Christ

"But in your hearts revere Christ as Lord. Always
be prepared to give an answer to everyone who
asks you to give the reason for the hope that you
have. But do this with gentleness and respect."

—1 Peter 3:15

Evangelism simply means sharing the good news of God's love for the world through Christ. But in today's world, sometimes it comes across differently. What comes into your mind when you hear the word "evangelism"?

- ☐ A silver-tongued television preacher smiling at the camera and asking for money
- ☐ A sweating preacher who is flailing and yelling at his congregation
- ☐ A red-faced person who is arguing obnoxiously with a skeptic about the Bible
- ☐ Putting Christian bumper stickers on your car
- ☐ Turning off all your friends by being preachy and weird
- ☐ Other (write on blank line below):

_____

The sad but true fact is that many Christians, for many reasons, don't talk about their faith to non-believers.

Primary Reasons Christians Don't Share Their Faith[5]

Reason	Example
Fear	"I'm scared of what others might say; how people might react."
Lack of training	"No one ever showed me how to talk about spiritual matters. I wouldn't know what to say!"
Minimal contact with unbelievers	"I mostly spend time with my Christian friends."

5　"Successful Witnessing," *The Compass*, www.cru.org/content/dam/cru/legacy/2012/01/successfulwitnessing.pdf.

Reason	Example
Shaky theology	"God is in control; he knows who is going to become Christian, so I don't need to say anything. Besides, who am I to foist my views on others? People have to find their own way."
A lack of concern	"I've got a lot going on in my life; I really need to focus now on my schooling/career/etc."
Losing sight of the power of the gospel	"As if my pitiful words and life could make a difference!"
Disobedience	"Bottom-line: I just don't want to do that."
Forgetting what successful evangelism is	"I have talked to twelve people about Jesus, and none have become Christians. So obviously I'm not called to evangelize."

And yet, a careful reading of the gospels shows that a disciple is a person who follows Jesus—to *know* Jesus and his teaching; to *grow* more like Jesus; and to *go* for Jesus, serving others and making new disciples. In this lesson we're looking hard at that third aspect of discipleship: going out into the world with Jesus. And specifically, talking about the gospel—doing evangelism, witnessing, sharing your faith, etc.

Bible Study

1. Have you ever tried to have a spiritual conversation with someone who was not a follower of Jesus, and if so, what happened?

_____

_____

_____

_____

2. If you are reluctant to talk to others about spiritual matters, what are *your* reasons?

_____

_____

_____

_____

_____

The apostle Peter wrote his first epistle to believers who were being persecuted for their Christian beliefs. If ever there were a group of folks tempted to be "close-mouthed" about Jesus, this would have been the group. And yet, in 1 Peter 3:13–18, we find a challenge for them to verbalize their faith:

> "Who is going to harm you if you are eager to do good? But even if you should suffer for what is right, you are blessed. 'Do not fear their threats; do not be frightened.' But in your hearts revere Christ as Lord. Always be prepared to give an answer to everyone who asks you to give the reason for the hope that you have. But do this with gentleness and respect, keeping a clear conscience, so that those who speak maliciously against your good behavior in Christ may be ashamed of their slander. For it is better, if it is God's will, to suffer for doing good than for doing evil. For Christ also suffered once for sins, the righteous for the unrighteous, to bring you to God. He was put to death in the body but made alive in the Spirit."

3. Before we look at it more deeply, what jumps out to you from this passage?

_____

_____

_____

_____

_____

Evangelism Myths and Truths

Based on the passage above, work your way through the following chart, reflecting on the wrong notions many believers have about evangelism and how this passage refutes these evangelism myths.

Evangelism MYTH	Seeing the good news as GOOD NEWS!	Evangelism TRUTH
Sharing your faith depends on having a slick, prepared speech.	**"in your hearts revere Christ as Lord..."**	Sharing your faith depends on a surrendered heart.
You have to know a ton of theology.		You have to know Christ as Lord.

Evangelism MYTH	Seeing the good news as GOOD NEWS!	Evangelism TRUTH
It's the pastor's job.	**"Always be prepared to give an answer…"**	It's the job description of every disciple.
Witnessing is an activity.		Witnessing is a way of life.
I prefer to let my life do the talking.		We need to add words to our good deeds and humble, loving attitudes.
Nobody is interested in the gospel.	**"to everyone who asks you to give the reason for the hope that you have…"**	People are interested in a life that's being transformed by the gospel.
Christians spread the gospel best by inviting Christians to religious gatherings.		Disciples spread the gospel most effectively by breaking out of their church groups and permeating the rest of the world.
Evangelism means confronting people—usually strangers—in a hard-hitting, and usually awkward, offensive, and abrasive way.	**"But do this with gentleness and respect…"**	Evangelism means loving the people God has placed in your life until they ask you why. And then, with great sensitivity, gently introducing them to Jesus.
A witness should "have it all together."	**"keeping a clear conscience…"**	A witness should be authentic and real, sharing his or her own struggles.
We should use whatever means are necessary to get the message out.		We should always be honest and ethical in our interactions with unbelievers, treating them with the same respect we want to receive.
Success in sharing your faith means that a non-Christian prays "the sinner's prayer."	**"so that those who speak maliciously against your good behavior in Christ may be ashamed of their slander."**	Success in sharing your faith means that God works in hearts in his way and his time, using our witness as he sees fit.

4. As you look at that chart, would you say your understanding of evangelism has been based more on myth or on truth? Why?

_____

_____

_____

One of the best and easiest ways to share the gospel with others is to simply tell the story of your spiritual journey. The Bible word for this holy habit is "witness." What's a witness? It's someone who has experienced something and who gives testimony about that experience to others (1 John 1:3). A witness has seen something with his own eyes. She's heard something with her own ears. A witness is nothing more than a truth-teller.

> "It is not our work to make men believe: that is the work of the Holy Spirit."—D. L. Moody

You don't have to be a theologian or pastor to learn to tell others about your own experience with Christ. Your testimony is just a succinct telling of how you met Jesus and how He has altered and continues to transform your life. It means sharing the ups and downs of your journey of faith.

Sharing your spiritual story is a valuable skill. It's an effective tool for several reasons:

- ▶ Who can argue with a changed, authentic life? People can debate the Bible or quibble over theology, but no one can deny that something significant has happened to you.

- ▶ Your personal testimony can be adapted to all sorts of unique situations.

- ▶ God often uses the story of a person's spiritual journey to pave the way for deeper discussions of the gospel.

So how to do it? How can you become adept at "sharing your testimony"? Here are some basics to get you started.

5. First, take a few minutes to read Acts 26:1–31, the apostle Paul's testimony to King Agrippa about his own encounter with Jesus. What stands out to you about Paul's witness here?

_____

_____

_____

_____

Do you notice how Paul spoke simply, logically, and chronologically? He began by speaking about his life *before* he met Christ on the Damascus Road (vss. 4–11). Then he related the circumstances surrounding his actual encounter with Jesus (vss. 12–20). Finally, he shared how his life changed *after* believing in Christ (verses 21–23).

That's an easy and clear outline to follow in preparing our own testimonies. Let's do it!

Writing Your Testimony

6. Answer the following questions lettered *a* through *f*. Then, take these answers and copy them to a separate sheet of paper or type them into your computer. Make whatever adjustments are needed for clarity and flow. The end result will be a concise and clear rendering of your personal testimony.

On the lines below, jot some notes and recollections about your own life prior to placing your faith in Christ. Perhaps you struggled with one or more of the following. And by the way, it's okay if these struggles continue to affect you. It's your *growth, trust, and persistence*—thanks to the strengthening of Christ—that matter.

- ❑ Feeling far from God
- ❑ Gnawing inner emptiness
- ❑ Lack of peace
- ❑ Fear of death
- ❑ Family dysfunction
- ❑ Longing for meaning in life
- ❑ Traumatic childhood hurts
- ❑ Feelings of insignificance

- ❑ Loneliness
- ❑ Feeling unloved
- ❑ Insecurity
- ❑ Immense guilt
- ❑ Desire for control
- ❑ Addictive behaviors
- ❑ Lack of purpose
- ❑ Emotional instability

a. Describe yourself before you met Christ in a personal way.

_____

_____

_____

_____

_____

_____

_____

Oftentimes people try without success to solve their own problems. Perhaps this is your story as well. Maybe you looked for answers to the deep needs of your heart through a job, money, fun experiences, or popularity—even being religious? Maybe you thought academic success or athletic achievement or romance would "save" you.

b. Describe some of *your* failed attempts to fix your own problems.

_____

_____

_____

_____

_____

Now, recall the circumstances surrounding how you were drawn to Christ. What made you consider him as the solution to your deepest needs?

c. Identify the specific events that led to your trusting in Jesus. If this was a long-term process, summarize it, but don't leave out important details.

_____

_____

_____

_____

_____

d. State clearly the steps you took to put your faith in Christ. If God drew you to himself through a particular Bible verse, share that verse.

_____

_____

_____

_____

_____

However you describe this life-changing moment, make sure to make the gospel clear. This includes the following truths:

▶ "I realized I was a sinner, separated from God."

▶ "I saw that the penalty for sin is death."

▶ "I understood that Jesus paid the penalty for my sins."

▶ "I put my trust in Christ alone and what He did for me."

Now very concisely, talk about your life *since* coming into a relationship with Jesus. Your goal here is to show the difference that Christ is making in your life. You don't need to show one-hundred percent victory over every difficulty. Simply sharing your confidence—through examples—that the Lord is walking beside you through the problems, will help your listener understand.

e. What are the biggest changes that have happened in your life?

_____

_____

_____

_____

_____

Be sure to conclude with a statement along the lines of, "And, of course, in addition to the amazing benefit of being accepted in this life, I also have the promise of heaven." A statement like this often leads to a deeper conversation of spiritual matters. Your friend may ask, "How can you say that? How can *anyone* say that? How can you know *for sure*?"

f. Write your closing statement.

_____

_____

_____

_____

_____

_____

"I look upon this world as a wrecked vessel. God has given me a lifeboat and said, 'Moody, save all you can.'"—D. L. Moody

Take-Home Reflections

Top Ten Testimony Tips!

▶ No two testimonies are alike because no two lives are. Don't try to copy someone else's story. God can and will use your own unique experience to speak to others. Be real. Be authentic. There's an old Yiddish proverb that says, "If you try to be someone else, who will be you?"

▶ If you met Christ as an adult, you may have a distinct *before, how,* and *after.* If you trusted Christ as a child, you may not be able to report radical changes in behavior; nevertheless, you ought to be able to point to some concrete ways Christ is changing you now or has changed you in the past (in attitudes, goals, challenges, desires, etc.).

▶ Avoid Christian clichés. Many Biblical words and phrases that are meaningful to believers (saved, sin, lost, born again, live in your heart, washed in the blood, sanctified, etc.) are meaningless to unbelievers. Translate Christian jargon into normal English.

▶ Avoid controversial statements or subjects. For example, going off on a rant against alcohol may turn off a skeptical person.

▶ Don't criticize specific churches, individuals, or groups.

▶ There is no need to share a lot of the seamy details of your life before meeting Christ. Be discreet.

▶ Keep your testimony warm and personal. Don't get preachy and wordy. Make it a point to say "I" and "me" rather than "you." This is your story, and yours alone. God deals differently with each person.

▶ Practice sharing your testimony with a spouse, child, parent, Christian friend, or small group until it becomes second nature. Then ask God for opportunities to share your testimony with non-Christian friends and acquaintances.

▶ Don't bore people with tons of unnecessary details. A succinct summary—three to four minutes at absolute most—is sufficient. You want to arouse curiosity. You want, when you're done, people asking for *more* details rather than thinking, "I thought he or she would *never* shut up!"

▶ If you can, include a meaningful Bible verse. God's Word is far more powerful than anything we might say. It has the power to change hearts and lives (2 Timothy 3:16–17). If you quote a verse, make sure it's one that speaks about the hope that Christ brings or about the free gift of the gospel (John 10:10, Ephesians 2:8–9). It's usually a good idea to do this from one of the more modern, easy-to-understand translations like the *New Living Translation* (NLT), the *New International Version* (NIV), or the *English Standard Version* (ESV).

Life Application

An important part of discipleship is learning how to apply God's truths to your life. Below are just a few ways you can start thinking about what you've learned and apply it to your daily life.

1. Memorize our memory verse, 1 Peter 3:15:

   "But in your hearts revere Christ as Lord. Always be prepared to give an answer to everyone who asks you to give the reason for the hope that you have. But do this with gentleness and respect."

2. Read through the suggestions in "How to Create Opportunities to Talk About Your Faith," on the next page. These suggestions help you weave your testimony into everyday conversations.

3. Wrestle with one or two of the questions in the right-hand column.

   ▶ How can a rich, authentic relationship with Jesus—and submission to his Lordship (1 Peter 3:15)—make a difference in how we share our faith?

   ▶ Which is more important: "walking the walk"— Christian living—or "talking the talk"—telling others about Christ? Which are you better at and why?

   ▶ Why is it that some Christians have no meaningful contacts with unbelievers?

   ▶ Why would Christians get defensive when skeptics attack our faith?

   ▶ Does Peter's command to respond "with gentleness and respect" mean that we can never say "hard" things to non-Christian friends?

   ▶ Make a list of five people with whom you'd like to discuss spiritual matters. Pray for them. We should always talk to God about people before we talk to people about God.

How to Create Opportunities to Talk About Your Faith

▶ Don't spend all your time with church people! Build relationships with those who don't know Christ! Move toward them in love. Love them because God does. Love them with no strings attached. Win the right to be heard.

▶ Don't condemn unbelievers for living like unbelievers. That's what they are! Their biggest need isn't a lifestyle change—it's Jesus! Accept them as they are. Many of them are leery about judgmental Christians. It's the Holy Spirit's job to convict them of sin and repentance, not yours.

▶ Open your life. Talk about everyday stuff (family, hobbies, job, school, friends, children, relationships, etc.). Listen attentively for expressed needs such as family problems or stress in school or at work. For example, if your friend says, "I'm really worried about my son . . . " maybe you can sympathize and tactfully share how Christ has helped you in a similar situation—or how he brought you through your own difficult teen years.

▶ Discuss personal struggles and needs— both past and present. "Did I ever tell you how I survived my divorce?" "We're going through a rough patch financially, and it's nerve-wracking, but you know what? Never in my life have I felt abandoned by God. He has always provided for us."

▶ After sharing something Christ has done or is doing in your life, ask a question like "Have you ever experienced anything like that?" or "Does that make sense?"

▶ Don't argue. Absolutely refuse to debate. No one ever got dragged kicking and screaming into the kingdom of God! Today may not be God's timing.

▶ Never "dump the truck." Better to say less, and have them ask for more, than to say too much and have them looking for the nearest exit.

▶ Piggyback off contemporary situations and news stories. Ask thought-provoking questions. For example, when a friend brings up how so many politicians seem to tap into and prey upon voters' fears: "Why do think people are so afraid? What are the things that scare *you*? What do you do when you feel fearful?" After listening thoughtfully, maybe you can say something like, "You know, I can certainly relate. The world is a pretty scary place. But that's something my faith has helped me with . . . "

▶ If it's clear your friend is uncomfortable, end on a positive note. Communicate love and acceptance. Allow the Holy Spirit to set the pace. He opens and closes doors of opportunity.

274

Topic 30: Missions

Embracing God's Heart for the World

"But you will receive power when the Holy Spirit comes on you; and you will be my witnesses in Jerusalem, and in all Judea and Samaria, and to the ends of the earth."

—Acts 1:8

In 1916, a young Irish woman by the name of Irene Webster-Smith went to Japan with the Japan Evangelistic Band (JEB) and began to minister to prostitutes. Eventually, she decided that it would be better to prevent girls from becoming prostitutes in the first place—or in her words, "Erect a fence at the top of the precipice rather than driving an ambulance at the bottom." To that end she began to adopt unwanted babies and began the Sunrise Home. Her work continued until 1940, when she was forced to leave Japan at the advent of World War II.

Following the war, when General Douglas MacArthur was supervising the rebuiliding of Japan, he personally invited Irene to come back and minister to war criminals who were to be executed. Irene was able to lead fourteen of these war criminals and some of their guards to Christ.

In her last years, Irene, who was known as *Sensei*, worked with InterVarsity Fellowship, teaching Japanese college students about Christ and founding the Ochanomizu Christian Student Center at Tokyo University.

1. When someone brings up the topic of *missions* what sorts of thoughts and ideas run through your mind?

_____

_____

_____

_____

Perhaps you've heard of the Great Commission of Christ. This biblical passage is what gets Christians and churches thinking about the global task of making disciples.

The Great Commission

> "God has made you for global purposes. God has made you for something very large."—John Piper

"All authority in heaven and on earth has been given to me. Therefore go and make disciples of all nations, baptizing them in the name of the Father and of the Son and of the Holy Spirit, and teaching them to obey everything I have commanded you. And surely I am with you always, to the very end of the age" (Matthew 28:18–20).

2. Do you think Christ's command to "make disciples of all nations" means we all need to pack up our belongings and move to foreign soil? Why or why not?

_____

_____

_____

Some believers regard cross-cultural ministry as "one more thing the church does"—an optional program, sort of like the men's softball team or the hand bell choir. Others cringe from guilt at the "m" word, because they're not involved. Still others feel they have no way to contribute to God's global cause.

In this session, we hope to demonstrate, first, that making disciples of all nations isn't a side venture of the church, it's our reason for being! Second, we want to explore some very practical ways ordinary followers of Jesus can have a worldwide impact, often without leaving their own zip code!

Let's begin!

276

Bible Study

God has a heart for the nations of the world.

The New Testament Greek word commonly translated "nation" is *ethnos* (Matthew 28:19). This is the word from which we get our English word "ethnic." That's the idea—a distinct ethnic group, people, or race.

> In North America, there are more than 1,430 distinct people groups and almost 147 of these are considered "unreached."

We tend to think of nations as political entities or geographical areas marked by lines on a map. But God in his Word always focuses on groups that share a common affinity and self-identity—cultural background and language. Think of the Kurdish People, spread out across Turkey, Syria, Iraq and Iran; the Choctaw Nation in the United States; or the Maasai Tribe who spill out of southern Kenya into northern Tanzania.

> An unreached people group refers to an ethnic group that lacks an indigenous, self-propagating Christian church movement.

After God created the world (Genesis 1–2) and mankind sinned (Genesis 3–9), we see the rise of nations. These distinct peoples—with divine help—begin to spread out across the earth (Genesis 10–11).

Then, in Genesis 12, we see God choose one man and give him remarkable promises:

"The LORD had said to Abram, 'Go from your country, your people and your father's household to the land I will show you. I will make you into a great nation, and I will bless you; I will make your name great, and you will be a blessing. I will bless those who bless you, and whoever curses you I will curse; and all peoples on earth will be blessed through you'" (Genesis 12:1–3).

3. What reason does God give for blessing Abram (later called Abraham)?

_____

_____

_____

_____

_____

Clearly, since humanity's "fall" into sin (Genesis 3), God's desire has been to rescue and bless all peoples. God has a heart for the nations of the world! Carefully read and consider the following passages from Genesis to Revelation:

▶ "I will make your descendants as numerous as the stars in the sky and will give them all these lands, and through your offspring all nations on earth will be blessed" (Genesis 26:4).

▶ "May your ways be known throughout the earth, your saving power among people everywhere. May the nations praise you, O God. Yes, may all the nations praise you" (Psalm 67:2–3, NLT).

▶ "God blesses us, that all the ends of the earth may fear Him" (Psalm 67:7, NASB).

▶ "All the nations you have made will come and worship before you, Lord; they will bring glory to your name" (Psalm 86:9).

▶ "Praise the LORD, all nations; laud Him, all peoples!" (Psalm 117:1, NASB).

▶ "This gospel of the kingdom will be preached in the whole world as a testimony to all nations, and then the end will come" (Matthew 24:14).

▶ "He said to me, 'Go, for I will send you far away to the Gentiles'" (Acts 22:21, ESV).

▶ "Is it not written: 'My house will be called a house of prayer for all nations'? But you have made it 'a den of robbers'" (Mark 11:17).

▶ "Moved by the Spirit, he went into the temple courts. When the parents brought in the child Jesus to do for him what the custom of the Law required, Simeon took him in his arms and praised God, saying: 'Sovereign Lord, as you have promised, you may now dismiss your servant in peace. For my eyes have seen your salvation, which you have prepared in the sight of all nations: a light for revelation to the Gentiles, and the glory of your people Israel'" (Luke 2:27–32).

▶ "After this I looked, and there before me was a great multitude that no one could count, from every nation, tribe, people and language, standing before the throne and before the Lamb. They were wearing white robes and were holding palm branches in their hands. And they cried out in a loud voice: 'Salvation belongs to our God, who sits on the throne, and to the Lamb'" (Revelation 7:9–10).

4. What do you see here in all this talk about nations, peoples, and Gentiles?

_____

_____

_____

278

5. According to the passage above from Revelation 7, where is history headed?

_____

_____

_____

_____

_____

6. How would you summarize God's desire, his heart, for the peoples of the world?

_____

_____

_____

_____

_____

Cultivating a Missionary Heart like God's

God doesn't call every believer to move to a foreign country. But he does want us to think about the world, pray for its needs, and do our part in fulfilling the Great Commission—even if it's a behind-the-scenes role. There's an old saying that some can go, most can give, and all can pray. The more we learn and engage, the more we'll sense our heart beating for the nations.

Here are thirty-one simple, doable, and creative ways to be a "World Christian" right where you are now.

- Read the book of Acts in one sitting. Imagine traveling with Peter or Paul, doing evangelism, discipling believers, planting new churches.

- Discover a wealth of information about reaching the unreached people groups of the world at www.joshuaproject.net.

- Offer to serve on your church's missions committee, or on a long- or short-term missions team.

- Get a whirlwind short-course in the history of world missions by reading Ruth Tucker's missions classic *From Jerusalem to Irian Jaya.*

- Get a list of church-sponsored missionaries. Memorize their names and where they serve. Find out their birthdays, anniversaries, etc. and fuss over them on those special days.

- Take the life-changing Perspectives on the World Christian Movement course. To find out about classes in your area check out www.perspectives.org.

- Get your passport or make sure it is up to date just in case you have the opportunity to go on a short-term mission trip.

- Every chance you get, invite furloughed or retired missionaries into your home for dinner. Let family members and roommates rub shoulders with disciples whose hearts beat for the nations.

- Identify culturally diverse people who live in your neighborhood. Reach out to them by inviting them over for dinner, asking them to go on a picnic, etc. In short, pray that God will enable you to develop a redemptive relationship with your neighbors.

- Begin asking the Lord of the harvest to send out workers into his harvest (Luke 10:2). Pray that some, even from your own church, would be thrust out into places of effective ministry among the unreached.

- If you're an empty nester, single, or a family with an extra bedroom in your home, inquire about missionary couples or families on furlough. Offer to host them whenever they pass through your area.

- Fast one day a week. Use those meal times to pray for an unreached people group. Give the money that you would have spent on groceries that day to a missionary working to plant a church among an unreached people group. If you estimate two dollars for breakfast, three dollars for lunch, and five dollars for supper, that would be ten dollars a week or forty dollars a month that could be spent supporting missions.

- Put an acrylic photo holder in the center of your dining table. Put a different missionary picture or prayer letter in it each day. Make these servants of God, their activities, and needs a regular part of your family's daily dining experience.

- Buy a small globe and make it a dining table centerpiece. At supper each night, discuss a different country. Learn the capital cities of the world.

- If you are financially able, don't sell or trade in your old car. Instead, donate it to your favorite mission agency for use by missionaries who are home on furlough and must make frequent trips to visit their supporters.

280

▶ Email a missionary you know and love. Ask, "If I could buy you any two books to help you in what you're doing, what two titles would you want?" Order those desired resources and mail them to the missionary.

▶ Take a picture of your Sunday school class, family, or small group holding up a poster that says, "We love you and are lifting you up!" Mail it to a sponsored missionary family.

▶ If you have an area in your city where different ethnic groups live (Chinatown, little Havana, a Hispanic neighborhood, etc.), gather a friend or two and go on a prayer walk through that neighborhood. A "prayer walk" is just what it sounds like. You walk and pray at the same time—for the salvation of those in the area who don't know Christ, for workers to reach out to them, for believers in the area to be strong witnesses, etc.

▶ Get an international cookbook from the library and one night a week, try cooking a dish that would commonly be served and eaten in another country. Allow your whole family to experience life from a different perspective. For extra fun, check out a

"travel videologue" about that country from your public library. These DVDs, usually 60 minutes in length, can give you a whirlwind, "up close and personal" peek at places and peoples around the globe!

▶ Make an appointment with a financial advisor about getting out of debt and living by a budget. For some, this is a long, slow, difficult process. For others, it requires only a minor adjustment in lifestyle. For all, it opens up new opportunities to live for the kingdom and to allocate more resources to eternal ventures.

▶ Start reading up on "International News." Many believers ignore these stories because they claim they don't understand political developments taking place around the world. The irony is that we will *never* come to understand global events until we make the effort to get informed.

▶ Consider offering your professional services (dental, medical, legal, accounting, etc.) for free to missionaries on furlough.

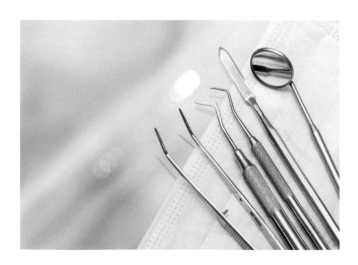

▶ Visit an ethnic market in your community. Take your children and allow them to experience the different sights, sounds, and smells. Better yet, once every three months or so, visit an ethnic restaurant in your city.

▶ Have a garage sale and donate the proceeds to a missionary family in need. They get necessary funding. You get a de-cluttered attic, garage, basement, and closets!

▶ Get a copy of *Operation World*, the definitive prayer guide to every nation. This resource looks at the world country by country, gives a brief glimpse of what God is doing in each place, and suggests ways believers can pray. Find out more or get other resources at www.operationworld.org.

▶ Look at the labels on your clothing. If your shirt says "Made in Malaysia," pray for that country—for God to open eyes and hearts there, for the church there to grow and be strengthened and emboldened, for missionaries working there, etc.

▶ Set your watch alarm to go off daily at a certain time, as a reminder to pray. For example, set it to beep at 2:22 P.M.

When it does, pray for two workers in two places for two minutes.

▶ Surprise a missionary family with a care package filled with goodies and hard-to-find items. Make sure you first find out about customs requirements and restrictions—you don't want your gesture of love to cost your overseas friends an arm and a leg!

▶ Minister to a missionary family on furlough. Take them to lunch. Bring them a batch of cookies. Offer to provide childcare for an evening. Take him golfing or fishing. Take her shopping. Give the family a gift certificate.

▶ Almost all universities have sizable international student communities.

These bright and influential visitors are often very open to your friendship. Many times the wives and children of such graduate and doctoral students lead lives of isolation and loneliness. If you live near a university, contact the International Student office and find out how you can reach out to these future leaders.

▶ Invite international students into your home and your life. Help them with English. Inform them about local customs. Have them teach you a song or authentic dance from their homeland. Or have them plan a native meal of two or three dishes. You buy the necessary ingredients; they come over and cook and tell you about their lives and culture.

The point is, whether you're a young professional, a small business owner, or a stay-at-home mom, you *can* play a role in God's global and eternal cause—right where you are. Every disciple can be a World Christian. Little acts of faithfulness can and do make an eternal difference.

7. What are some things you'd like to explore in terms of becoming a more missions-minded "world Christian"?

_____

_____

_____

_____

_____

_____

_____

Take-Home Reflections

World Missions: By the Numbers

(as of 2016)

7,300,000,000	People in the world
865,000,000	Muslims with no gospel witness
550,000,000	Unreached Hindus
275,000,000	Buddhists who haven't heard of Christ
4,190,000	Full-time Christian workers
16,761	Distinct people groups
6,500	Languages in the world
900	Number of churches for every unreached people group in the world
105	People who die every minute
1	Life you have to give

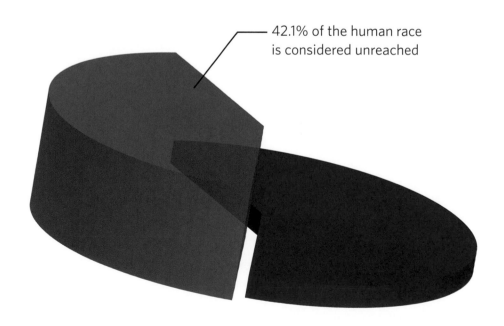

42.1% of the human race is considered unreached

Life Application

An important part of discipleship is learning how to apply God's truths to your life. Below are just a few ways you can start thinking about what you've learned and apply it to your daily life.

1. Memorize our memory verse, Acts 1:8.

   "But you will receive power when the Holy Spirit comes on you; and you will be my witnesses in Jerusalem, and in all Judea and Samaria, and to the ends of the earth."

2. Learn about the 10/40 Window:

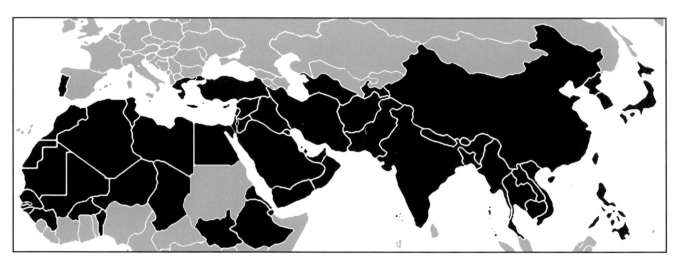

   Within the rectangle formed between ten degrees north and forty degrees north latitude lies much of Asia, the Middle East, and North Africa.

   This land area is home to almost 5,500 unreached people groups and some three billion individuals. This is where most of the world's Muslims, Hindus, and Buddhists live. Many have never heard of Christ's love and sacrifice for them.

3. Ponder these words:

   "Most men are not satisfied with the permanent output of their lives. Nothing can wholly satisfy the life of Christ within his followers except the adoption of Christ's purpose toward the world he came to redeem. Fame, pleasure, and riches are but husks and ashes in contrast with the boundless and abiding joy of working with God for the fulfillment of his eternal plans. The men who are putting everything into Christ's undertaking are getting out of life its sweetest and most priceless rewards."
   —J. Campbell White

   Journal your thoughts on a separate sheet of paper.

4. Pray, asking the Lord, "What is my specific role in fulfilling the Great Commission?"

Appendix

How to Create a Flexible Discipleship Program

Making disciples isn't like making widgets.

We can't mass produce followers of Jesus like cars on an assembly line—nor should we try. Life is fluid, people are unique, and life's challenges vary from believer to believer.

Maybe your group can't commit to a 30-week study right now. Probably the members don't even need some of these lessons right now, but they'll be more relevant six months or a year from now.

Recognizing these realities, *Rose Guide to Discipleship* is designed to be flexible and adaptable. Here's how to tailor a discipleship plan that fits the needs of your group:

1. Have your group members complete the "Discipleship Snapshot" (also here in the Appendix). On that self-assessment, they'll simply indicate their ten preferred study topics by ranking their top ten choices from ten to one (with ten being the subject they want to explore most) out of the thirty topic choices. Note: The instructions say to rank all thirty topics. Let your participants know you only need their top ten.

2. Have the math whiz in your group add up the group's responses.

3. Decide how many weeks you'd like to meet. (Note: Most small groups have the best experience with studies broken down into four- to eight-week modules).

4. If, say, your group decides it can only meet for six weeks, pick the six topics with the highest overall number of votes.

Guidelines for Disciplers and Group Leaders

How good and gracious of God to let us play a role in the spiritual growth of others! Here are some important truths to keep in mind as you embark on leading a discipleship group:

▶ God is the primary agent of transformation in a person's life. You can't rescue or "fix" anyone. See yourself, instead, as a human instrument in God's hands. The Holy Spirit alone knows what is best for each person. Trust him to work his will (not yours) in his own timing.

▶ Your job description is to be pure, available, and yielded to God. You are to be a conduit of God's love, grace, and truth. Your role is to ask God to work in your group members' lives—to believe that he sees and knows the deep needs of their hearts, to trust that he is at work, even when you can't see it.

▶ Though you can't save anyone or *make* anyone grow in the faith, you can:

✦ Pray	✦ Share the gospel
✦ Observe	✦ Open your heart and life
✦ Come alongside	✦ Pass on your experiences
✦ Engage	✦ Invest time
✦ Accept	✦ Teach skills
✦ Invite	✦ Remind
✦ Ask good questions	✦ Encourage
✦ Listen	✦ Challenge
✦ Model	✦ Gently confront
✦ Love	✦ Be gracious and merciful
✦ Serve	

In short, you can do a *lot!*

▶ Those who happen to be in your discipleship group are ultimately Christ's followers, not yours. They should imitate you only to the extent you are imitating Jesus. Don't try to create clones of yourself. Everyone's personality is different. Each person approaches faith and life in ways that you might not.

▶ The spiritual success or failure of those in your group is not—ultimately—your responsibility. Your responsibility is to be faithful. *God is in charge of outcomes.* Don't take credit for "dynamic" disciples; don't shoulder excessive blame for "followers who falter or fail."

Discipleship Leader MYTHS (and TRUTHS)

MYTH	TRUTH
Has it all "together"—has few weaknesses or failings—and works carefully to hide such flaws	▶ Knows he or she does NOT have it together and never will this side of heaven! ▶ Is real, honest, and open about shortcomings . . . and is trusting God for transformation in those areas over the course of a lifetime. ▶ Has compassion for others too, knowing the Christian life is a marathon, not a sprint.
Must be a Bible **scholar**—ideally with knowledge of Greek and Hebrew	Must be a Bible **student** steadily growing in his or her understanding of the Word
Super Shepherd! Has deep, lengthy personal interaction (via email, phone calls, lunch visits, etc.) with everyone in the group, every week	▶ Works to create an environment where group members care for one another—each one using his or her gifts. ▶ Does not want to pressure others about their life decisions but leaves that to God.
Seldom asks for help from others	**Insists** on help from other believers
Must have a big, fancy home	May or may not have a big, fancy home. If not, it's no big deal! Fancy doesn't matter, and if the home is too small, then other group members can take turns hosting meetings and socials.
"One-man/one-woman show" ▶ Dominates discussions ▶ Makes all the decisions ▶ Does everything him- or herself	Encourages participation ▶ Delegates ▶ Decentralizes the ministry ▶ Divvies up responsibilities among group members according to gifts and passions
Has all the answers	▶ Realizes he or she does NOT have all the answers ▶ Is both teachable and willing to learn
Entertainer—responsible to make sure everyone is happy and having a good time	**Encourager**—responsible to challenge group members to continue to grow and serve
The goal of the group is a good weekly meeting with lots of "God-information"	The goal of the group Is healthy *community* that spurs *spiritual maturity* and leads to *outwardly focused ministry*.

Minding Your *Ps* and *Qs*:
How to Have Great Discipleship Discussions

Pre-Meeting

▶ **P**rayerfully **p**icture the **p**ossibilities—What if God used this upcoming meeting as a catalyst to change hearts?

▶ **P**erspective—Instead of seeing your discipleship prep as a project, one more "to do" on your long list, view it as a personal imperative. "I need to grapple with this topic or this passage; and then, out of my struggle, facilitate an honest conversation."

▶ **P**repare—Read, examine, ponder; no shooting from the hip or winging it.

▶ **P**ersonalize—In two ways:

1. In the sense of internalizing the truth, living in it, and wrestling with it. It's one thing to examine a few Bible verses; it's another thing to let those truths examine you. Speak and share from your life, not just from your lesson plan.

2. In the sense of adding your unique imprint; can you think of a better question that fits your group better than the one provided? Ask it instead!

▶ **P**ress and **p**rod your group to come prepared.

At the Meeting

▶ **P**rime the **p**ump—Get 'em going. Ask fun, warm-up questions, non-threatening icebreaker type questions to get people talking; this is less necessary as groups get to know each other.

▶ **P**roven **p**rocess—We're not just filling thirty to forty minutes with "God-talk." We're trying to bring eternal truth to bear on everyday life. When handling Scripture, always move from "what do I see" and "what does it say" to "what does it mean" and "how do I live this out?" Remember that Jesus' disciples—even after three years with him—were still learning the basics and messing up a lot. If you as a leader show up, lead the group, and love the individuals, that is enough. God will do the rest!

▶ **P**articipation—Pull others in. Involve the whole group. Absolutely resist the urge to lecture. Go around the circle and ask people to give a short update about whatever they want. Limit this to three or five minutes. This allows the quiet reserved people to have a chance to be heard. Don't assume they don't want to talk. Allow people to say "Pass" if they aren't up for sharing.

▶ **P**atience—Don't be afraid of silence. Sometimes people need time to think and process before they are willing to share.

▶ **P**ush for honesty—On the first question, you should share first and set the pace for authenticity and vulnerability. Thereafter, have others go first and you go last. Disciples aren't created from polite, superficial, religious chit-chat.

▶ **P**ull out the "take home" truth. Interesting theological facts and Bible trivia don't really do much for us, but an understood and applied Scriptural truth can change our lives. What's the truth about God, the promise to bank on; the sin to avoid, the godly action or character quality to cultivate, etc.?

▶ **P**ress for participants to complete the life application—What does this look like in everyday life? What are we going to do about this? Determine to be doers, not listeners only, of the Word (James 1:22).

▶ **P**ray it into your lives.

▶ **Q**uestions—Keep them relevant, open-ended. Avoid "yes or no" type questions. Go for "how" and "why" questions.

▶ **Q**uiz—At the end of your time or at the beginning of the next time, review. Ask: So what did we learn? How did we do?

▶ **Q**uit on time—It's better to stop in the middle of a great discussion, than to drag on until all you hear is crickets. It's also okay to end early.

[Leader's Note: Copy these sheets and hand them out to each member of your group; then read and discuss.]

What to Expect in a Discipleship Group

Something very powerful happens when Christians who are eager to grow in their faith commit to:

▶ "Do life together" for a season.

▶ Gather regularly to open God's Word and wrestle with what it means to follow Jesus.

▶ Trust the Spirit of God to bring about transformation in and through them.

Here's a list of five things you can expect if you participate in a discipleship group:

1. **You'll be surprised.** When we dig deeply and ponder prayerfully, we discover things about God, about walking with Christ, and about ourselves that we never knew. Disciples should be curious and open.

2. **You'll be transformed.** Jesus promised that those who are spiritually hungry and thirsty would be satisfied (Matthew 5:6). Disciples can expect to know God better and grow in the faith.

3. **You'll be encouraged.** Nothing is more inspiring than being in a group where the members are experiencing transformation and are being used by Jesus to make an eternal difference in the world. Disciples must be committed and faithful to build each other up in the faith.

4. **You'll encounter resistance.** The enemy of our souls doesn't want us growing in the faith. He will pull out all the stops to oppose, distract, and tempt us. Disciples have to be wary and persistent.

5. **You'll be corrected.** The more we study God's Word, the more we realize that many of our notions about life and the spiritual life are simply wrong. Disciples need to be humble and teachable.

If you are up for all that, here are five important challenges:

1. **Be committed.** The old saying is true: You get out what you put in. Show up. When you miss a group meeting, others can't benefit from what God is teaching you. But don't just attend. Merely showing up to meetings doesn't lead to growing up in the faith. Study. Ponder. Wrestle. Then come prepared to participate.

2. **Be authentic.** It's always tempting to try to make ourselves look better—more spiritual, more solid, etc.—than we really are. But no one benefits from that kind of dishonesty. You don't need to share your deepest secrets, but be a truth-teller even when the truth is hard or ugly. Often one member's transparency and vulnerability can set the tone for an entire group. Be that person!

3. **Be trustworthy.** Help make the group a safe place. Adapt the "Vegas philosophy": *What's said in the group stays in the group.* Don't blab the secrets of others. There's no quicker way to kill a group.

4. **Be realistic.** Groups aren't heaven on earth. You won't "click" with everyone. Some nights the discussions will drag—or you'll come away with more questions than you had when you showed up. That's okay. Remember discipleship is a lifelong process, not an eight- or thirty-week program. Hang in there. Long journeys take a lot of little steps.

5. **Be prayerful.** Jesus said, "Apart from me, you can do nothing" (John 15:5). Without the presence of Christ, your group will be a mere meeting. But if, in a spirit of faith and surrender, you summon and submit to the infinite power of God, who knows what might happen?

[Leader's Note: Copy these sheets and hand them out to each member of your group; then read and discuss.]

Discipleship Snapshot: A Self-Assessment

Jesus began his ministry with the call to "Repent and believe the good news" (Mark 1:15). From those who answered this call, Jesus hand-picked a group of *disciples* (Mark 1:17). He invited these students—that's what "disciple" means—to follow him so that he could teach them, change their lives, and through them, change the world (Matthew 28:18–20)!

The ministry of Jesus shows us that his disciples are those who follow him—to *know* Jesus and his teaching; to *grow* more like Jesus; and to *go* for Jesus, serving others and making new disciples.

This brief self-assessment is meant to give you a general sense of where you should focus first in your journey of discipleship. Simply rank the thirty statements below, from one to thirty (with one being the topic you most want to focus on, and thirty being the issue you feel the least need to wrestle with right now).

Know: Disciples learn. They get a handle on certain basic truths.

_____ Learning the amazing good news of Jesus (Topic 1)

_____ Establishing a relationship with God (Topic 2)

_____ Knowing what it really means to be a new creature in Christ (Topic 3)

_____ Being sure I am right with God—that I actually have eternal life (Topic 4)

_____ Following Jesus—the nuts and bolts (Topic 5)

_____ Knowing the kind of life change that's possible for disciples (Topic 6)

_____ Understanding the mission of Jesus (Topic 7)

_____ Answering common questions about the Bible (Topic 8)

_____ Learning what God is really like (Topic 9)

_____ Getting a clearer view of Jesus (Topic 10)

_____ Hearing what the Bible says about the Holy Spirit (Topic 11)

_____ Figuring out how church fits in to following Jesus (Topic 12)

Grow: Disciples change. They gradually become like Jesus.

_____ Dealing with the struggle to love others (Topic 13)

_____ Experiencing joy and peace in life (Topic 14)

_____ Strengthening my relationships with others (Topic 15)

_____ Understanding the rare traits of faithfulness and gentleness (Topic 16)

_____ Battling temptation (Topic 17)

_____ Knowing the truth about forgiveness (Topic 18)

_____ Coping when life is one big struggle (Topic 19)

_____ Keeping on when you feel like quitting (Topic 20)

Go: Disciples act. They engage in practices that can change the world.

_____ Clearing up misconceptions about worship (Topic 21)

_____ Dealing with a noisy, frantic, and jumbled life (Topic 22)

_____ Digging into the Bible for yourself (Topic 23)

_____ Building a richer prayer life (Topic 24)

_____ Figuring out what God wants you to do (Topic 25)

_____ Understanding fasting (Topic 26)

_____ Hearing Jesus on money and giving (Topic 27)

_____ Using your abilities to bless others (Topic 28)

_____ Having spiritual conversations (Topic 29)

_____ Making a global difference (Topic 30)

Discipleship Participant Form

Name:

_____

Address:

_____

_____

Phone:

_____

Email:

_____

How did you hear about this discipleship group?

_____

_____

_____

Explain a little about your spiritual journey since childhood:

_____

_____

_____

_____

_____

_____

What do you hope to get out of this group?

_____

_____

_____

_____

_____

Is there anything you want the leader and/or group to know?

_____

_____

_____

_____

_____

_____

Are there any things for which you'd like prayer at this time?

_____

_____

_____

_____

_____

_____

_____

_____